Her mother said,

"If you are so fed up, then for God's sake go down to the village hall youth club and get a boyfriend like your older sister Rosie has!"

These were the mother's words to her restless sixteen-year-old daughter when she was again a little bored of the few TV programmes and a dull radio during that winter's Friday evening, in their bungalow in sleepy South Woodham Ferrers, in 1966.

Her mother expected her to return with a nice smart white-collar lad with a tidy car,

not to return with a biker.

But Pamela, as always, did it her way...

This book is dedicated to The Bear, 'Edwina', Micky Craven, striking Pamela and to my older Brother, who sadly passed just before this book was published.

Images

Front cover: *At Essex Way Jaywick, 1965 & 1964.*

Rear cover: *Myself astride my 1959 Velocette Viper, some fifty years after the Mods and Rockers riots of Clacton and elsewhere.*

The Journey of a Biker

An exciting journey through the Rock and Roll Sixties in the Essex countryside

Peter Williams

The Reality of it all.

The Book Nut Publishing

First published 2021

The Book Nut Publishing

South Woodham Ferrers, Essex.

©Peter Williams 2019

The right of Peter Williams to be identified as the Author of this work has been asserted in accordance with the copyrights, Designs and Patents Act 1988.

All rights reserved. Without limiting the rights under copyright reserved above, no part of this publication may be reproduced, stored, or introduced into a retrieval system, or transmitted, in any form or by any means (electronic, mechanical, photocopying, recording or otherwise), without the prior written permission of both the copyright owner and the publisher of this book.

A catalogue record for this book is available from the British Library.

ISBN 978 0 9957 9205 0

Typesetting by The Book Nut Publishing

Printed by Lulu

First Edition

In Search of my Shangri La

Winter of 1966.

Many, many months later, whilst reviewing the past events and considering the current situation brought on by my impatience and stubbornness, I am leaning on the evening coffee bar of the unusually quiet South Woodham Ferrers Village Hall, head in cupped hands and my mind is in the doldrums without a current girlfriend, just my Vincent motorbike as company during that winter's evening, when I was startled by a very sudden and dramatic 'Splash', and a very cold wet soaking to my head and face. *'Oh, what now I think to myself, Drat, it's a cold winter's night and I am soaked through. What now, who has dared to chuck cold water over me?* I cleared my eyes, fists clenched and arm muscles tense, expecting a fight or full-on confrontation with a visiting bad lad or a Mod, and there, giving me a verbal lashing, was a sure fire talking but very attractive, well-proportioned and well-dressed 5ft 6-inch brunette, a brunette that I had never previously had the pleasure nor indeed the displeasure, of knowing. I had occasionally previously noticed her and reasonably assumed that she was a no-go to a biker, an unapproachable type of girl. She was a girl who held her head high and was assertive, often holding court among other girls and usually casually leaning against the hall's centrally mounted wall radiator with a couple of girls each side of her. In the summer she was often to be seen in the village very admirably in a miniskirt and occasionally bare feet, with her own very noticeable driven charisma and never with a local boyfriend, an out of reach stunner, or so I thought.

Apparently, she was part of the South Woodham Ferrers Carnival Queen Court. Whatever does she want of me, it can't be the bike, can it? And surely not the way I dress, nor for more confrontation... maybe she's just mischief.

This no-nonsense brunette had ambushed me, telling me in no uncertain terms whilst looking me directly in the eyes, that this coffee bar might not have music nor the coffee, tea, nor Cola tonight that I had requested, but it does indeed have cold water and plenty more of it, If I want it. I have just met Pamela, Pamela Mary that is. Our eyes, in a moment of shock were fixedly aligned and I just hoped that I could calmly break the deadlock. Do I run or pick up the gauntlet, this girl is certainly no shrinking violet, more of a striking rose, complete with some threatening thorns. After all I'd been through, I was in for the challenge. No more fairies for me, after all, I'm a biker and can take on anything (within reason) including this daredevil girl. What would the future hold?
(Continued later in book)

The *Sixth* Sense

Most of us are lucky enough to have the five senses, the magical senses of hearing, sight, smell, taste, and touch.

Indulge if you will, and enjoy with me my Sixth Sense, my enjoyable and fortunate strong sense of memory.

Immerse yourself with my memories of possibly the best decade ever to be a teenager, in the sunny and exciting south east of England, during the vibrant and colourful sixties... memories of fun, excitement, mischief, motorbikes, police chases, superb music and the beautiful Essex Coast and Countryside

Foreword

We were only trying to enjoy ourselves at a time when this country and its people were rather short of money and happiness, many having lost homes and members of the family and being left with very few recent happy memories after the second recent devastating war with Germany. However, Germany, even with its European-wide production plants and vast expendable slave labour lost again. Again, we won, with some help from our friends but at an unbelievable cost. War scars were deep, many, and obvious.

We trusted that the world had learnt a lesson as we looked to enjoy the future and ignore wherever possible, the devastating past.

The key to an enjoyable life is happiness and fun, which I think we eventually achieved, as you will see in this book.

Looking back, I will let you be the judge.

I thought that writing this book was long overdue in my grand plan of life, and that it would be relatively easy to accomplish with the strong memories that I have. The first twelve thousand words were based mostly if not totally on my sometimes-crazy motorbike days and took just three months of my spare time to write, and I thought that my initial writing would be enough with the excitement told to avoid the accusation of being boring.

However, my wife Pam, Pamela Mary that is, and one of my daughters, Hazel, who had listened to my rarely exaggerated but often doubtful stories over the years and after reading my initial twelve thousand words, insisted that I needed to write at least four times as many words, to do my memories sufficient justice. I thought, Oh no! That will take forever, and I don't think that I can find enough memories, material nor inspiration to attempt it. I soon considered abandoning this part of my grand plan, and just enjoy my exciting memories alone in my dreams, or when visiting long-off nostalgic memories whilst sitting in my armchair, during the long winter evenings or when there is some dribble on the TV that is keeping Pam amused. They (Pam and Hazel) however both said that listening to my tales over the years had given them much laughter and disbelief, and Pam retorted that I should never give up the writing and that I would do the teenage lads and bikers of the sixties Essex a disservice if I didn't put my sometimes funny, crazy and often unbelievable memories to paper.

So, I have had to write beyond my initial mad bike memories and included so much more of the rather varied and interesting events of the nineteen fifties and sixties that I have experienced. I have made a deliberate attempt to avoid the book appearing to be an autobiography, but more of a 'would you believe it' casual record of the fun and emotions that so many of us youngsters experienced when the country was trying to forget the war, and the tales that if not written now will be lost to posterity. I also accept the candour that I have used in places may seem a little blunt or less than delicate, but it is a true reflection of *as it was* at the time and is therefore impossible to alter.

Mostly factual, rarely anecdotal and never totally imaginary nor false, here are some of my memories. I have tried my very best to be accurate without exaggeration and not to offend anyone. If any of my subjects seem to be scallywags, then they probably were scallywags and maybe still are, if they are still alive. Typically, of teenage boys throughout the generations, most of us got involved with a little mischief, usually harmless and never with any ill will nor ill intent. Out in the countryside it was very rare that we would come across a lad with real bad intent and if we did, he would be shunned and avoided. We could find enough fun without him spoiling it or getting us into deep trouble.

As a reminder that most of this book is written from memory and hopefully totally accurate, I will follow the lead of an ancient English scribe, Bede, who completed in 731 AD, his *Ecclesiastical History of England.* In compiling it he realised that most that he wrote, being totally historical and with little written records besides the enormous works of the Monks in the Monasteries, were indeed often legend and hearsay. He therefore pre-texted his book with the statement *'it is said'* and so I pretext and qualify this book here with the appropriation of *'it is said'* and *in the best of my memory* in the same vein to give the best realistic review of the many previous interesting events.

It is said, *and how it was.*

As I write I realise that some of the events and attitudes that I write of, that happened some sixty years ago, may offend and upset some readers. This was not my intention, the content of this book is just a record of *how it was,* **to the best of my memory.** *Or it is said* in legend, **here-say or local stories.**

To be loyal to the truth I cannot and will not re-write the past just to be politically correct, it would be wrong to. Since the period that is the basis of this book, some things have unfortunately changed for the worse with the passing of time just as some things have changed for the better, what was acceptable then may not be now and so in places it may make challenging reading, but...

Some of us have been fortunate enough to experience both time periods that have made us a little sadder but to our advantage, a lot wiser.

The more I wrote about my evolving memories, the less that I struggled to recall them, the more they came to life, sometimes most vividly, and writing this book eventually became self inspirational and a joy to write and revisit those long-forgotten memories. Each evening I would revisit an incident or character or event that had lain dormant in the depths of my brain until some fifty years later, the grey matter brings those memories back to virtual reality again. Viva the Sixties, Viva Jaywick, Viva the Bear, Viva The Blinking Owl, Viva Clacton Pier, Viva Southend's Golden Mile, Viva the music and Viva the unforgettable mini skirt that was everywhere you went, and *Viva* a world that was in transition from unhappy wartime memories to exciting and futuristic designs and space programmes, and so much more. I now realise what a really good time we youngsters had in the sixties and how fortunate we were to be born into them. Two years and a half or so later, after much soul searching, smiles, laughs, doubting my own memory to the point where I find that in actual fact that the subjects and events of my memories did actually happen, unreal as they sometimes seemed, I have done it, I did not give up and I have written this book. It is a testimony, almost a bible, of the Essex teenage sixties, and I hope that you read it without wanting to put it down nor to use it as a door-stop, nor use it as a medical tool instead of a bible to get rid of a ganglion, use The Bible. It's bigger, sacred, and therefore more effective.

So here goes, this book is a history, a catalogue and a celebration of that magical period. After all, said Pam, my long enduring wife, time is running out on bikers of my age and if I delay writing this book, they'll all be dead before it's published, and then none of the sixties generation will enjoy my eventual masterpiece, if indeed I really do manage to complete it. So let's hope this madcap collection of memories gets to them before the grim reaper does.

Was it Shakespeare who said "The pen is mightier than the sword"?

I have on occasion added a verse, a lyric or a few lines from a suitable piece of music of the time, sometimes adapted to add to the exciting or sad sense of the occasion as a musical accompaniment. Such verse is listed in the index at the back of the book.

Viva the Sixties!

With the background of continuous lively rhythmic, romantic and sometimes melancholic music, from the top twenty issuing out of portable radios, car radios, out of terraced houses with the windows wide open in the summer months and from dance halls at weekends all year round, there was always a popular song to match the mood that you were in, or whatever you were doing. People at work, particularly in factories, workshops and on building sites, would burst into spontaneous song at the slightest provocation of a favourite 'pop' (popular) song playing from the portable radio, and some of us motor cyclists would sing our hearts out, when inspired, to an invisible audience when we were travelling and revelling at the excitement of speed. Eventually the BBC TV and ITV switched into this mania with the introduction of the Oh Boy!, Ready-Steady-Go! and The Six-Five Special TV pop music shows that often went live around six o'clock on a weekend evening. Typically there was no introduction to the television programme, just a sudden full-on blast of music as the curtains raised on the Oh Boy! by a band, The Rockingham X1 headed by a line of very loud and splendid saxophones dishing out a Scottish Wonder called 'Oots Mon' 'There's a Moose, Loose, aboot this Hoose' as an opener, or 'The Six Five Special's coming down the line, The Six Five Special's right on time'. Eventually BBC Radio was forced into transmitting pop music on the radio for more than its meagre one hour a day by the infamous but very popular ship based Pirate radio stations and Radio Luxemburg. What a way to kick start each weekend. They were probably the very best years ever to be young. Such memories, such fun and so lucky to be able to remember them . . .Oots Mon!

Memories . . .

I closed my eyes,

drew back the curtains,

to see for certain,

what I thought was true,

And what I saw,

was so surprising,

as the dreams were rising,

Any dream will do . .(1)

So indulge with me with my dreaming memories . . .

PART ONE
THE START OF MY WORLD

ONE OF MANY 1946 WAR PRIZES

I was born as one of the 1946 'Victory' baby bulge children immediately after the end of WW2 on Canvey Island, Essex, when a mass of children were born to the returning military who naturally celebrated the end of the six years of massive international conflict, with their war weary families. So many of my friends share the same birthday month as me, February, it is clear what happened. The earliest that I can clearly remember was in 1950, when as a four-year old child exploring the snow-covered garden in our freshly moved into house in nearby South Benfleet, I found the cold extremely unpleasant and the ice crust on the snow added to the snow's normal soft fascination. I approached the inviting chicken hutch that most families had back then due to wartime food shortages and extended rationing. I could hear the hens gently brooding away inside and became inquisitive. Being just four years old I was small enough to climb through the small hutch door and escape the bitter cold outside. There were four or five dark red hens but no cockerel as the fox had killed it during the previous night. It was warm and cosy in there with the friendly nature of the brooding hens on their nests, and before long I snuggled up and fell asleep to the sound of the roosting hens. Maybe an hour or so later, I awoke to my Mum and Auntie repeatedly calling my name, they couldn't hear my quieter return call as they didn't come near to the chicken hutch and went indoors out of the cold. I eventually climbed out of the chicken hutch and went indoors where I was greeted with mixed emotions as not only did I smell strongly of chickens and was covered with straw and feathers, but I was still alive. My dear Mum had been out searching for me with my visiting Aunt after not finding me in the house.

After an extensive search of our large secretive garden, they walked to the local shops in the snow and worryingly reported me missing to the local constable, assuming the worst in the severe winter weather that day. Imagine their relief when I walked through the front door, feathers, dust, dirt and all.

I think at this point, a casual look at my family's history before I was born will add a slice of almost forgotten history that was just before modern times.

At the turn of the nineteenth and twentieth centuries during the end of the Victorian age, this country was really marching forward in the world with the British inventions of radio, electricity, railways, the early motor cars, maritime navigation, and shipbuilding, such as the Titanic and many other engineering products making Great Britain, very 'Great' to the outside world but only really noticeable in the major British towns and cities where industry was based.

My Great Grandfather, like many Welshmen, left impoverished Aberystwyth on the Cardigan Bay of Wales in the nineteenth century, with his pram full of essential possessions on the long walk to London and hopefully a better life. After arriving in London and after a while of improved circumstances and after opening a hardware and general shop in the hectic and dirty East End of London serving Whitechapel and Mile End, he, like so many others, was tempted by the Midland Railway Company's joint promotion with a local landowner Frederick Hester of low cost home ownership on Canvey Island, Essex. It was near a railway station at Benfleet on the mainland that was within an easy hour of London. Interested people bought a very small plot, or maybe two adjoining plots of land on the Island from Hester's Company and then bought or supplied their own home to be placed on that plot. The 'homes' were often no more than a shed, a shanty house of timber and asbestos construction, or a disused railway carriage body from the Midland Railway Company, which was more robust, more weatherproof and a little warmer. My Grandfather (on my father's side) became the first drainage and sewerage engineer on the new Canvey Council and eventually lost his life at work due to pneumonia while inspecting and planning Canvey's first drainage system. My family became some of Canvey Island's pioneers. My uncle Harry was one of the first builders on the developing island and he had one of the very first telephones on the island, to the point that his phone number was Canvey 9, a number that he kept until he emigrated as late as the nineteen sixties to Australia for his wife's health, who was in need of a better climate than that of damp Canvey. Harry's son Chris grew up with the renown Prout brothers on the island and was instrumental in building the first catamarans in the UK with them. Chris, a talented Jazz musician now also resides in Australia where he continues designing and building leading catamarans and playing his jazz trombone on the Sydney Harbour cruising ferry boats.

My Grandfather on my Mother's side had a busy coal round business in Shepherd's Bush, London at the beginning of the last century. The military requisitioned his horses for the awful battles in the Great War and he consequently lost his living. He turned to furniture and antiques dealing as well as house clearances due to the devastation caused by war, difficult times indeed, for everyone. Many people suffered so much more.

My father owned one of the Canvey Island's first bus companies and he had a small fleet of omnibuses including a horse drawn open bus, which was very much like a large farm wagon that could carry upwards of twelve people with seats and a rear entrance up a short flight of steps and then through a central door/gate. This was for the seafront service as the council did not allow motorised vehicles along the mile-long grass promenade in the early motoring years and so it was drawn by Dolly the Horse and/or depending on demand, Jimmy Riddle another horse that got his name for obvious reasons. Dolly and Jimmy were full size but gentle work horses that were walked at the beginning and end of each day to and from their stables at the Winter Gardens at the far end of the Island by the beach bus driver and a helper, often my older brother. Further motor-buses were added in the nineteen twenties including ex London Transport Ford Model T and some ex London Transport Chevrolet buses. My father named one of his buses after a national heroine known as Grace Darling, a lighthouse keeper's daughter who played a significant part in the rescue of the survivors of a shipwreck. She was alone in her bedroom near the top of the Longstone Rocks Lighthouse on some dangerous rocks off the coast in the North East of England in 1838 when she spotted a passing paddle steamer, the 'S S Forfarshire' hit rocks in a storm and break in two, sinking slowly overnight with ninety two people aboard. There was no radio back then and she roused her father and together they rowed their small open rowing boat as the sea was too rough for the proper lifeboat to be launched during that storm lashed autumn night, to the slowly sinking wreck from the exposed lighthouse. They arrived to rescue the very few survivors before the larger land based rowing lifeboat from North Sunderland, (Seahouses) could get launched, much later, and then all life would have been lost. Lifeboats did not have engines back then and were often out of action due to launching difficulties in stormy seas. Her heroism gripped the nation and not only did she become a national heroine but the event caused the creation of the National Lifeboat Institute that is run by volunteers to this day. William Wordsworth dedicated a poem to her and she became known as 'The Maid of the Isles' and *'The Girl with the Windswept Hair'* Her story is epic, in that storm lashed night. . . .A dramatic painting is on the internet. . . .*She never gave up.* ,

There was continual acrimony between the various taxi operators who would wait in the taxi rank outside Benfleet railway station to the point where foul play was often used as the taxi-men not only had to compete with each other but also against the bus operators. One of the mischievous goings-on was always against the first taxi in the taxi line up. The plot was to wait until the cabbie in the first cab left his cab to have a cup of tea between trains or use the toilets at which point the taxi-men in the following taxi queue would tilt the back of the first taxi, invariably a lightweight Ford Model T briefly, and put a couple of bricks under the back axle on the pavement side and then go back to their own cabs and innocently wait to watch proceedings. Eventually the driver of the first taxi would return from his nature break and sit in his taxi awaiting the arrival of the next train and hopefully a fare (customer). The train arrives, some passengers depart the train and usually there would be one of the passengers that would climb into the first taxi in the rank and ask for a journey onto the island. After starting the engine the driver would engage first gear and release the clutch, but hey ho, the car would not move as the pavement side rear wheel would just spin in the air due to the action of the back axle differential. The passenger being dismayed that the taxi didn't move would then move onto the next taxi, that might also have been mischievously sabotaged and the first taxi driver had now lost his fare, such high jinks amongst grown men.

Back on Canvey the buses were kept busy in competition with other small bus companies on the island by transporting dwellers, holiday makers and visitors to the Island's three social clubs to the mainland and railway station at nearby South Benfleet crossing the muddy creek that was maybe fifty feet wide at and around low water, when there was often a passable broom-way that was swept clear of riverbed rubble by a council workman, and some stepping stones. The buses would regularly cross this broom-way until the returning and rising tide came through the wooden floorboards of the primitive buses at which point it was declared that this was the last bus of the tide until the eventual falling tide some ten or so hours later allowed the buses to wade through again.

Chevrolet, realising the publicity that the wading buses were drawing eventually placed a photo of one of the buses pushing its way through the water with small bow waves at each front wheel and appearing to be at sea with the caption 'Chevrolet,- it always gets through' on the front cover of a national motor magazine between the wars.

There was always a period after the last bus when the replacement eight-passenger wooden rowing boat ferry could not reach the customers queuing on the seawall until it was near high water when the ferryboat could be rowed right up the wall and the waiting queue. The answer was the loose laying on the slippery angled mud of scaffold planks, from the muddy seawall to the water's edge maybe twenty feet away, or use the stepping-stones if exposed. There was no street lighting, nor light pollution nor shelter within half-a-mile, and often at night it could be cloudy and moonless, if not raining, cold and rather windy, a nightmare scenario for walking the planks.

Often at the end of a weekend the visiting Londoners would catch one of the many buses from their shanty holiday chalets or from one of the active clubs on the Island, of which my Dad owned one, The Premier Club in Foksville Road, and travel the three miles or so to the station for a train home to London's East End during the Sunday night.

Happy days if it was low water and the bus driver was brave enough to wade his bus and passengers through the unlit shallow water to the station on the mainland in the pitch dark that often existed, but not so happy if the tide was on its way in, flooding the bus and plank walking became necessary.

If walking the planks were the only way home, the fun would begin.

Late on a summer's Sunday night one or two dozen if not hundreds of visitors could be queuing, many of them drunk and singing and being very merry as only a London East Ender knows how, but when it was his time to walk the loosely laid planks without hand rails to the ferry boat, more likely than not, he (or she) would lose their footing and balance on the planks and fall with much jeering and hilarity, face down into the pungent Thames creek mud. Others would try to help and often get mud covered and fall into the awful mire themselves.

One can only imagine the displeasure of some of the well dressed passengers already on the approaching London bound steam train from Southend-on-Sea as it pulled in to Benfleet station, when their single compartment door was flung open and a mud covered, singing, belching, stinking, drunken East Ender announced that he was going to join them for the remainder of their journey to Romford or beyond to the East End, Happy Days, Happy Days indeed.

At weekends, particularly in the summer, if the Island was cut off after the last ferry by an evening tide, the three clubs on the island would carry out an island 'lock in' after drinking up time to the advantage and entertainment of so many. My Dad's club had three full size snooker tables and a stage where my Mum would sing to a piano or lead a sing-along, creating an oasis of pleasure during those long desolate pre-TV damp island nights. Typically, in an evening my mother would play the Grand Piano to dancing in the dance hall or sing this duet from the operetta 'The Desert Song' with my Welsh descended father;

> *Blue heaven, just you and I and sand kissing a moonlit sky. A desert breeze whispr'ng a lullaby, Only stars above you To see I love you. . . .Oh give me that night divine and let your arms in mine entwine, the desert song calling, its voice enthralling Will make you mine*(1)

The damp island evenings then turn warm.

One evening, as a response to a complaining publican on the mainland who was having quiet nights during summer high tides, the nearby Southend-on-Sea Constabulary took action and spoilt the party. A force of officers dressed as holiday-makers landed onto the island during the day and before the evening tide went out and they made their way to the three clubs, and twenty-five minutes after final orders they pounced and a few licensees lost their licence. Fresh licences were applied for and granted, however, a lesson was learnt as everyone was reminded that the island was still part of the UK even when isolated at high tide, and the island was now less fun at late evening, unless you watched the shenanigans of the ferry passengers tip toeing the planks over the mud in the dark.

The make-up of the Islanders

Families had endured so much during WW2, six years of national crisis, hundreds of thousands of lost lives, mostly young men and boys, with so many other hardships and a depression, before our country destroyed the German war machine for the second and hopefully final time in recent history. Ironically after the war that our people had decisively won, our country was again left virtually bankrupted in the process but left proud but on its knees after such a sustained but necessary effort, but would not give up. There were tens of thousands of terribly bombed houses, streets, shops and factories in almost every English, and some Scottish, Welsh and Irish major town with some cities almost totally destroyed, such as Coventry, Hull and the East End of London. The skies above Canvey Island, where I was born, were often the turning point for incoming German bombers whose goal of London, before the invention of radar, was only in their sight if they followed the Thames and it's oil refineries, glistening in the moonlit night sky, when suddenly approached by RAF Spitfires and Hurricanes from Biggin Hill, Hornchurch, Rochford and North Weald, the bombers would turn quickly and try unsuccessfully to outrun the RAF by returning to Germany after unloading their unused bombs all over the Thames Estuary to gain more speed to escape which was often fruitless. This caused much damage to Canvey Island and Westcliff-on-Sea. Due to this excessive bombing, Westcliff in particular, became uninsurable, which collapsed local property prices and led to the Westcliff property purchases by the Jewish community who understandably took the view that they had little to lose if Germany won the war, then Westcliff's property, as so many other property prices, would totally collapse and we would all be losers. Hitler however, totally misjudged the British peoples' resolve, and thriving Westcliff-on-Sea now has the largest Jewish community and Synagogue in the UK. It took some forty years after the end of WW2 before a German new-car dealership was accepted in the Southend-on-Sea area. Memories and wounds truly run deep especially in this heavily bombed part of England.

 Canvey Island sits mostly below sea level in the Thames Estuary, surrounded by seawalls built of mud and heavy Thames clay, containing marshes drained by dykes, built by the Dutch in the seventeenth century. The drained marshes became damp and therefore very cheap pastures for cattle and sheep and attracted low cost housing usually built of wood to prevent the weight of brick and concrete sinking into the marsh clay. Eventually brick built houses were introduced in the twentieth century but were usually built on individual concrete rafts to give stability. The people who lived there loved the estuarial fresh air and accepted any shortcomings as being eminently preferable to living in the noisy, dirty, hectic and industrious East End of London from where most of them had 'escaped'. They included my parents, who loved the island's communal way of life and were proud to call themselves 'Islanders'. In 1952, my parents, who had themselves migrated from Whitechapel in London's East-End, from where they had a hardware store in New Cross in the twenties, moved us as a family to adjacent South Benfleet on the higher mainland.

 We moved off the Island with its dampness that didn't help the avoidance of bronchial, rheumatic, and pneumonia health problems that came with the damper living conditions of a sea level, salt marsh air island existence. The move to 'Nymphase' on Vicarage Hill, South Benfleet where my younger sister Marion Brondwyn was born, soon became an unforeseen blessing.

The earliest memories I have of the Island are in 1950 when as a four-year old I can clearly remember the island's long wild grass, marsh reeds, wild flowers and fluttering white cabbage butterflies together with golden corn fields waving invitingly and gently in the warm and friendly summer breeze, there was always a breeze on the Island. There were very few trees, maybe due to the soft damp soil that had too much sea salt in its water table. With so few trees you would notice the very few birds beside wild fowl on the island but in particular the frenetic call of the Skylark hovering high above its nest and young in the long grass. There were no true meadows on the Island just marshland and saltings for the little livestock, mostly sheep farmed there.

I remember once we had moved off the Island to Benfleet trying to get off the Island after a day's return outing there in the car. The very long queue of cars queueing to get off the Island at the end of a summers day stretched sometimes two miles to beyond the Red Cow pub. The hold-up on almost every summer's day was caused by the operation of the Colvin Sliding Bridge over the creek and the nearby railway crossing gates being the only connection to the mainland at that time. Navigational rights made the bridge busy letting slow moving sailing craft through, be they pleasure yachts or Thames Barges or Smacks, which if fighting the tide may even be slowly travelling backwards over the creek-bed while actually sailing forward through the moving tidal water. There was also the weekly council rubbish boat that collected domestic rubbish from the many houseboats that were tied up bow-on to the Benfleet-side seawall. Just as bad a hold up was caused by the nearby railway level crossing. All Island traffic had to cross the creek bridge and then the railway crossing over the very busy London, Tilbury and Southend Railway (LTSR). The large, heavy wooden railway gates were worked manually and remotely by one of the signalmen in the adjacent and overlooking railway signal box. On a warm summer's day they would have the sliding door-windows of the signal box open, and would often be seen sitting down having a breather after the exertion spent working the big wheel inside the box that opens the gates after the passing of several trains in a short space of time. They were often fed up and exhausted and the patience of the motorists on both sides of the gates would run low and there would often be much motor horn blowing as frustrated motorists wanted the gates opened. This would be followed by the signalman giving the 'V' sign to the motorists, a bit of loud bad language, and the eventual opening of the gates, this was almost a daily ritual.

THE CANVEY FLOOD 1953

My parent's action was unbelievably fortuitous, maybe they were clairvoyants, as very soon after we moved to Benfleet, Canvey and much of the East Coast of East Anglia was flooded in the calamitous 1953 East Coast Floods. We had luckily moved to the higher mainland and avoided a nightmare. The swollen North Sea had burst Canvey's sea walls and put almost the entire Island under water. Whilst nearly ninety islanders lost their lives, most of the Islanders survived but were left totally desperate and homeless. The flood happened during a February winter's night, a true living nightmare, as most islanders were asleep and without the luxury of hourly weather reports on the radio and virtually no television and their radios switched off for the night, a majority were unprepared for what was to come. They were soon to be dramatically awakened by the flood water and would soon be sitting wet and cold during a winter's night on their shanty bungalow roofs, many with children and some with babes in arms, calling forlornly for help. A few people a mile or so away on the mainland heard their distant cries, but they assumed that a party was going on, how wrong they were. The calamity was caused by a rare combination of a very high spring tide that was pushed higher by the unrelenting and violent storm force 12 northerly wind, which the Beaufort Scale classes as a Hurricane, forcing down a storm sea surge from Scandinavia down the huge funnel shaped North Sea towards the River Thames with a low pressure area over the south east of England sucking an unusual amount of this seawater towards Canvey and an equally unstoppable amount of rainwater coming down from the Cotswold Hills west of London trying to escape through London to the North Sea through the Thames Estuary. The meeting ground of the two raging water flows was the further funnel shape, relatively shallow and restricted area of the Thames around Canvey Island. Canvey's very basic sodden clay seawalls just burst in places under the immense pressure of so much turbulent water. The Island's sad story deserves the better justice that is in the various books that are dedicated to the event, there were many tragedies. On a national scale, it was a tragedy of epic sadness and bad luck.

On daybreak of that February morning I awoke as a child in my parent's house that sat high up Vicarage Hill in adjacent Benfleet to much desperate discussions going on downstairs and outside in the garden, I peered around my bedroom curtains to see a strange mixture of horses, chickens, dogs, and cars, carts and trucks in our large garden, as relatives and friends who still lived on the Island had no choice but to escape to the dry mainland and knock on doors in the middle of that cold winter's night and seek salvation. Those who could not escape the island spent the night out in the open on the roofs of their lightly constructed timber and asbestos bungalows in that freezing winter night. They were surrounded by what was now a wild open sea and hoped for rescue in the total darkness with no phone, no heat, and no moonlight in the rain-clouded night, nor protection from the biting winter wind. There were many who were unable to climb onto the roofs of their homes as ladders were not normally a necessity on bungalows and consequently drowned in the icy cold muddy salt water. Many more did not survive the overnight ordeal on the roofs and died of hypothermia. A tough lot was an Islander, a very tough lot indeed. The modern generations have no idea just how bad things can be.

A few days later as a seven-year old, I walked alone down to the local Benfleet railway station and climbed the footbridge that spanned the railway's level crossing to have a look at the flooded island. It was a strangely unmoving sight, an unpleasant, depressing and sorrowful sight, it was a totally overcast day with low grey cloud that met the calm, clay-brown lake of floodwater at a misty and indistinguishable horizon at an unjudgeable distance. There was no sight of any people or anything else at all moving, no lights, no life, and little hope, just grim desolation . . . Eventually the entire population of the Island was put up in the nearby empty army barracks and local schools, until the Island and their homes were habitable again many, many months later in the year. Like all of the other Benfleet and Canvey school children, I was displaced from our school by the occupation of the flood victims and therefore went without schooling from February, right the way through to the Autumn Term some seven months later, just as in the 2020 pandemic school lockdown.

Our school, the rather large St Mary's in the High Road, Benfleet, took many of the now homeless people. Each classroom became the home of one or more families. The military supplied stoves, iron beds, pots, pans, camping type cutlery and crockery, and steel cupboards, and whatever else was available. Heavy grey bed blankets were supplied to each family and to those Benfleet house owners that turned their homes into mini guesthouses to help out. The flood could not have come at a worse time for the Islanders and the rest of the affected part of eastern England. Due to shortages caused by the war, food rationing with ration books existed until around 1954, nine years after the war had ended. Most cars, trucks and motorbikes were of old pre-war construction or design. Money was still in short supply after the war that we had ironically won. TV was virtually non-existent, but the radio served an unforgettable motivating background in every home, broadcasting much needed soothing medleys and melodies from orchestras and crooners and some jazz from the thirties to cheer things up. The down on their luck islanders, refused to give up.

My parents received blankets and suchlike to help our needy visitors and my mother still had some of the military blankets nearly fifty years later. I often used one to keep warm in the extremes of winter, as we, like so many others had no double-glazing, central heating, nor loft or cavity wall insulation back then. Bedrooms were cold, very cold on a windy winter's night, with unblocked and unused bedroom fireplaces drawing what little heat there was out of the house and drawing replacement colder air into the house around the badly fitting wooden doors and windows. They were never a tight fit in their frames, as an allowance was built in to allow for heat expansion in the summer, or swelling from the damp in the rainy seasons of spring and autumn. The cold wind drifting through the house would gently hoot almost to a mysterious rhythm throughout the draughty house and you would eventually, as a child, drift into sleep, thinking that the house was haunted. Fitted carpets were almost unheard of, instead there would be a heavy dark patterned rug covering most of the wooden floor of each room which was often Oak planking and nearly always with shrinkage gaps between the flooring planks. On a windy day it was not uncommon to see the centre of the rug rise and fall nearly an inch or so in a slow pulsating rhythm as the wind tried to inflate the house through the airbricks below the damp course, if there was one, making the house even colder. House owners often would block up the airbricks or any unused chimneys, usually one in each room including bedrooms, to retain what little heat the house had. Blocking the airbricks or chimneys, would often lead to problems with the fabric of the house in later years. Trapped dead birds and their collapsed nests decayed unpleasantly just behind the fireplace's temporary shuttering, caused chimney fires or smoke blowbacks if ever the chimney was returned to service without it first being swept clear.

In 1954 our family moved to Wickford just eight miles away, and watched the building of the new Hanningfield Reservoir nearby. There was a twice-daily routine of our road being virtually cut off as the vast number of trucks and navvy's buses made their way from accommodation in Wickford town to the construction site in the Sandon Valley at Peasedown, near South Hanningfield. Peasedown was a hamlet that was lost under the water to the reservoir's needs. It was claimed when built that the reservoir would hold enough fresh water to give every person on the planet a pail of water. Not only did the hamlet of Peasedown go under the reservoir's water, but so did a large piece of construction machinery that could not be removed because of its immense weight and its muddy location, so it was encased in a concrete coffin and left there for archaeologists in a future millennium to rediscover and muse over. Also and sadly, the very palatial 'Fremnells' country house was lost, its masonry, brickwork and fabric being committed to becoming part of a large baffle wall at one end of the reservoir, even though many tried to save it, unfortunately the English Heritage movement was yet to be properly formed. Historically the notorious Guido Fawkes (Guy Fawkes) spent much time at the Fremnells with his cronies planning the destruction of The Houses of Parliament of 1605.

Our new house was rather draughty, never cosy, and the military blankets from the Canvey Island flood support became a much-needed blessing. The military blankets had a tough woollen edging, a red wool edging and the blanket came from the Army, dark blue wool and the blanket was from the Navy, and light blue wool told you that it was from the RAF. Was the Navy's the warmest? well maybe and maybe not, but two were even better than one regardless of colour. Those of us that survived the damp cold winters and were not wiped out by pneumonia became a healthy lot. I did unhappily catch pneumonia after hypothermia whilst carrying out a paper round in the very cold January of 1958 at the age of twelve which laid me off school for the best part of three weeks and gave me very worrying hallucinations and out of body experiences. I was knocked for six, the doctor visited me three times a week and on one occasion when I was really low he looked me in the eyes and said, *don't give up lad*, you're nearly there.

Fortunately, after a struggle I recovered, truly Darwin's survival of the fittest theory in action, but it was nothing much to be proud of, I was just happy to have survived to enjoy what was to come, my teenage years. We did not have the modern highly insulating clothing fabric back then, and we just got cold, very cold. We would actually look forward to going to our old Victorian schools in the winter mornings as they were a haven of heat with their underground coal fired boilers and the huge cast iron classroom radiators that were just seriously too hot to touch. Junk food did not make us obese as due to rationing there weren't any Junk food shops, and basic food was hard to get, so junk food was an unknown alternative future food supply. Fish and chips wrapped in newspaper was the only fast food, and as you added the copious amounts of salt and vinegar the ink from the newsprint added flavour and black stains to your hands, but it was a delicious and warming experience. So many people continued the practice brought on by the war of turning their gardens into vegetable plots or smallholdings with a few chickens and a Howard petrol driven rotovator that was actively marketed in the daily press for a few bob monthly. With two pints of fuel it would easily plough and turn your garden ready for the planting of cheap seeds to create good quality low cost food. Like so many other housewives of the time, my Mother would pay the milkman a few bob each December, to chase and catch one of our chickens, break its neck and hang it in the out-house ready for us children to pluck it ready for Mum to gut and clean it before putting it into the oven, in time for Christmas. Plucking a chicken was a necessary but very unpleasant annual task, but the end result always tasted delicious, especially in the time of the shortages.

As time passed by, the British people felt a little happier. From America the Teddy-Boy style arrived with the colourful long Drape Jackets with deep sponge soled 'Brothel Creeper' shoes and bootlace ties with Brylcreme quiff hairstyles. Accompanying that style, also from America was the guitar centred Rock and Roll bands of Bill Hayley and The Comets and their likes, who led a change in the core music direction to a new generation of singers such as Tommy Steel, Cliff Richard, Buddy Holly, Elvis Presley and many others. Eventually this combination of cheerful entertainment helped the population forget most of their wartime and flooding memories, and enjoy seeing a previously disappointing life change to a new future with new hope.

HOPE SPRINGS ETERNAL

And how to fund my future

Many lads like me, would supplement their meagre pocket money with paper rounds or farm work for those who lived in the countryside, or community and shop work for the town lads. Money was very much in short supply to most of us and it was clear that I would have to make my own way in the world as Mum was not well off with four children to raise after Dad had died from a spin off from pneumonia, a winter problem that continued to plague everyone until central heating and modern house building methods saved our collective health. The idea of one day owning my own house seemed like an impossible dream. As a Boy Scout I had enjoyed the 'Bob a Job week' each year and found that the ability to earn money for various jobs hugely satisfying and decided that it was within my capabilities to earn a 'bob or two' for myself when the scout campaign was over each year. To improve my financial situation I cycled 13 miles on a paper round before school each day and on Saturdays too. I enjoyed the colourful spring, summer and autumn early mornings with the fresh air, traffic quietness and dawn chorus bird call, but whilst the dark winter mornings were exciting they were especially spiteful in January with frozen fingers, a frozen nose and a chilled feeling during the entire round. I also had a small job printing building plans for local builders and architects at a local estate agent after school each day, printing as required, sometimes four days a week but rarely less than two using a seven feet high xenon plan copier.

WICKFORD JUNCTION

During the Saturdays I would visit the local railway station, Wickford Junction, where I had an interesting if sometimes arduous job where I would empty and wash out railway livestock wagons that had been shunted into the station's livestock dock siding in the goods yard. These wagons had just been used by animals, such as cattle, horses, pigs and sheep in transit to and from local farms or the weekly Wickford Livestock Market. The Station Foreman, Bert, would then pay me 2/6 (22.5p) out of the stations casual labour float for each wagon emptied and washed out. The casual labour float included petty expenditure, which included a small weekly sum for the station cats' food. The cats, Ginger and Sooty kept the station and freight yard reasonably free of rodents, mice and other vermin. They had individual territories, Ginger patrolled the London bound side of the station and Sooty the Southend bound side, which were conveniently separated by the sheer platform edges, the twin railway tracks and the many signal and points control rods that radiated from the signal box to the extremities of the station, the freight yard and approaches and ran between the platform tracks to their destinations. They had a good out-door life as was evident by the fact that they were both more than a little plump. In the winter they were more noticed as they would seek the heat of the roaring coal fires in the cosy signal box on the London side (Ginger), or the staff room (Sooty) on the Southend platform, by queuing at the doors awaiting a passing member of staff to let them into the warm inviting shelter from the cold and the chance of a few tit-bits from staff member's sandwich boxes.

An unusual event that happened several times each week was when the branch line train from Southminster would arrive with several aerated crates of gentles (maggots) from the various River Blackwater area bait farms that were unloaded onto the London bound platform to await being transferred to the next London bound train's Guards Van on their way to fishing tackle shops throughout the country. Each crate would contain many thousands of maggots that could not keep still and would make quite a lot of screeching noises between them that always attracted the attention of Ginger. Ginger would closely inspect the crates whilst trying to understand this wriggling, noisy cargo and standing on his rear legs, trying to communicate with them as though he was mute, shaking his jaws and teeth with a quick quiet and repeated 'kack kack kack' noise. Live fowl and game was also crated and left on the platform and sent by passenger or mail trains in a similar way.

The inside of the mostly red brick Victorian signal box was the most fascinating part of the station. It was positioned close to the end of the London bound platform just south of the station so that its' crew had the best visual and physical control of the entering and leaving mainline and branch line traffic. You entered it from a seven feet high flight of wooden steps and once inside and having taken in its wonderful museum style atmosphere, you noticed it commanded an uninterrupted view through its three walls of slide open and walk through latticed windows, of the station, the branch line bay platforms, goods yard, livestock dock and the approach lines from London, Southend and the Southminster branch line. Unless it was inclement weather one of these large sliding windows was often left partly open to give the signalmen easy access to a balcony with handrails that served three sides of the 'box so that they could communicate with the crews of passing trains or swop single line control keys/tokens with trains entering or leaving the single line branch to Southminster and Burnham-on-Crouch. There were several noticeable clocks all ticking majestically away and so much polished brass that it was almost overwhelming. There was an impressive bank of maybe forty man-sized levers painted in blocks of colours, white, red, and yellow, blue and black, denoting their group but individual purpose. The entire building was a place of constant activity and a busy bustle with high and low pitch bells and gongs that individually rang when a fresh train entered one of the

Wickford Box Sections, also a stand-to oak desk with a daily events and movements diary that every five minutes or so would be occupied by one of the signalmen writing yet another report. As it was the nineteen fifties, this was so pre-computer and pre-electronics that it was fabulous. Above the levers that controlled signals, points, and ground frames and interlocks was a panel plan of the railway towards the next station in each direction, which had lights that covered each mile or so section that lit up and extinguished when a train entered or left that section accompanied by the sound from one of the bells or gongs, low or high pitch depending on the trains' direction. We didn't have private movie cameras then, but a one-hour film of its activity would make a very interesting viewing

For obvious safety reasons it worked with military precision but there were however two train accidents at Wickford in a short space of time, one of which seemed to be caused by a misjudgement by one of the signalmen.

The first accident was apparently caused by a misunderstanding by depot staff between the use of vacuum and air brakes on a rake of eight empty coaches being pulled by a relatively new 800 HP diesel freight locomotive, coming down the long five mile descent from Billericay on a regular empty carriage turn after attention at the Stratford railway works. Soon after leaving Billericay the driver realised that the mixed brakes could not restrain the train that was slowly gathering more and more momentum as it went down the incline towards Wickford. At a time when there were no mobile phones the driver could only continuously blow his horn as a warning all the way down the five mile hill, hoping to clear Wickford station and junction for his out of control arrival. Fortunately some residents at line-side Ramsden Bellhouse heard the frantic loco horn and phoned ahead to the station where staff promptly evacuated the station and emptied an electric passenger train that was standing at the Southend bound platform. Eventually the runaway train passed the 'caution' distant and 'stop' home signals in sight of the station and at the last moment the diesel locomotive driver and second man seeing that a collision with the stationary passenger train was now imminent and unavoidable, leapt from the loco and tumbled into the gravel of the adjacent freight yard while the train was still travelling at an uncontrollable speed and there was a heavy collision. Much damage was done with the electric passenger trains coaches ending up in a vertical zig-zag formation and contacting the overhead electric power lines, tripping out the power. To what I remember, the driver broke a leg in the fall, and the second-man suffered some cuts and bruises. Matters might have been considerably worse. The second train accident was an unusual derailment by the rear half of a Southend bound electric passenger train possibly due to too early point switching.

An eight-coach electric passenger train with some passengers on board left Wickford station bound for Southend during the day. It would appear that the signal man, possibly blinded by a London bound train passing his box at the same time of his view of the departing Southend train, switched the forward facing branch line points to the 'open' position moments too early and before the Southend bound train had totally cleared them with the net result that the rear end of the eight coach Southend bound train joined the parallel branch line to Southminster whilst the front coaches carried on heading towards Southend-on-Sea. As the forward section of the train correctly carried on towards Southend, the driver was oblivious to the fact that the rear section of his train was now heading towards Southminster whilst the two tracks ran parallel. Eventually, after some distance from the station the lines diverged and one of the centre carriages whose front bogie was heading for Southend-on-Sea and whose rear bogie was heading for Southminster, tried to do the splits and became derailed. A line-side hut was destroyed along with damage to line-side equipment, fortunately no staff or passengers were injured.

However there were some casualties in the emergency services that were dashing at speed to the attendance of a train crash of an unknown size and nature. A relatively new fibre-glass bodied fire engine from the Basildon Fire Station had a front corner to front corner crash with an elderly Austin Horsebox travelling in the opposite direction through a pair of sharp bends on the Nevendon Road in Wickford. Unfortunately three of the fire-crew were injured. The elderly wooden horsebox won the conflict and the body of the fibre-glass bodied fire engine was badly damaged.

Due to my casual jobs of wagon cleaning together with the paper round and the copying of builder's plans, I had now experienced and enjoyed a 'work ethic' life style, which would benefit me and stay with me for the rest of my life. Bert, the station foreman, would also benefit from my efforts as he, being a very large fit man, would push the large overfilled railway barrow loads of muck, in his uniform up two steep hills to his cheerful new bungalow near Shotgate a mile and a half away, where the mixture of straw and manure was sold off by Bert to the local horticulture club, of which he was an active member, if not the secretary. Bert was a very broad shouldered solid individual with a gruff voice and a square chin who had the mannerism of a Regimental Sergeant Major. He wore his railway cap with the peak flattened down over his forehead and eyes so that he was forced to walk head and shoulders back and thereby look down at you. Equally so, you were forced to look up at him behind the peak of his cap that gave him a very commanding military air. However, even though he was a no-nonsense individual, he was a kind-hearted gardener. He controlled the junction station with few short commanding gruff words and a rod of iron whenever Station Master Mr Gordon was absent or off duty, which seemed often. In the fifties, Wickford Station was a moderately busy junction on the old Great Eastern Railway route from London Liverpool Street to Southend-on-Sea Victoria. It had two through, and two bay platforms, with water cranes to fill up the steam engines, a goods yard, cattle dock, a reservoir served by a weir on the adjacent upper reaches of the River Crouch and a water tower with a busy, complex and active Victorian signal box. There was also a locomotive servicing bay and siding which consisted of an inspection and ash drop pit, an engine dock, a water supply crane and a manually operated locomotive turntable. On the main line that served the two through platforms each week-day, there were usually three passenger trains an hour in each direction to London or Southend, an early morning daily newspaper supply train, followed by a milk train and a Royal Mail train from London, a mid-day fast Royal Mail train to London and a general freight train, again daily, in each direction. Occasionally there would be a locomotive or rolling stock running-in turn from the vast locomotive and wagon and carriage-works at Stratford to Southend-on-Sea and back which would park in the refuge siding for a mid trip inspection, and to await a clear road after the passing of more important traffic before continuing its journey. The Essex railways were undergoing major modernisation in the late fifties. At Wickford, steam locomotives carried out the medium size freight turns on the main line with some modern 800 horse power diesel electric freight locos usually on the branch to Southminster. After 1956, the main line passenger trains were totally powered by overhead electricity. After 1958 the Southminster branch line passenger trains were two, three or four carriage diesel multiple units whilst the Bradwell Nuclear waste train was usually headed by a new express English Electric Diesel Electric locomotive of 1750 horse power as a sign of the modern age. However, the midday mail to London from Southend was still the province of one of a rapidly dwindling fleet of Sir Nigel Gresley's colourful Sandringham express steam locomotives, that carried such evocative names such as 'Framlingham Castle', 'Sandringham', 'Audley End', and 'The Suffolk Regiment', which were kept beautifully clean and in tip top order at the Southend Victoria loco shed, for such duties and stand-by duties in their later years before their unfortunate scrapping. They had a lovely three-cylinder rhythmic exhaust beat that barked six beats to each rotation of the very visible driving wheels due to their double acting pistons, as they smartly accelerated away after a delayed stay at Wickford. At Wickford they would have been picking up mail and crated poultry, and maggots/gentles from the Southminster branch train as already said. The mail and parcels train was keeping an essential lead over a following electric passenger train that spent less time at each station and left Southend fifteen minutes after the Mail Train's departure. This was a well timed daily cat and mouse chase where the cat never quite caught the mouse until it could overtake the mouse whilst the (mouse) Mail train was busily spending valuable time loading and unloading parcels at Shenfield Junction, for onward transit to East Anglia. The maintenance crews and footplate staff of Southend Victoria ensured that the steam loco's had no deposited ash, a clear grate, a clean chimney, good quality coal and softened water so that their last years, whilst still shining in a lovely green, would be glamorous years. With their large six feet eight inch diameter wheels, among the largest in Britain, and a good fire, they could fly with the six or seven-van mail train.

As well as the main line activity, there were also crates of homing pigeons that would arrive on the mail or passenger trains from pigeon fanciers from often never heard of towns deeper in England, and it was the responsibility of the station staff to release them to fly home. At the time we had the new electric trains served by the overhead wiring carrying 1,500 volts DC above the platform areas and the staff, worrying about pigeon fatalities if the birds hit the wires, would release the pigeons from a nearby field and watch them circle a couple of times to find their bearings and then fly off, usually to the north/north west. The seventeen mile-long branch line to Southminster and Burnham-on-Crouch was served by an almost hourly branch passenger as well as a daily freight service and often a twice daily heavy sand train from the Southminster quarries and Burnham-on-Crouch and a daily Nuclear waste train in each direction as already mentioned to Southminster for the Bradwell-on-Sea Magnox Nuclear Power Station. The line went deep into the beautiful Dengie Hundred Peninsula, an area that seemed to be my Utopia, an imaginary place between dreams and reality that was to be an influential part of my later life.

THE BEAUTIFUL DENGIE HUNDRED PENINSULA

The attractive Dengie Peninsula is surrounded by The River Crouch, The River Blackwater and beyond the windswept easterly Tillingham Marshes, the North Sea. The River Blackwater serves the historic town of Maldon, home of many active Thames Barges, and serves the boating centres of Bradwell, Maylandsea, St Lawrence Bay, Tollesbury, Mersea Island, Brightlingsea and St Osyth. Then there is the River Crouch which is possibly Britain's senior yachting river with three major yacht clubs at Burnham-on-Crouch and a further six or more further upstream.

The remote and tidy village of Tillingham is where the huge walking Martian war machines are said to have marched through the small country High Street after first landing on the nearby Tillingham Marshes in H G Wells book and Orson Welles's film 'War of the Worlds'. At nearby Bradwell-Juxta-Mare, also on the marshes is Saint Peter's Chapel, Saint Peter's on The Wall, also known as Saint Cedd's, an ancient large stone barn built a long time ago from reclaimed stones from the now undersea Roman Fort of Othona, from which the nearby village of Althorne gets its name. Saint Peter's is said to be the first Christian Church in the south of England, which was built by Saint Cedd on his way down what is now the North Sea from Lindisfarne Island off the Northumberland coast.

There is a wonderful view of The River Crouch from the Southminster branch train just east of North Fambridge station, where the railway track and 'low road' to Burnham-on-Crouch both run parallel with the river and share the same spectacular view. This section of river is called Long Pole Reach, an indication of the long poles used to steady Barge foresails when running downwind and downstream from Battlesbridge on their way to the estuary and eventually The North Sea and on to The River Thames. Before the advent of the motor vehicles, hundreds of large flat bottomed Thames sailing barges often crewed by no more than one man (the skipper or bargee) and a dog or a young boy, carried loads of Essex hay for London's vast horse population and returned full of London's horse muck and maybe more which was spread onto the clay based fields and marshes to break down the heavy clay and introduce nitrates into the marshland to help generate yet more hay for London, truly early recycling on an industrial scale. These man and a dog barges had no electricity, no radio nor radar and certainly no satellite navigation and often no engine. The art of navigation was planned by the method of dead reckoning. Dead reckoning was achieved using a compass, a lead line, the knowledge of the stars, an accurate timepiece and the dog barking from the bow of the barge as it passed various farms, especially in the dark. The barking dog making the livestock respond and the barge skipper therefore knowing, in the often fog bound rivers, exactly where he was by the response of the cattle, sheep, chickens, geese or pigs and their farms disturbed by his navigational dog.

This straight stretch of the River Crouch at Fambridge has a very special place in aviation history. It was the testing arena of the initial and famous Supermarine Seaplane, the forerunner of the famous Spitfire of World War 2. It was here that its attempts were made for the Schneider Seaplane Speed Trophy, before further development and then being relocated to The Solent in the nineteen thirties. Experimental flight was being carried out at Fambridge as early as 1909 and it became the very first aerodrome in the UK, known as Pemberton's Field. Not only was Supermarine based there, but so also was an early flyer and aircraft designer, Handley Page.

During February 1909 the first experimental flights were carried out there and a hundred years later on February 20th 2009, a Spitfire, performing aerobatics passed overhead to celebrate the centenary. At the same moment a Memorial was unveiled in the very small associated village of South Fambridge to mark the event. The seaplanes were passed over the riverbank from the river and then moved to a large corrugated-iron hanger of the project that stood at South Fambridge, on the south bank of the Crouch, whilst wheeled aircraft used the grass runway. Eventually, after relocation of Supermarine to The Solent, rust took its hold of the eventually long abandoned hanger, and in the early nineteen eighties it was demolished to make way for a small community of modern houses called Pemberton's Fields after Noel Pemberton-Billing whose vision created the aerodrome. A memorial stone now stands there and the mews were named in memory of the Supermarine and eventual Spitfire design team.

Further seaward on the same bank is the site where King Canute's historic Battle of Assandun in 1016 AD was fought, in the falling fields just east of Ashingdon Church in the direction of Canewdon Village, notorious for its history of witches. Canewdon is not named after King Canute but after Cana and Cana's people, an ancient local lord that Canvey Island was also named after, who pre-dates the Danish King Canute by some four hundred years. Canvey was documented by Alexander Ptolemy, the Greek geogropha at the time of the eventual Roman Conquest of Britain in AD43, nearly a thousand years before King Canute's victory at the Battle of Assandun, Canvey Island was part of a group of five flooding low marsh islands from Vange, stretching towards Shoeburyness, that was occupied by people known as Counus' or Cana's people who were associated with Boadicea. Was there a Counus who has been wrongly thought of as Cana, allowing for a language corruption from Counus, or are they the same tribe whose name was misspelt with passing generations, or two different leaders? What appears to be clear however is that Canewdon and Canvey were not named after King Canute. However, King Canute of Denmark did win the very bloody Battle of Assandun (Ashingdon) but with help of a traitor from the English (Saxon) side. It was an epic battle and deserves its own story.

Ashingdon Church was rebuilt to honour the battle. Stigund, appointed by Canute, was the first priest of this rebuilt church that the Saxons originally built in 970 and Canute rebuilt in 1020 as a Minster, Stigund was promoted in 1052 to be the Archbishop of Canterbury, such a high office achieved from such a small but significant Minster.

On the opposite north shore of the river, near to the Southminster railway line at Creeksea is The Cliffs, a pretty, low cliff area at which is said to be one of the three places in England that claim to be where King Canute sat and commanded the water to recede. With a large local tidal range typically of seven metres, and the extra effect of low and high pressure atmospherics and North Sea surges, strong winds and an extra wet winter's rainfall, anything is possible, but again, who knows? *It is not said.*

Between South Woodham Ferrers and Maldon is the small hilltop village of Purleigh, from which parish, the great, great grandfather of George Washington the first President of the United of States of America, Laurence Washington was the rector until, *it is said*, that he was disgraced for local womanising and subsequently emigrated to The New World, America, for the continuance of his influential dynasty. His story is displayed inside the delightful old English pub, The Liberty Bell, commonly known as the Purleigh Bell. It is well worth a visit. His remains are said to be buried in the churchyard of All Saints Church, Maldon and a reference to his connection is depicted in the elaborate stained glass Washington window in this Church of England situated in the nearby ancient Maldon High Street, coincidentally, overlooking the American influenced Wimpy Café. Due to this fascinating American connection the only pub in the charming little village of Purleigh is called ' The Purleigh Bell' as in the American 'Liberty Bell' as an acknowledgement to George Washington, but not as in Church 'Bell' in respect of the adjacent fine and supposedly haunted Purleigh Anglo Saxon church, nor as in 'Belle' being a French thing of beauty as many Essex villages have French names from our dual Kingdom history, nor indeed as in

Ship's 'Bell' as is commonly the case, as many Essex pubs are built from locally supplied surplus ships' timbers. These timbers became available after the defeat of The Spanish Armada and later the fall of Napoleon and The Battles of Trafalgar and Nile, which drastically reduced the need and building of so many wooden warships for the Royal Navy at Maldon and nearby Harwich. Naval auctions were held at Harwich for the disposal of unused timbers and the scrapping of battle worn warships and some, fine and pensioned off ships whose heavy shaped and sometimes ornate timbers will be seen to this day in the construction of so many Essex public houses, including The Liberty Bell at Purleigh, and many town houses in the historic towns such as Billericay and Maldon, from where some of the Pilgrim Fathers emigrated. Typically, to build a wooden warship would require maybe upwards of two thousand trees, Nelson's HMS Victory, albeit being a capitol ship, took eight thousand trees alone, to build. The Harwich Naval Auction also disposed of for salvage, Charles Darwin's and Captain Fitzroy's famous ship, The Beagle, which took them on the epic voyage to South America that was the basis of his theological writing 'The Origin of the Species'. The HMS Beagle was sold after completing four circumnavigations of the World to create some of the first and finest charts for the Royal Navy, some of which are still used today and playing a major part in Darwin's Theory of Evolution and the almost universal reliance of English Sea Charts and the creation of the essential English Longitude navigation standard. After extreme use and many voyages and those four circumnavigations, HMS Beagle eventually sadly ended up as a customs officers' accommodation hulk for the look out for smugglers and was tied up to the sea wall in a remote mud berth at the nearby quaint village of Paglesham on the River Roach, before eventually being sold for salvage. Some of its large wooden knees that supported the deck from the hull still exist. Until recently they formed part of the structure of the ancient boatshed in Paglesham that was visited in December 2003 by the World's media and the UK's Mars expedition Mission Director Professor Colin Pillinger to coincide with the planned moment when the UK's

'Beagle 2' landed on Mars and to have a bizarre twenty-first century celebration on Christmas Day at that remote 19th century mud berth. They almost found hard actual carbon physical evidence of the Beagle (1) in its final mud berth that still exists, and received a radio signal from Beagle 2 as it approached Mars. Initially the probe did not appear to survive its distant landing as no signal from the Beagle 2 after landing on the surface of the planet was received. However, twelve years after the unrecorded landing, in January 2015 it was spotted intact and on the surface of Mars by the American NASA 'Reconnaissance Orbiter'. It found the Beagle 2 sitting there with possibly one of its solar wings jammed by the landing impact preventing it's data transmission to earth and just waiting for an astronaut to casually wander along one day and plug in a USB stick and recover all of the information that it had gathered on that long inter-planetary journey and then while sitting in the Martian sun, before repairing the solar panel that had prevented so much priceless information being transmitted to earth.

Charming old Maldon is as important to the historic and continuous timekeeping of this planet and the solar system as Stonehenge is. For many thousands of years Stonehenge has proved and continues to prove to us that our planet, Mother Earth, has not moved from its exacting and critical solar orbit by the exact positioning of its stones to shed a precise sun-beam on the critical Heel Stone at the mid-summer solstice which occurs during June 21st of each year. The Druids with their amazingly accurate reasoning and construction abilities created such a perfect alignment of giant Heel Stone and rocks from Wales and elsewhere that NASA, Jodrell Bank in Cheshire and Goonhilly on The Lizard in Cornwall, cannot disprove. With all of their modern technology we can only doff our hats to the Druids and ask how did they do it?

Just as much a harbinger of solar timing is the High Tide of the River Blackwater turning every alternate Saturday, as the church bell at the top of Quay Hill welcomes in midday, as it has done for the thousand or so years since the church was built.

Each spring, summer and autumn weekend I would ride my bike to some destination that was two or three hours away from home at Wickford, giving four or five hours of return cycling and sufficient time to enjoy the views or company at the turning point. Often it would be to visit my sister at her house 'Florence Ville' in Mayland, on the peninsula. It always seemed a compelling ride with plenty to see, whether it were the wartime defensive relics or the beautiful countryside views. There would be so many shades of verdant green, golden crops, summer blue skies, and puffy white summer clouds with little wind nor rain, a benefit that is peculiar to this region. There was always an abundance of sunshine and the many fragrances or drifting ozone from the salt marshes and sounds of countryside nature itself. Wild flora abounded everywhere with the vetch, cowslip, cornflower and celandine swaying in the soft summer breeze with the musical accompaniment of soft buzzing of the bees and the excited call of the hovering skylark together with the crakeing sound of foraging pheasants hiding in the tall crops, gently mooing cows or noisy crows in distant high Elms, so wild life and livestock live in harmony. With the occasional soft droning of a distant tractor at work or a rattling combine harvester and away from the noise of traffic and bustling towns, with Stansted and its jets being a spoiler of maybe a decade or more in the future. A summer cycle ride alone through the Dengie countryside was a delight with none of the worries, pressures, responsibilities and goals that would come in later life. I often thought that an easy laid back life, such as this on the Dengie Peninsula could and should, go on forever.

I would eventually cycle home to Wickford after such an enjoyable day that was not yet over. Just three miles from Wickford I climbed the final long rise from bustling South Woodham Ferrers to Rettendon and as I breasted the summit at Rettendon Turnpike, suddenly, and very suddenly, there, on the huge western horizon over nearby Runwell would be a most fabulous sunset and the huge golden orb of the sun slowly and gracefully slipping behind the vast horizon as a smiling goodbye from The Dengie Peninsula and a reminder that I must return before the summer and early autumn pass before the evergreens stay green and everything else goes through the most remarkable shades of red, gold and brown. With the weeping willows and silver birches dancing beautifully in the late summer breeze and are eventually replaced by the falling leaves and the occasional chill winds of mid November, events that heralds the approach of winter. Winter, a time when the picture-postcard Burnham-on-Crouch High Street with its Wisteria adorned cottages, now became a chocolate box snow scene, and air frosts are turning the golden autumnal roadside woodlands into winter wonderlands.

IS THIS EAST ANGLIA'S SHANGRI LA?

The peninsula's rolling hills, spectacular sunrises and sunsets, crop growing farmland, salt-marshes, rivers, harbours, marinas and huge East Anglian blue skies with the sparse summer cumulus cauliflower shaped fair weather clouds floating and drifting a'high towards the coast like ancient sailing ships floating in the sky, or the chains of thunder storm carrying anvil shaped Cumulonimbus clouds marching forever eastward and onwards, make it the only unspoilt and thereby mostly unknown sparkling gem left in the south east of England. It is truly a kaleidoscope of colour. The focal centre of the Dengie Hundred surprisingly is not a major centre but a small village that is really no more than a very small hamlet named Dengie. It is however the name of the historic administrative district of the peninsula, the Dengie Hundred, which covers an area of approaching three hundred square miles. There are mixed views as to why such an area was deemed a 'Hundred' the most likely being the ability of the local laird or land owner back in deep history to raise a 'hundred' fit men to be men at arms in the case of civil war or other strife, to support the King. But maybe it is because I can think of a hundred memory glimpses of the area.

PART TWO

I see my Shangri-La...

in my paper round.

THE DECISION IS MADE

However, out of the dreams and back to the reality of busy Wickford with the need to earn some pocket money as money was still very tight some twelve years after the end of the war. In the summer of 1958 I was given a six mile (return) paper round six days a week and occasionally on a Sunday from Harringtons Newsagents in Station Avenue. This resulted in thirteen miles on my bike or bikes before reaching school each day. Tuesdays was the most hated day of the paper-round week as my 'sack' of newspapers more than doubled in weight due to the vast number of ladies weekly magazines every Tuesday. So intense was the paper round, 25% of which was on unmade roads, that I had two bikes, one that was virtually thrashed on the paper round, and another that was used for the daily seven miles return school journey and another seven miles for evening classes. The houses that I delivered to were mostly of pre-war stock if not Victorian or Edwardian, with gates, hedges, dark damp corners even after sunrise, and muddy unlit paths or drives. The first day of this particular round was during a bleak and uninspiring mid November, the beautiful golds and reds of the autumn fall were now being replaced by the unattractive drooping black thicket and blackthorn of the hedgerows, bitter winds, dark mornings and jack frost hardly putting a smile on your face to compensate. In fact quite the contrary, you started asking yourself why you got out of bed so early and to what end. After an hour or so doing the round on a major housing estate at Wickford, my route took me away from the Belmont area after summiting the highest part of Wickford and skirted a six acre ploughed field before rejoining the few residences in Oak Close. After making that muddy short cut just after twilight, I returned to a section of the London Road, which I was not so familiar with, and after crossing the road I went to my next delivery address of that section of road, 'Shangri La' of London Road. I was gobsmacked, its frontage stood bold and beautiful in the bright rising autumn Sun and for once I was spellbound. I gingerly pushed my laden bike along its U-shape drive of loose white marble granite chips in a manner that hopefully would not awaken the occupants as I felt as though I was intruding its grandeur and quietly put the Times broadsheet newspaper that had been ordered through its large letter box in its twin broad golden oak front doors. I was almost embarrassed to be there in such beautiful surroundings. In a town consisting mostly of dull and unloved pre-war housing, here was a recently built beauty of light yellow brick with the modern 1960 style large panoramic windows adorned with huge white drape lace curtains, a chimney-less low pitch roof, and to add some natural beauty there was a seven feet high, five feet in diameter mature Pampas Grass gently swaying in front of each front window. A magnificent 'Shangri La' of a house, and not by name alone. A desire to own such elegance one day seemed well out of my future reach but that desire would drive me for all of my future years and would stay with me for the rest of my life. I was determined that a stunningly lovely dwelling such as this placed somewhere in the Dengie Hundred or similar, will be my achievable Shangri La, and not a pipe dream Utopia. I now knew what I wanted in life and somehow would find a way to get there, no matter how long, even if I would lose direction in a few wayward years in the passing of time, I was determined that I would get there, and never give up. I could see my hopeful future.

However, I was also spurred on by the then current Mini/Jaguar E-Type/British Motorbike boom and revolution of 1960 and I wanted to one day own a scooter, or motorcycle and then a car, and eventually maybe, a house as beautiful as 'Shangri La' that sat high up London Road, or in the Dengie Peninsula, and so I needed to save money. . I had discovered and understood the work ethic of life and was going to carry on the paper round, the evening printing and shovelling manure from railway wagons until I could find a better way to earn more. The paper round, printing and wagon cleaning, were the only likely ways to get on the ladder, but how many rungs would I be able to climb? Only time would tell.

I enjoyed school and fortunately was always one of the top achievers in the top class of each year. Due to the baby boom effect, my particular year was intense with five classes of up to sixty pupils in my class with an even mix between boys and girls. I attended Wickford Secondary School which was an overcrowded Comprehensive Secondary Modern School covering all subjects other than foreign languages. Foreign Languages were available only by evening classes. I attended three evening classes weekly and also attended the local RAF 1474 Training Squadron. In the summer months four or five of us including Dennis Strong who in later life became the brains and drive behind the popular Tropical Wings tourist attraction in South Woodham Ferrers, would go bus chasing on our bicycles in the late evenings after evening class. The evening buses would go to Billericay or Rayleigh and we would ride in their slipstreams, pedalling very hard on hill climbs or if the driver rarely opened it up downhill to around 30 mph. An hour of that chasing after a long day of paper round, school, and evening class kept me very fit and I slept deeply, very deeply and had weekly evening piano lessons to boot. My week was very full, and with so much cycling it was no wonder that I wanted a scooter or motorbike as soon as I was old enough to get a provisional motorbike license. I achieved my wish, Hello scooter, bye-bye pedal bike. No more midnight bus chasing nor time for the school Chess Club, the pace of life quickened.

To add to the adventure, and before I was old enough to get a provisional motorbike/scooter licence which at that time was sixteen years of age, one of my school-friends, Peter Bird invited me to a bit of fun after school in the brickfields near to his home. I went there and he had a snorting old oily, ugly, frighteningly noisy but wonderful worn out, BSA 500 pre-war motorbike. It was great fun charging up and down the various tracks on this at a momentum well in excess of a pedal bike's speed, and with no effort at all, just hold tight and pray you don't fall off. That evening more than anything fired up my passion to one day get a powered two-wheeler but not a squeaky smoky little moped.

Not all days were good days though as I struggled to create my financial future I needed some kind of sanctuary when the chips were down and there was no one like-minded to turn to. My Dad had died when I was young, and poor old Mum had enough on her plate with six children, four of whom were still at home in the late fifties, not to want to counsel me with my woes. At times like this I could always have a comforting talk with our dog, a black spaniel that always had a listening ear. And often sneaked upstairs and jumped onto my bed late at night, which was frowned on by Mum but encouraged by me.

> *Walk tall, walk straight and look the world right in the eye,*
> *That's what my mother told me when I was about knee high,*
> *She said son be a proud man and hold your head up high,*
> *Walk tall, walk straight and look the world right in the eye,*
> *Walk Tall. (3)*

For sanctuary I would turn to the piano and drift into the oblivion and distraction from worrying matters that music allows you to do. I would often play music from Strauss if I was feeling cheesed off, the mellifluous 'Tales of The Vienna Woods' was sure to set the mind at peace, If I was happy then 'The Harry Lime Theme' would match my mood and if I was frustrated however then 'The Dambusters Theme' would let go a lot of my anger, Mum's poor old piano really took a thumping with this piece as with the left hand on the bass (Forte) keys I played the introduction that simulated the rolling, pulsating and increasingly loud harmonic thunder of the approaching Merlin engines of the Lancaster bombers, getting louder and louder and louder until with a crescendo, Bash, the theme starts. What the neighbour's thought in the non cavity wall semi-detached house I never knew. Maybe they were partially deaf, or maybe back then, just a dozen or so years after the war's end, they just relished and reminisced in the thunderous noise of the conquering RAF being relayed on the piano next door. Either way, the piano was my escape route. I needed something as an escape as an alternative to administering violence to an innocent dustbin or a window that dared to reflect my anguished face. I did that once, breaking a window and got little satisfaction, but I did get a bill. The GCE examinations were not offered at the school, the alternative offered were the Royal Society of Arts (RSA) exams, covering English, Maths, Geography, Science, Technical Drawing, History, and Wood and Metal work. I fortunately achieved thirteen passes in these subjects, many with merits. Even though I was very good academically my heart was in the nuts and bolts world of my Meccano set and mending my bike and drawing intricate technical items for the fun of it, typically a cross section of a main line diesel electric locomotive or a section of the Forth Bridge. This led me to my first career as a Heavy Goods Vehicle Apprentice Mechanic and an array of motor cycles that culminated in a powerful and stunning Vincent motorbike. Then later in life owning an exciting and relatively exotic Italian Lancia Dealership when Lancia's incomparable Integralis, were World Rally Champions for an amazing seven years, but never a banker. Maybe from some viewpoints I made the right decision, but.

Due to the overcrowding at the Secondary School, our entire second school year of pupils and staff were bussed out to a new and partially vacant grammar school some five miles away namely 'The Rayleigh Sweyne'. The Wickford secondary second year of two hundred or more pupils were collected each morning at the Wickford School gates by a collection of very colourful green and yellow brand new Bedford Duple Vega coaches owned by Ashdown's the Vauxhall dealer from Danbury, some ten miles away. Occasionally there would be a substitution in the fleet by an awful drab, old pre-war Guy Otter single deck coach that was always very dirty, from Cambell's of nearby Pound Lane, Pitsea. It stank of cigarette ash and damp and had a depressing dark interior with a dark brown flock seating material and dirty windows It was noticeably slower and noisier than the modern Bedfords as the driver struggled with its noisy and clunky, agricultural gearbox. The Guy's tyres were always covered with awful brown Essex clay with mud splattered on its bodywork where it had been parked in the field in Pitsea that was its depot. It was like its namesake an Otter that had just crept out of a muddy creek after an early morning frolic covered in Pitsea Thames mud. All of us kids would welcome it with a chorus of boos and disdain when it approached and would jostle position to get into one of the smart modern Bedford Duplex with their panoramic roof windows, radios and light and airy interiors. The School Year started 9.00 am Thursday 4th September 1958 and promptly ended the following afternoon. 3.00pm Friday 5^{th}1958, after just two days, and we never saw that school at Rayleigh again because...

THE WICKFORD FLOOD

Autumn 1958

At the time I was living with my brother and sisters in my Mum's nineteen twenties semi-detached house alongside Brock Hill on the way out of Wickford. The house sat high overlooking the fields at the back and the road at the front and was therefore draughty as well as being tired, and small, it was cosy in nature even if it was cold in the winter, but it was our home. The next day Saturday 6th I was woken rather early in the morning by an unusual amount of traffic and trucks passing my bedroom window, so dramatic was the traffic flow that I quickly dressed and ran out and spoke to one of the slow moving truck drivers, who said that due to an almighty overnight storm. The Town Centre of Wickford was unusually and deeply flooded by the River Crouch and all traffic was being diverted. I hastened to the newsagents to do my daily paper round and what confronted me was unbelievable. Most of Wickford's medium sized town centre was flooded by four feet of water where more than three inches of rain had fallen overnight in just ninety minutes. The narrow and sleepy River Crouch was unable to cope not only with Wickford's rain, but also to take the excess water coming down from the high villages of Crays Hill and Ramsden Heath and the large hilltop town and surrounding meadows of Billericay, some five miles away that came down the Crouch Vale to Wickford on its way to the sea. The problem was the Crouch's meandering nature through the flat parklands and fields of Wickford and hundreds of years of unattended overhanging trees causing beaver type log jams and huge floods of backed up water.

To add to the drama, a green Eastern National Bristol double deck bus of route 251 which was the hourly prestige Southend-on-Sea to London Wood Green service, sat stationary and marooned in a rising six feet (approximately two metres) of floodwater at the London Road/ High Street, Halls Corner junction which is situated next to the convergence of two Crouch tributaries and a weird railway reservoir built to serve the many steam locomotives of the area. The bus engine had failed the previous evening after consuming flood water and failing like an abandoned Sunbeam Talbot car that was also trying to wade through the flooded junction. Upstairs were sixteen rather unhappy passengers who had no option but to seek refuge there in the rising floodwater, during the previous late evening. They had stayed there all of that autumn cold damp night, with no heating nor lighting and only the comfort, or lack of it, of the rather basic bus seats to sleep on as it did not have the more luxurious coach seats. The bus driver was sitting crouched up on top off his steering wheel, where he had been all night, as he could not escape the rising water in his small cab, a true drama in the dark.

The stout local Police Sergeant, Sergeant Adams arrived and muttered, "what the hell do I do with this situation" to which I suggested that he should contact the local builders, Carter and Ward Ltd, who had recently purchased an amphibious DUKH type army landing craft, that I saw trundle through the High Street in a small convoy of ex military vehicles that they had purchased earlier in the week, and ask if they could launch a rescue mission to the stranded bus passengers with it. Unfortunately he was told that it was not immediately serviceable. Hearing of the passengers' plight however, Silva Carter of Carter and Ward roused their mechanics and asked them to, if possible ignore their own flooding problems and report to the flooded workshops on this unscheduled Saturday morning, to make the DUKH usable as quickly as possible, which they did without a second thought, and within a couple of hours or so the DUKH landing craft was in action and helping the relief effort.

VIC PLIOPA.

The unavoidable delay was too much for some of the elderly passengers to endure. Fortunately, step forward a certain Victor Pliopa. Vic was a well-known and popular market-stall greengrocer, a very tall but likeable Latvian immigrant. *It is said that* Vic had arrived on our shores by escaping his motherland by joining the Latvian army, enlisting into their border guard, and then jumping the border to the next country of Estonia and repeating this process several times over until he eventually arrives several years later at Harwich, as a persecuted political immigrant. Once here and virtually penniless, he wouldn't give up and he opened a 7 day a week fruit and vegetable market-stall in Romford Market and soon after, another stall in the Wickford Broadway, renting a pavement-side plot of land from my family, much to the dismay of the local five and a half days a week greengrocers. Unfortunately, his stall, like most other High Street properties, had no flood protection and when Vic went to open his stall that sat on the junction of The

Broadway and Southend Road and backed onto the river, for business that Saturday morning, he found nothing but flood-water and devastation. All of his fruit & veg' was floating amid other flood debris and ruined stock and was drifting down the Broadway on the now ebbing tide and stream towards Battlesbridge and eventually The North Sea beyond Burnham-on-Crouch.

Vic, having experienced and overcome so much hardship in his impoverished Eastern European homeland did not stand and moan, but instead using his tall 6ft 6"height and wide frame, waded slowly into the cold floodwater surrounding the forlorn bus. With others I watched in amazement as the rubbish strewn water now flowing fast, was up to his shoulders by the time he arrived at the bus and he took off the marooned passengers one by one and carried them on his broad shoulders to much applause to the small un-flooded area of the High Street, nearer to what was then, Woolworth's.

All that is but three elderly and frail ladies, who understandably were too scared and modest for such a rescue aboard this gallant foreigner's shoulders, they were later rescued by the now serviceable DUKH. This was later accompanied by a small fleet of rowing skiffs/boats commandeered by the police from Lake Meadows, of Billericay. The town's shops and their stock were ruined, and for some years later, muddy high water marks could be seen four or five feet up the wallpaper of many of the shops until their walls had dried out and were redecorated. Where did this leave me with yet again after the 1953 and now 1958 floods, no schooling, and I wanted some exam results to get a career.

FINAL SCHOOLDAYS

Well, my new school of only two days, the Rayleigh Sweyne, unfortunately had been built on an ancient uncharted and dried up riverbed, and consequently also suffered the same storm and was flooded the same weekend as Wickford, and therefore was closed due to the extensive flood damage it had sustained to the walls, timber frames, electrics and parquet flooring. The result was that I, and all my year of two hundred, had several weeks off school having fun and adventures with my mates until a remedy was found. Essex County Council eventually found the answer and managed to bring forward the completion of a new and therefore vacant infant school on a small hill in Church Road, Basildon, 'The Bryn', for the 'Wickford two hundred' to accommodate.

Infant school it certainly was, with very low desks, low seats, low toilets and very easy climb stairs with low banisters. The Wickford school geography teacher, a corporal punishment advocating Welshman by the name of Mr Richards, became its head teacher, and consequently an Eisteddfod, an annual Welsh Arts and Music Festival, was planned for the pupils for the summer at the Bryn. (Bryn is Welsh for the 'Little Hill'). The Eisteddfod went off well with most of the students taking part including a piano rendition of the Blue Danube that Mr Richards asked me to play, happy-days indeed for Mr Richards, he had created a Welsh culture centre in what was then a culture-less Basildon.

Ashdown's again supplied their smart Duple Vegas for our daily transport to the Bryn, and unfortunately the scruffy and sad old Guy Otter of Cambell's, still made its occasional and very unwelcome appearance.

For their eventual third fourth and fifth years, the 'Wickford two hundred' were finally settled in Wickford's new Beauchamp's school, a brand new secondary modern purpose built school, near Shotgate, a school for one thousand pupils with no more bussing out, nor flood risks. I failed my eleven plus and also my thirteen plus exams, but Mr Lovelock, our class and mathematics teacher said "Whatever you do, don't give up!" Apparently I was border line on passing in both cases, my maths teacher said that as I was a victim of the post war baby boom, and examination paper marking standards had been tightened as there were not enough grammar school places to fulfil the normal GCE pass rate. I was rather cheesed off with this and took up and passed, all of the thirteen RSA options that were available to improve my future chances. I then felt partly sated of my feeling of not getting into a grammar school. I felt that I would now have enough academic proof to get somewhere.

In my final school year, which was an optional fifth year, I was advised by Mr Lovelock, also the school careers master or 'bullet-head' as he was affectionately known due to his polished baldness, that due to my grasp of arithmetic and mathematics, that I should take the London option of insurance or banking when leaving school which offered a lucrative future. I however, maybe wrongly, rejected his well-meaning advice because I had a feeling for adventure, rather than many more years at a desk, as was the recent eleven years at a school desk. I yearned for a 'hands on' mechanical future.

The major mechanical employer in the area was the Ford Motor Company at Dagenham and I approached them for an apprenticeship. I attended Ford's Apprenticeship Selection Process at Chadwell Heath, which involved technical ability and awareness, attitude, state of health, verbal examinations, and varied practical tests. On successful completion I was offered one of the sixty places available to the more than six thousand applicants, but unfortunately Ford did not have the vacancy that I was looking for, rebuilding and overhauling engines. As they said to me, "we only build new engines, we don't overhaul them". They did however offer me a complete choice of other vacancies including the much sought after tool-making, but again, maybe wrongly, like Mr Lovelock's banking recommendation, I declined, and looked further into engineering and the motor trade for an exciting future.

THE SMOKY CITY AND THE SUNSHINE COAST

During my early teenage years I spent many a Saturday enjoying a visit to London by catching one of the new electric trains that left Wickford three times every hour for the forty-minute journey to London Liverpool Street. The old Great Eastern Railway's Liverpool Street terminus was a noisy, dirty, hectic but a thoroughly irresistible eighteen-platform piece of railway Victoriana. In 1959, steam locomotives still reigned supreme in East Anglia, and in the chaotic inner suburban services to the north and east London which all terminated in Liverpool Street. Many lads held the same fascination of it all as I did, and would spend meagre pocket money and paper round money most weekends just travelling to London, or 'The Big Smoke' as it was laughably known. We would marvel at the giant Meccano type one-hundred year old bridges built of masonry, steel or iron latticework or by suspension or bowstring construction, as well as the vast overall unsupported roofs of Paddington, Waterloo, or St Pancras railway termini or the huge Scotland bound locomotives at Euston or Kings Cross or the total confusion of Clapham junction. There was also the magnificent Cathedral styled masonry of St Pancras station or the National Natural History or Science Museums in Kensington, added to this was the Tower of London, Tower Bridge or other London Bridges whose foundations were built underwater with the use of incredible *submersing* wooden Victorian Casson chambers. There was also the attraction of the many steam locomotive depots around London. I visited them all and often, my favourites were the Old Oak Common loco depot that served Paddington and consequently had the Great Western Railway locos that all had attractive copper chimney tops and were known for speed and stamina on the expresses to the West Country and Wales. I also had a liking for Kentish Town Loco Shed that served St Pancras and whose locomotives covered the Midland and North Country expresses. However, everywhere was draped in what appeared to be a widow's lace of black soot which appeared to be so thick at maybe an inch deep on ledges and wall tops, indeed anything that was not vertical. The foul soot even hung onto the many porous vertical brick or masonry surfaces, and it seemed that it would be there for absolute eternity unless we had a winter of continuous acid rain and also if the councils could continually clear the street drains of the excessive amount of thick soot that such an acid rain would wash off everywhere. Both challenges seemed impossible and very, very unlikely. The awful dirty black soot blanket seemed to be here to stay and if you sat on a wall you were likely to end up with soot stained trousers and a roasting from Mum. As factories nationwide shut down their factory chimneys at week-ends, Monday, with its temporary cleaner air, became the traditional national wash day, but during almost any day you could see the white sheets of each household flapping and billowing in the gusting breeze as they hung tentatively from the windows and balconies of the many, many Victorian tenements that overlooked the smoky London termini. Coming from the country, as I did, I often wondered how the London women endured their immaculate clean laundry linen getting so absolutely spoilt within minutes of being hung outside by the filthy smoke being continuously belched out by the dozens of hard working steam locomotives that visited the many platforms below, every hour of every day. A typical example was a very large and powerful steam locomotive that left Kings Cross at about 11.30 every morning with a large train of some fifteen well-filled coaches heading for distant Newcastle. Being a large train it would stand for loading at the very longest platform, which not only was long but also offered an almost straight piece of track to the entrance of The Gasworks Tunnels on the way out of the station. This straight stretch was important to help avoid unwanted locomotive wheel spinning and train stalling on the alternative curving track from other platforms with their many crossovers, as it struggled with its task to pull its heavy and long train from a dead stand to an acceptable 10 mph slow struggling trot, to prevent the entire train stalling inside the long Gasworks tunnel. This would be a huge embarrassment to the railway company and passengers, and the near asphyxiation in the tunnel of the locomotive crew at the head of the train as well as delaying the entire days services to and from 'The Cross' as it was known. Matters were made worse as that particular platform was always used earlier in the morning by a huge experimental diesel locomotive that spilt and leaked diesel fuel and engine oil onto the track as it sat idling readying itself for the 10am Flying Scotsman service to Edinburgh. The locomotive was called 'The Deltic' which was built and owned by English Electric/Napier and loaned to British Rail for long term testing and appraisal on the route from London, Kings Cross to Edinburgh. The Deltic had two huge almost indestructible Napier two stroke diesel marine engines each built in a triangular format and without cylinder heads but with three crankshafts, six in all, that were used extensively in motor torpedo boats and was the only locomotive of any sort that could match or nearly match the very reliable, fast and powerful steam locomotives of designers Gresley, Peppercorn and Thompson, whose capabilities of hauling very heavy trains at high speed over very long distances to the north, were legendary. The Deltic was claimed to be the most powerful diesel locomotive in the world, but it leaked oil as diesel engines do, both sump and fuel oil.

So, moments before the allotted time of the 11.30 Newcastle departure, the fireman of the steam locomotive at the head of the waiting train ensured that the loco would reach maximum boiler pressure of 225 lbs per square inch, and its safety valves would 'pop' to an accompanying tremendous rush of steam and noise as the excess steam pressure escaped into the atmosphere and deafened the station's loud speaker system. Exactly on time, the guard frantically waved his green flag whilst fiercely blowing his whistle maybe fifteen loaded coaches away at the far end of the platform to make himself heard followed by a brief blast of the locomotives whistle, followed by a longer shriek from the smaller stock movement shunting engine that was trapped and unhooked at the far rear end of the train, deep in the station after pulling the empty coaches in earlier. The activity that followed was almost theatrical. The lead locomotive driver could clearly be seen trying to gently move the over-sensitive regulator with enough control to give a very slow pull away to the train and to avoid a dramatic and sometimes uncontrollable wheel-spin, that if uncontrolled could lead to significant damage to the loco's motion and valve gear. Often the loco's large wheels would slip on the Deltic's previously spilt diesel fuel that had leaked onto the track an hour or so earlier and run wild with a virtual volcano of steam, smoke, noise and some of the valuable contents of the fire rocketing with great force more than fifty feet into the London sky from it's chimney, with the soot and embers landing on the washing that was hanging out to dry. The driver would be seen fighting with the regulator, engine brakes and valve controls and get his stationary but runaway charge properly under control to avoid self-destruction. The wheels could be rotating at twenty miles per hour whilst the loco and its train stood motionless and then with a heavy and very deep thump, thump, thump, the engine would eventually get a grip on the rails with the help of some sand dropped onto the track immediately in front of the locos driving wheels controlled by the fireman, and climb out of the station on its long fast run up North, with the thumping and valiant struggle of the stock movement loco echoing in the huge arched roof of the station, at the rear coming into earshot from the bowels of the station, getting ever louder as it pushed with all of its might to ensure the successful on-time departure of this monstrous train. There would then be a sudden total drop in this noisy event as the loco at the head of the train was now muted as it entered the Gasworks tunnel and the stock movement loco after exerting so much energy pushing the train out of the station from the rear through the uncoupled buffers, suddenly reached the departure end of the long platform and braked to a sudden stop at the shunt low level ground signal as the departing train vanished with increasing haste into the smoke filled tunnel and headed for Newcastle some three hundred miles away with a vanishing thunder of the locomotive now deep in the tunnel only being heard by the loco's crew and the passengers in the first few coaches. Many, many times daily a similar event happened at The Cross, and the giant steam engine often in charge of the 11.30 to Newcastle was ironically named 'Tranquil', yes Tranquil, so inappropriately named it seemed when it lost its feet and filled the air with its volcanic efflux, but it was named like so many of its A3 class, after a racehorse that ran at the Doncaster Races, the town where the engine was built along with so many others, named after race horses or wildfowl. We all loved the dramatic and living being that was a steam locomotive, but we knew that combined with the awful yellow London Smog of the period and the thick soot on the buildings, that the Government's Clean Air Act of 1956 and Smokeless Fuel Zones would soon make their future replacement sadly inevitable and necessary unless an answer was found.

THE WORLD'S FIRST POLLUTION LAW, 1285 AD

It may come as a surprise to know that King Edward 1 started the fight against London's bad air when he banned the burning of sea coal back in the city in 1285 after many years of bad air related deaths and extended the ban in 1306.

Sea coal produced little heat and created a lot of soot and sulphur that mixed terribly with London's river mists and atmospheric fogs at the time and caused a lot of incurable illness.

Unfortunately, as deforestation with the growth of London eventually caused a huge shortage of available wood to burn, residents and businesses, even though aware of the risks of bronchitis and other ailments, continued to burn this cheap, easy available and low quality sea coal fuel. King Edward, after fining people heavily for breaking the ban eventually turned to the death penalty for law-breakers. However, realising that this was reducing the number of taxpayers, and needing as many taxpayers as possible to fund his wars with Scotland, Wales, France, and his attendance to the ninth and final Crusade, he decided to stop enforcing the law and ignore the problem, and so pollution continued and got worse.

With the Industrial Revolution, hundreds of years later, pollution increased until a high in 1860 London, when illness was rampant. Cows were dying in the fields around London and in 1952, with the addition of carbon monoxide from the relatively recently invented and popularised petrol driven cars, four thousand Londoners died of smog until the Clean Air Acts were passed and there was a seventy per-cent increase in sunlight in London.

The smog was made worse by unwanted mists that were often created in the autumn from the evaporating salty dampness stored in the Hackney and Barking Marshes and would creep eerily as if by stealth with the incoming tides into London's crammed East End overnight, penetrating into the already damp shanty buildings that pre-dated Charles Dickens' dank London of Oliver Twist by five hundred years, and causing much illness and death.

The fogs, caused by slowly falling low clouds just added to the problem of the river and marsh mists. *As I write this book in 2020, more than seven hundred years after King Edward's determined air pollution commission and legislation, we seem to be no nearer his goal.*

LONDON'S RAILWAYS

During the winter months we found that the warm underground trains, and the steam locomotive heated over-ground carriages, were a welcome release to a day at home that didn't have central heating, double glazing, loft insulation nor cavity wall insulation. The same can be said of the Victorian schools with their coal fired basement boiler rooms and cast iron radiators that were just too hot to touch. Many of us could see the benefits of this free and enjoyable warmth and would stay on at school for extended learning in the winter's late afternoons rather than suffer the chances of pneumonia and frozen fingers away from the protection of the hot school radiators.

After an always interesting and almost addictive day in London and on the return home on the Southend-on-Sea electric service we would always be overtaken at Stratford, Goodmayes or Brentwood by one of the many East Anglian expresses to Norwich, Harwich, Lowestoft, Great Yarmouth or 'The Essex Coast Express' to Clacton and Walton-on-the-Naze, the sunshine coast. These expresses with red and cream coaches would pass us at full flight often behind an immaculate green Gresley Sandringham steam locomotive that was in its proud but final years. The driver always had a smug smile and a slow almost regal wave to us electric train passengers as his well loaded steam train with the locomotive's large high kicking driving wheels spinning, outpaced the bustling new electric train or some of the recently introduced Diesel Electric locomotives. Most electric suburban services at the time were limited to 70mph whereas the Diesels were usually limited to 90 mph. At that time, however, British Rail were still promoting the Norwich steam hauled express service out of Liverpool Street that scheduled at three figure speeds (100mph plus) outside of London's area restrictions and into Suffolk, behind the superb and not so old Britannia Steam locomotives. However, the electric and diesel locomotives and trains had the benefit of being like a car, just turn a key and press a button and even when cold, they would work virtually immediately whereas the evocative steamers would need many hours daily preparation in the sheds for fire dropping, ash removal, clinker clearing, fire building and lighting and then time passing before there was enough boiler pressure before it could start to take on the world. During this period the tender would be filled with maybe six thousand gallons of water and six tons of coal. An express engine could consume forty gallons of natural water an hour and one ton of coal every fifty miles, depending how hard they were being driven. There was no actual mechanical limit to their top speed, which was totally dependent on the quality of the coal, the internal cleanliness of the boiler and flues, and the fitness of the fireman. The Kings Cross Scottish expresses would change loco crews on the move midway in their four hundred mile journey through a novel corridor through the tender to avoid crew fatigue slowing the train on their seven hour journey at speed. Whereas the Great Western Railway had the virtual monopoly of high output anthracite coal from the Welsh coal mines which was easy steaming, easy shovelling and high in calorific value to give the Western trains a timekeeping and speed advantage against the neighbouring railway companies to the West Country, Wales, the West Midlands or Liverpool.

The Eastern Region of British Rail also owned some ships that took freight wagons or passengers from Harwich on a six-hour journey over The North Sea to The Hook of Holland, such a service was known as The Hook Continental. Or even further was the service to Oslo in Norway and Gothenburg in Sweden called 'The Scandinavian' with a sea journey of nearer twenty-five hours. Due to occasional poor weather conditions and a sometimes boisterous North Sea, the Hook Continental and Scandinavian London bound services may well be running an hour or two late. These were prestigious and well-loaded services, that carried senior government, military or industrial passengers and a lot of baggage. They were always handled by one of Harwich, Parkeston Quay's, top locomotives and crews and given top clearance on their run to Liverpool Street to try and recover some of the lost valuable time at sea. It has been often unofficially said by loco crews that occasionally these trains broke the region's London area speed limits, *it is said* often reaching 100 mph down the Brentwood Bank and along the well maintained flat level stretches to Ilford, and also out as far as Witham and Kelvedon. Due to the ships delays in rough weather on the North Sea, the trains often still reached Liverpool Street 'behind time' after a top speed dash to London from Harwich. It was difficult for management to reprimand the drivers for speeding as it was impossible to reach London ahead of schedule in rough weather and many of the loco's had no speedometers. The old tradition was that drivers drove their train at a speed determined by the scheduled timetabled passing time of the large station clocks that predominated on the platforms edges back then, and the fitness of the fireman. The large clocks were not there so much for passengers' information but more for the accurate timekeeping of the train drivers. If the train was behind schedule, then exceeding the maximum speed was catered for. The drivers knew the maximum safe speed and the speed restrictions well. With the steam locomotives being so dependable, powerful, almost indestructible and running on home grown low cost fuel (coal) and water that was free, hard high speed running to catch up with lost time was encouraged. The railways had their own collection and storage systems of water, with this free natural resource, low cost coal, and steam locomotive construction costing less than a quarter of the cost of an equivalent power diesel locomotive to build, why then were they being replaced by the much more expensive diesel locomotives? The steam locomotive had two problems, one problem was its partial blame for the awful London killer smogs, which few thought the Diesels would, the other problem was that it would take many hours to service the steam locomotive before its daily roster. All of this needed plenty of men to work very early in the morning readying the locos for the day's work at the depots. Water was easily loaded by water cranes at the end of platforms and at depots, and some express locos could fill up on the move at 60 mph on some busy long distant routes using half mile long water troughs set between the rails every seventy miles or so, and a retractable water scoop below the tender collecting up to four thousand gallons, on the move, in one go! Whereas coal was loaded by expensive loading gantries that would lift a twelve ton coal wagon, invert it and send its' load down shoots to the waiting locos. So the modern Diesel, even with its four times the price to build, won the day. The difficult coal supplying miners unions were replaced by the difficult Arabs holding the World to ransom with the price of a barrel of oil. London got rid of its soot but it was replaced by the obnoxious, poisonous, diesel fumes and soot. Sixty years after its sudden large-scale acceptance on most of Britain's railways and roads and the epic period of the London smogs, the diesel was still falling foul of the Clean Air Act, and contributing towards the London's and the worldwide pollution problems.

It is ironic that we were convinced by the German industries that the diesels were a lot cleaner than they actually were. The diesel was always nicknamed 'the dirty diesel, a name and reputation it deserves and may live with forever. Diesel exhaust emissions create micro-particles that can block the linings of ones lungs, and that can eventually prove fatal.

We now (2020) seem to be left with a choice of controversial or impractical wind-farms, solar panels, Nuclear Power, tidal energy or the worrying problems of fracking

After King Edward 1st's initial clean air act of some seven hundred years ago and all of our latest technologies, surely there must be a way to benefit from our vast coal reserves. Or should we continue passing energy profits to the European or Chinese owners of our energy suppliers. Here is a chance for our UK universities to shine. Just pulverise, liquify, vaporize and reconstitute it into a gel and find a way to burn coal or its by-products cleanly. The potential profits would be enormous and the technologies we could export. Our country's fortunes would be reversed to an unprecedented level. The USA and Germany are reviewing the case of coal so why not us, we have universities.

JOCK THE SCOT (Mac) and a Freight Train Ride, 1961

Home at Wickford was nearly a two-mile bike ride from the town centre and the station. Occasionally my heavily used paper round or school commuting bikes would need their not very robust, exposed and unusual gears repaired. Occasionally I would leave the faulty bike at the cycle shop next to the station in the morning after freewheeling down the hills from home. I would then clean out some railway livestock wagons to earn a few bob during the day, and then collect the repaired bike in the afternoon to ride it home. Sometimes due to lack of local spares the bike would not be ready and so I had no option but to walk home, maybe a mile through the pre-war housing estate and Swan Lane and then another mile through the attractive countryside of Brock Hill.

The timing of my walk home in late afternoon would often coincide with the returning home of one of the local railway staff at the end of their shift at the vast Stratford Depot, some forty minutes away on the new electric trains.

One particular individual was a freight train guard who was known locally as Jock the Scot, I knew him as his true name of Mac, he was fit but slight in stature with heavy eyebrows over his deeply furrowed eyes with a rather quick step, cutting quite a sight in his dark blue hard-wearing uniform complete with a Great Coat that was rarely buttoned up and a peaked hat with a dark blue enamelled badge proudly declaring 'GUARD' which he wore cocked, as a Tam o' Shanter. He walked with a crooked frame due to the immense weight of his 20kg staff kit bag on one shoulder that he held strongly onto as if it was full of precious metals. The bag was more realistically a very tough heavy black leather railway staff box case that carried a high powered dual aspect lamp, a powerful white light torch, a red flag, a green flag, two whistles, some fierce matches, some tough leather gloves, a cleaning rag, a stick of chalk, a length of lamp-wick, a large flask and a big sandwich tin and last but not least, a pack of cards and two sets of darts! Altogether it was very large, difficult to carry, and very heavy, but he swiftly and incessantly strode to his home at a pace that was difficult to keep up with, proudly declaring that he came from the western lowlands of Scotland from where some of the quickest marching light infantry/rifle troops of the British army came, and that they could outmarch any European battalion. One hundred and forty paces per minute he boasted, or one hundred and ninety if they were on the double, *with* a rifle and kit. No wonder I had difficulty in keeping up with him "Where have you been today Mac"? I would ask. "Mchh" came the shrift reply," Mchh?" I would reply. "Ne, Mach lad, March!" he descriptively eventually said, this time with assertiveness, "March?" I replied, I am almost running to keep up with you Mac. No, "MARCH, came the repeated reply, "it is a large marshalling complex near Lincolnshire" was his final answer. Mac had acted as a guard from the Stratford marshalling yards with a long slow moving freight train on its daily schedule to March, some one hundred and twenty miles north. "Mch yer sassenach," he finally jested. A few weeks later, Mac invited me to enjoy a day's experience on a freight roster, which I happily accepted. Bring some sandwiches and a warm coat, and make sure it's a warm coat he added. It was an early start on one of the first passenger trains of the day out of Wickford bound for London Liverpool Street and then de-training at Stratford which is a major junction serving the Stratford freight yards and depot. We then travelled by London Transport's Central Line underground service to nearby Leyton station which was at one end of Stratford's yards, and there, in the yard were several freight trains, awaiting the signal to leave the yard to their various destinations, no diesel locomotives in sight just the steam locomotives at their fronts with a gentle gush of rushing steam from escaping boiler pressure from various parts of the locos and awaiting a responsible guard and the clear road signal to go. The scene was dirty, with black coal-dust, black puddles and grey ash everywhere, smoky and noisy but totally motivating and awesome. There was a full blue autumn sky, but you could barely see one quarter of it as it was almost continuously masked by drifting smoke, steam and dust of a Victorian if not Dickensian atmosphere that would soon come to a sad end with progress and the passing of steam. It was most certainly safety first, watch your footing, I was told, and be ready to grab something in the very likely event that you tripped or slipped. You were certain to get rather dirty and needed to have your ears and eyes wide open at all times. I was now transported from a schoolboy's white collar world into this unfamiliar but wonderfully addictive dirty, noisy, man's world, full of the wafting smells of soot, anthracite, coke, coal, steam oil and sulphur. I just didn't want to leave. With the background chaotic noise of clanging buffers and the busy squealing locomotive and wagon wheel flanges on the many tight curves in the yard, the slow chuffing and occasional barking of the steam shunting locomotives and the, whistles blowing, men shouting, clacking points and signals rattling with the distant thunder and ground tremor of an

East Anglian express dashing through nearby Stratford Junction, regulator and whistles wide, full of gusto after surmounting the long heavy climb out of Liverpool Street some five miles away with its loaded train. Is it any wonder that I eventually pursued a life in engineering but not deskwork. A career in the Heavy Goods Vehicle and the Motor Industry and Motor Cycles, rather than the suggestion of working white collar in banking or the insurance sectors of The City when I left school the following summer.

Banking, the chosen career by my careers master at school, long term may well have been the wisest and most beneficial future life for me, but on *that* day, there was just no contest, mechanical mayhem won, hands down. I was hooked. I was going to form my future in the man's world of engineering.

Moments later, Jock, after clocking in at the depot's scruffy wooden office where he was assigned a train, led me to a long rake of forty or so mixed and empty, goods wagons and stainless steel lined milk tankers headed by a powerful looking J19 six wheeled heavy duty black, and unappealingly grubby fifty or more years old freight steam locomotive. It had the attractiveness of a large hippopotamus at rest, large, dirty, stubby, top heavy, hissing, dripping dirty water from its underbelly, uncluttered but looking menacingly powerful tipping the scales at eighty eight tons or so and slowly breathing very deeply almost silently and looking ready to charge without warning. It was ready to take the empty wagon returns train to Ilford electric traction depot and works, a train that was going to be his responsibility to our intermediate destination at Ilford. Mac briefly climbed aboard the loco and planned the journey with the crew and then we walked and stumbled on the rough track-bed the length of the train, visually checking the couplings between each pair of wagons and making sure that each wagon had its handbrake off.

THE OLD GUARDS VAN

A den of promiscuity

At the far end of the train was our journey's accommodation, an old well-worn, unloved, dirty and ancient, four wheeled wooden Guard's Van (or Brake Van to give it its correct name). After Mac had heaved his heavy bag up high onto the van's platform floor we climbed up high with some difficulty to get onto and into it, where I studied this basic but rather important piece of rolling stock. It consisted of the accommodation of nearly seven feet square (or forty-nine square feet) with a couple of wooden bench seats, a heavily used office type rotating chair for the guard to view both directions from, bolted to one side of the centre line to the very worn floor, an old iron coal stove with an iron flue through the roof and panoramic windows and sliding door assemblies facing front and rear leading to open roofed balconies, and a general cupboard. Loads of dust and lose rubbish was on the burnt wooden floor in the centre of which stood a heavy cast iron pedestal atop which was a large hand-wheel that was the control of the very essential handbrake. Large colour magazine pages of naked ladies were pinned everywhere on the wooden walls with the odd double page spread brightening up the otherwise grubby and colourless interior of this fascinating old piece of railway railwayana where a guard might spend his entire eight hour shift, or more, often without any communication with the outside world. There were dozens of dart holes in the coloured pages and various parts of their subjects' anatomy seemed to have suffered considerably more than their arms hands and toes. Mac explained that often the guard, the van and its train may stand for many hours in a siding or freight yard waiting for more important commuter or express trains to clear a path for it, especially around the rush hours, and the guard needed something to keep him awake and pass the time. Portable radios were not yet commonplace and were not allowed when on duty but anyway would not be heard in the very noisy van when on the move and would wrongly hide the distant noise of the loco's whistle signalling when the driver was given the road and would cause sack-able chaos. So solitude with a roaring salamander brazier in the winter became part of a freight guard's life, and centre spreads came to the rescue. If no one had left a dartboard in the van then the centre spread girls became the target. Things now became clear and I understood why Mac carried two sets of darts in his large leather case. Often whilst a long standing in a predictable holding siding the fireman and driver would take it in turns to walk the length of the train to the guards van and enjoy a game or two of darts and a mug of tea from the locomotive's large hot water enamel jug and a rest until the engine whistle was blown to stop the game of darts as a green signal needed to be obeyed and the crew very quickly returned to their stations. My young eyes opened in amazement at these Playboy double pages spreads that were generally not easily available in the late fifties and well before the days of page three, here they were in full and glorious Technicolor. Mac said "They lasses get a wee cold from the draughts when we get a'rollin' so British Rail with its kind heart, supplies the salamander there to keep them warm, och aye!" And then proceeded to prepare this mobile gallery of artistry in a wheeled garden shed for the slow forty-five minute journey to Ilford. Hanging a red tail oil light to a bracket at the rear, and waiting a few moments to ensure that it didn't self extinguish, which would mean trimming the wick to get a brighter yellow flame and no black soot which would discolour the red tail lens. After a distant shriek from the engine's whistle, and a vigorous wave by Mac of his large green flag to the driver, Mac said, "That's it lad, we're off, get ready to hold tight." There was no motion, no motion at all, just the distant muffled chuffing of our engine pulling very gently away, I looked quizzically at Mac who could see my concern and said "nae worry lad, we will move in a minute or so...with a jolt".

While I am sitting there pensively in the silent but draughty wooden guard's van, I am only aware of a calamity of distant noises outside in the shunting yard, however I pick up on a rhythmic sound of striking, clattering metal that is getting more frequent, louder and nearer by the moment, "This is it" shouts Mac as he hastily tries to loosen the large brake control wheel in the centre of the van and with a violent jolt, I get catapulted off my seat and onto the burnt, dirty and unswept floor whilst Mac managed to cling onto the virtually ineffective handbrake wheel. A further attempt at loosening off the brake wheel caused Mac to explain... The job of a freight train guard is to protect his train, locomotive and crew from danger, be it a collision from a following train in fog, poor light, or in the case of a breakdown or derailment, or to control unhitched wagons. The breaking of a coupling chain between two wagons can create a disastrous set of consequences, especially as the locomotive crew have almost no way of knowing of a broken coupling in the dark or fog and little way of knowing of the event otherwise, especially on a loose coupled freight train. A loose coupled freight was by far the most common freight back then, and was a freight train where none of the wagons had dynamic brakes, the entire braking of the train on the move was done by the locomotive's brakes which were very much limited by the weight of the locomotive, and by the assistance of the emergency brake of the guards (brake) van. Most of the heavy freights needed a locomotive of more than 50 tons weight to get sufficient adhesion between the steel wheel flanges and the track, to slow the train down to a slow stop, especially in damp conditions when the loco's wheel sanders might be used to help adhesion. As an added safety measure, loose-coupled (un-braked) trains were limited to a top speed of around 30 mph. Most wagons were open wagons of ten tons carrying capacity and were linked to the next by a large wrought iron chain of three links, which fell slack when the train was stationary on a down gradient or on the overrun and snatched tight when the train pulled away or was climbing a hill. The danger was that as the train pulled away, one of the wagon chains could snap under the sudden excessive snatch load and the tail of the train would run free. Although unlikely it was more likely of chains towards the ends of a long, heavy train. When the train pulled away there would be an almost unavoidable opening concertina action of the wagons on their buffer springs once the entire train of wagons and not just the front wagons were in motion with a consequence that the snatch load between each wagon got sooner and more violent than the chain before it to a point that the rear wagon and guards van did not start moving until the locomotive and front wagons had already pulled away and were now travelling at maybe 15 mph and had travelled twenty five feet before the guard's van was catapulted into action, which was our experience. By careful use of the guard's van handbrake, the guard could compromise the awful recoiling snatch load to avoid any of the wagon link chains snapping.

The snatch load was so violent that the 'Salamander', a cast iron coal fired stove heater bolted to the wood floor in the centre of the van, would suffer an extreme reciprocating mass inertia stress on the often burnt and weakened floor mountings and break free, toppling over and if alight eventually setting light to the guards van that never carried an extinguisher nor a roaming yard guard to act as a fireman when the trains were parked up. Often in ones travels in the fifties and sixties, you would see a totally burnt out guards van in a station siding and wonder what had happened and why, it was unlikely to be arson, vandalism nor a lightning strike, it was either the stove broke free and toppled over or it got so hot that it would set light to the nearby page three and centre spreads pages that adorned the vans interior, and if the van was left typically unattended at the end of a shift, it would turn the van into a torch. Colour pages certainly risked becoming very hot property.

After a short blast of the distant loco's whistle and with the train ready to pull away, the locomotive crew, like the guard, trained at taking care with the couplings, had eased away very cautiously over the meandering track over the various points and were heading for the main line. The loco had pulled away some twenty seconds after announcing its intention on the departure warning whistle and before the both of us in the rear of the train were snatched off our seats by the sudden snatch departure as all of the chain links suddenly became taught. Soon we were settling down to the slow and steady mechanical rhythm of all the four wheel wagons calling out 'Clonk, Clonk, Clonk', in unison as they passed each rail joint every sixty feet throughout the journey, just as the monotonous sound of the Southend-on-Sea Pier train shouts to the coast as it commutes to its remote destination nearly two miles out to sea and back. Whoever designed that pier railway where the wheelbase of the coaches was identical to the length of each piece of track, making the very loud and repetitious donk, donk, donk, noise heard far along the coast and out to sea, and hammer blowing the entire pier's iron structure deeper into the mud and sand as the years went on, needed tying to the pier at low tide for his error.

Indeed in 2001 some of the Victorian cast iron support legs did suddenly sink into the sands taking the track's horizontal alignment down with them. The support legs have sand and water vents formed into the lower parts of their structures so that when the bottoms of them are exposed at low tide, the corrosive salt water mix can drain out. This system works until the vents are hammered permanently below the sand level by the pile driving effect of the train's donk, donk, donk and the vents are blocked. The seawater is trapped and corrosion begins. Southend Pier, bless it, was also handicapped by further bad design much more recently. In recent times alone it suffered three fires since the sixties, all of which I witnessed as I worked in the area at the time and a ship colliding into it in the seventies, events I mention in more detail much later in the text.

Back to the guards van ride... the clonking from the rail joints continue as we are travelling at about twenty-five miles per hour on the slow line amongst the suburban trains and there is a cold twenty-five miles per hour easterly headwind, so effectively we have a fifty miles per hour eastern gale whistling through our rattling old van, it is now obvious why the freight train guards are issued with such heavy duty winter great coats and why the vans have stoves. I look again around the van and see a small amount of coal and some tinder in a catchment tray for the salamander stove, it is cold and draughty enough to need the salamander's heat but too draughty to light it so we go without. Thirty minutes or so later we are approaching the Ilford flyover where we slowed to a near crawl as we climbed the steep gradient, and then descending the other side where we had a red signal and the locomotive at the head of the train gives a long blast of the whistle as a warning to Mac the guard sitting with me in the draughty heat-less guard's van that we are about to stop. At this point the guard would normally apply the big handbrake wheel in the middle of the van to prevent the un-braked wagons attempting to overrun the locomotive but it is virtually jammed and ineffective, possibly due to lack of use. This becomes a bit of a drama as Mac says 'Mind the recoil, Hold Tight'. Without an effective handbrake, the built up momentum or inertia in the wagons becomes a problem. Even though the locomotive at the head of the train is now stationery, the wagons continue to trundle slowly forward and when nearly all eighty pairs of buffers in a forty wagon train are compressed and the wagons have momentarily stopped, the kinetic energy within the buffer springs releases into a slow recoil action forcing the springs back to their uncompressed longer length and are suddenly propelling the wagons backwards at quite a rate, so we in the Guards Van are now travelling backward and upward on the flyover whilst our locomotive at the other end on the train is stationary. When the train of wagons has extended to its maximum length with all of the chains taut without the damping effect of the Guard's Vans brakes, anyone in the Guard's van will again possibly get thrown and one of the tough wrought iron chain links may well snap under the extreme tensile stress and set the now uncoupled train behind it, loose. So Mac, not for the first time said "Hold Tight again laddie" as the chains and the decompressing buffers start clanging more frequently and louder by the moment as the point of violent snatch approaches our refuge at the rear of the train and Bang! Yet again we are nearly thrown off our seats, very dramatic but at least none of the wagon chain links broke, possibly due to the damping effect of going briefly uphill, we could now sigh a relief for another day. Says Mac "I'll have to make a report of the

77

handbrake not working freely, the problem is that by the time the maintenance lads have decided to fix it, the van may be anywhere in the UK, Great Yarmouth or York, and they wouldn't be able to find it unless it is reported as a burn out, complete with it's photos of naked ladies, so sad!"

WE ARRIVE AT THE ILFORD MILK DEPOT

A green signal, a blow of the whistle, a wave of the guards green flag and the train restarts and slowly heads into a refuge siding besides the main line and opposite a milk depot, which will be the eventual destination of some empty stainless steel milk wagons that form part of our train of returning empties. At this point the loco is due to detach from its train, then continue light engine to Shenfield sidings where there was an engine dock and turntable were the loco can be turned, serviced and the tender topped up with water and coal if needed before it's return journey some two hours later ready for its next duty. With some Scottish cursing from Mac and assistance from the locomotive fireman the brake wheel in the van is slowly turned, but as there is some uncertainty of the brakes effectiveness, some of the heavier wagons in the train have their individual handbrakes 'pinned down' as a safeguard and a notice to this effect is chalked on the notice board inside the van for the next crews attention. Once given the road by a ground-frame signal, the purposeful looking but grubby loco sprints away now without any wagons, heading for Shenfield some ten miles away. Mac says, "be sprightly" and we dash, all eyes and ears on full alert, over the six busy tracks to the milk depot sidings on the south side of the busy East Anglian main line. We enter a dark cosy, wooden, almost Dickensian, cigarette smoke filled line-side 'Staff Shed,' where there was a small group of typically friendly railwaymen, all in dark blue dirty overalls or uniforms, who offered a fag and a mug of piping hot tea or, being a milk depot, a copious amount of warm milk. It was like a small workingman's club. The blue enamelled badges on their peaked caps told who they were, Fireman, Driver, Guard, Foreman, Shunter and so on. The two-hour wait for our returning heavy breathing hippopotamus soon passed by just listening to the banter and anecdotes of the men. The windows of the shed were filthy dirty from a mixture of London air, soot, smoke, steam, ash, coal dust and dirt filled rain. Even on a bright day you could hear and feel the thunder of the passing expresses, freights and suburban trains, but only catch a glimpse of their silhouettes, so dirty were the windows. The two hour wait gave me the opportunity to compare the dirty atmosphere here with that at the noisy smoky termini at Kings Cross and Liverpool Street, or the thick soot that lay inches deep on London's magnificent ancient buildings or the notorious killer yellow smog. I loved London, so exciting, so dynamic, and such wonderful buildings, but I could never at that young age, look forward to living there. The open countryside of Essex and the bracing fresh air of the cycle rides through the sunny coastal Essex was the only sensible future that I could imagine.

Two hours passed and there was a brief toot, it was 64646, our grubby but friendly six-wheeled deep breathing freight locomotive, waiting near the staff shed. The crew had replenished and turned it and returned, and were now coupling it up to a rake of loaded milk tankers. This time, in the absence of the general purpose un-braked wagons of the previous train, the brake pipe from the locomotive was connected to the leading tank wagon and we were soon ready for the off. I was invited into the semi-open cab for a cab ride, which I readily accepted and this was a whole new experience. The autumn daylight was now beginning to fall and the fierce and blinding bright yellow glow of the loco's fire inside the cab was mesmerising. Speed increased to maybe a mile a minute as unlike the previous train, this train now had dynamic brakes and only high-speed wagons and we were now on the main line and had to show a clean pair of heels to any following trains. The fire doors were closed firmly shut by the fireman to avoid a possible and very dangerous fire blowback or burst if we passed another train at speed through any tunnel like structures

At this point on an adjacent line, an express was approaching at speed. It was the hourly Norwich express from Liverpool Street. With a large green Britannia steam locomotive named 'Harold the Great" at its head and it was coming through the Ilford station after bursting out from under the rail flyover with much thunder at around eighty miles per hour. With a long howl of it's twin whistles to clear the platform edge there was a terrific blast of coal dust and ash filled air, noise and confusion as a sudden cloud of smoke from its chimney momentarily filled our semi-open cab. The passing of the express with its eleven well loaded carriages' mechanical clatter lasted for about ten seconds, when suddenly the suction behind the express cleared the smoke from our cab in an instant like a giant vacuum cleaner and the chaos had gone. I looked back at the rear of the rapidly disappearing guards van of the express that was being followed by some swirling wisps of smoke and steam and platform litter in its wake, like a pair of playful poltergeists giving chase in the vortex. As quickly as the express appeared, with our joint parting speed of around one hundred and forty miles an hour, with a rush, it was gone, still gaining momentum to storm the not too distant Ingrave Bank near Brentwood on it's very tight schedule to East Anglia, whilst no doubt some well dressed Frintonian passengers casually sip *afternoon teee'* in the First Class restaurant car! "Those Norwich drivers are such show-offs, they enjoy every moment of driving the crack expresses, lucky buggers!" shouts our dusky fireman above the mayhem, dramatically kicking open the fire-door again, full shovel in hand.   Such theatre.

Any thoughts of becoming a desk bound banker after leaving school were now totally gone, I was now hooked into a world of mechanical mayhem and would never look back.

We continued to rumble through Ilford, Manor Park, Forest Gate and Maryland stations with great elan and sense of occasion, with the superb lighting effects inside the cab as we momentarily passed at speed through the semi darkness of some wide over-bridges and stations and the heavily pulsating chimney smoke bouncing noisily on the over-bridges and entering the cab giving momentary semi blindness. I was sitting on the fireman's seat on the right of the loco and the cab was a little full with the loco driver, fireman, Jock and me. To give shovel swinging space to the fireman I was asked to sit tight to the side on the fireman's seat, which meant having some of my right-side leaning outside the ancient semi open cab and into the cold airstream. With the rattling and jostling of the busy loco giving a wonderful sensation of speed. At speed, the wonderful fire-glow pulsed rhythmically in colour between orange and white in time with the pumping action of the loco's pistons. The roar of the fire, muffling the rush of the wind and the sound of the fireman's shovel scraping the steel floor and in the background the brief but purposeful loud shouts between the fireman and the driver whilst the left of my body was roasting and the right of my body chilling, it was an experience never to forget. Above the fire door where you get a glimpse of the inferno when the fireman kicks it open to add more magical shiny black coal, there is a shelf, maybe the most important shelf on a train, on this shelf is a collection of white, randomly chipped enamelled metal jugs the contents of which being milk, tea and coffee, are kept nice and warm by the boiler, whilst a further large jug of water is kept boiling to top up more tea or the guards flask. A home from home maybe, but this machine was alive and on a hippo's adrenalin as it breathed heavily with its moderate load of laden milk tanks. I was no longer in a boys or teenager's world, I was for the second time in a day mesmerised in a man's world, a land of escape from being a youngster

. . . Freight train, freight train, go so fast, freight train freight train, go so fast, please don't tell them which train I'm on and they won't know where I've gone (4)

We then slowed through Maryland station and took the slow tight left curve, all six loco wheels squealing in protest down to Stratford

Low Level and then headed along the lines to the docks, our final destination, and sadly back to reality. The dream was over, but it wasn't a dream, just an unbelievable memory and experience.

The decision was made.

A future in an office was not for me

Ps. Mac, If you're still with us out there somewhere, then thanks a thousand for the once in a lifetime experience.

PART THREE

A NEW WORLD BEGINS

1960

A MAN ON THE MOON IS PLANNED

Very soon 1960 arrived, followed by ten years of the swinging sixties, and the popular and charismatic American President John F Kennedy taking office. During the following spring of 1961, I was travelling to Italy on a school-trip through the vast, colourful and surprisingly monotonous bulb fields of Holland, after crossing The North Sea by ship from Harwich. The train was the international 'Rheingold Express' that would take us all the way from The Hook of Holland, down through Germany and on to Basle in Switzerland passing the beautiful Lake Lucerne and then through the stunning Swiss and Italian Alps. We would then change to an Italian Express and then a local train from Milan to Finale Ligura our Mediterranean destination. Whilst travelling through Holland the train's public address system announced in French, German and then English that a Major Uri Gagarin of the United Socialist Soviet Republic had just become the first human-being to travel into space, after successfully orbiting The Earth in one hundred and eight minutes at 27,400 kph in the spacecraft, Vostok 1. This sudden and unexpected newsflash created a moment in time that I never will forget.

Later, in a defiant response, the American President, JFK claimed that America would have a Man *on* the Moon and safely back to earth before the decade was out, and according to the American media, indeed they did in 1969. Many of us saw the stunningly live TV of the Apollo lift off from Cape Canaveral. Hundreds of people watched it in full colour through the local TV shop windows as most of us still only had black and white TV at that time, it was a moment to remember. Its return journey was tracked by Jodrell Bank Radio Telescope in Cheshire, the World's most powerful of the time, however some people still doubt that the Moon was actually landed on, but I think they are just doubting Thomases, albeit there was not a representative from the Guinness Book of Records there to authenticate the event. But hey, who cares, we do have Wallace and Gromit in a 'Grand Day Out' and the Clangers with their Soup Dragon to give an enduring testimony to its likely-hood, so roll on the Sixties, without hope there is no hope, one must just believe in the future.

To add to the excitement of the period, a little later, a young Irish businessman Ronan O'Rahilly, whilst visiting The United States on a fund raising trip in 1963, discussed with President JFK, a vision of an American backed ship based Pirate Radio Station network around Britain but just outside British Territorial Waters. He proposed to name it after JFK's young daughter Caroline who was playing in The Oval Office at the time.

So, with so many others, I arrived in the sixties surrounded by mini-skirts, lively or soulful music, The Beatles, technical wonders galore, colour and enlightenment, the first man in space and a Man on the Moon Apollo programme, the Jaguar E-Type, Morris Mini, and the English Electric Lightning jet fighter (the fastest climbing aircraft in the world at the time) It was nothing more than two very powerful jet engines, an ejector seat for the pilot and a bit of streamlining and a fuel tank. It didn't actually fly nor could it glide, but was propelled as a rocket, it was a very rapid *projectile*. As it couldn't actually glide to a landing, it was more of a controlled crash-landing, the Russians and Americans couldn't catch it. In recent years over forty per cent of The World's surface of the school globes was shaded in pink, showing the large part of The World that was run by Great Britain. Great Britain also held world speed records on land (Bluebird CN7), air (Fairy Delta), water (Bluebird K7), motor cycles (Triumph), steam trains (Mallard) and invented the hovercraft (Cockerell), radar, and before the war the jet engine (Whittle) and television (Baird) and even earlier, radio (Marconi) Longitude (Harrison) and just about everything else by Trevithick, Brunel,

Watt, Stephenson, Isaac Newton and Faraday, Dunlop and Lanchester. What a great country in which to start my teenage years. And then before the decade was out, there was Concorde, a true time machine where you could leave London after breakfast and arrive in New York before breakfast... *Roll on The Sixties...*

THE RAF 1474 SQUADRON

From a schoolboy to a man

The swinging sixties had the precursor of the superb summer of 1959 of record sunshine and temperatures in the UK, which followed the terrible autumn floods of 1958. In 1959 there were plenty of good feelings with the introduction of the stylish new Ford Anglia with its reverse rake rear window, the incredible Mini which was like absolutely nothing before, the exciting two miles a minute Triumph Bonneville and Norton Dominator high speed motor cycles, and soon after, the stunningly beautiful 150 mph Jaguar E-Type as well as a huge dress revolution with the Carnaby Street fashions of Mary Quant's teenage girls styling, and the daring miniskirts. There was also the widespread growth and popularity of the transistor pocket size radio (Tranny). Like so many other lads I left the scouts and joined something a bit more adventurous, in this case it was the ATC, 1474 Training Squadron of the RAF. Flying lessons in an RAF Chipmunk and rifle shooting were given at North Weald aerodrome and gun drill, gun servicing, unarmed combat, first aid, Morse code, the principles of flight and map reading in detail were carried out in a typical RAF wooden mess hut building close to Wickford's town centre. The most challenging experience was to endure the ninety-minute induction lecture that was given by the affable and slightly over-fed Squadron Leader and his aggressive Adjutant in their smart Prussian Blue Officers uniforms. This was done within the Squadron Leader's office with all windows and doors closed whilst he got through four large cigars as only a man of his calibre could. With us newcomers suffering from watering eyes, sore throats and involuntary coughing, we were being continually scrutinised by the adjutant, also smoking a large cigar, but only one, that he made last for most of the introduction lecture, whilst he was looking for the weakest link or most likely outspoken troublemaker or insurgent amongst us. Rumour had it that he was likely to grab your balls if you were one of those fringe elements, so it didn't make sense to complain about the thick smoke. The smoke in that room was excruciatingly uncomfortable and then the next most challenging experience was to carry out under simulated combat condition, the strip, clean, rebuild and firing of an Enfield 303 or a Bren gun within twenty five seconds and in total darkness, a seemingly impossible time target. This was simulating a gun that had jammed due to overheating or ingress of sand or dirt at night in an unlit combat area. Many years later I still have the scarred knuckles to remind me of what was a frantic race against the stopwatch and a bawling Sergeant it was. Of equal importance was the unarmed combat training. The assumption is that your plane has downed in enemy territory and you are alone with your pistol and that you are confronted by an angry farmer, or worse, also you may well be injured or your pistol jammed. The theory is to use the weight and momentum of your opponent to your own advantage with little effort from yourself. To achieve this takes very sharp timing to suddenly drop as the opponent makes his initial lunge at you, grab one of his flaying arms and somersault him over your rather solid and crouched form by putting your knees or back into his groin to act as a very painful pivot. Unless you are unlucky, the assailant will lay there winded for a moment, the larger he is, the heavier he will fall and the more winded he will be, at which point you make your escape if indeed that is the best option. I ended up with much useful experience in the squadron and a ruptured right eardrum that was the result of rifle practice with the Lee Enfield bolt action 303 rifle. They were old and heavy but reliable and accurate, and could discharge some thirty aimed bullets per minute

We also practised parade ground marching and presentation of arms as well as the basics of radio technology and the use of radios, Morse Code and semaphore signalling.

I loved the days and evenings with the ATC mixing with new and old friends and I left without a really good reason other than I wanted to enjoy life on my motorbike and biker mates and local girls as I didn't feel that a commitment to the military, super exciting as it might have been, was really for me yet. Maybe when I would be a little older it would be different, but I was not yet ready to commit myself to a long-term adventure. Just as Mr Lovelock's suggestion of banking that I chose to ignore, maybe this was another missed opportunity, I'll never know.

A RATHER LONG CYCLE RIDE

To Mersea Island and Walton-on-the-Naze

Another summer came and my neighbour Leslie Ball and I decided to be a bit adventurous and go on a cycling/camping holiday for a week to Mersea Island before finally we got our driving licences and then mothballed our bikes. We found a campsite advertised complete with sailing dinghies at the east end of Mersea Island some thirty-five miles away. As the summer school holidays came, we packed some necessities, a tent and a paraffin camping stove and after pushing the laden bikes to the top of Brock Hill in Wickford where we both lived, we made our way across the top of the southern section of The East Anglian Heights on our way to Maldon which would be a good place to break the journey some fifteen miles away. We went through the villages of Downham, Rettendon Common and East Hanningfield before passing the picture postcard Lepers Colony with its thatched roofs that is run by a sisterhood of Nuns in Bicknacre, before continuing through Woodham Mortimer and Purleigh, and then finally to the ancient and fascinating town of Maldon. We stopped at Maldon for some refreshments on the extensive and scenic promenade alongside the still working Thames Sailing Barges, and then took a quick look at the rather intense and still existing railway system. At that time Maldon still had two passenger stations, East and West, two freight yards, a twin track tunnel, a magnificent and high brick arched steel rail viaduct over the River Blackwater, a rail triangle, a level crossing with a light traffic underpass, some port facilities, a loco shed and turntable, two large goods sheds, and a vast goods shed, a large signal box and a Jacobean styled Station building and house. Besides Baltic timber imports, and the export of fruit, vegetables and aggregates, much local produce was despatched from here each year. Eight thousand tons of locally grown green peas were handled each season and on July 11th 1891, nine hundred and twenty five tons, filling three hundred and thirteen railway wagons were sent to London in one morning and reached the hotels, canners and grocers by nine o'clock that same morning. That is a staggering number of hand picked green peas, where is progress since then. Empty fields, forgotten green houses and a railway that is nothing but an extinct fading memory but to a very few of us, where has all of that freight gone? We were not to know that within ten years, all of this would be history and totally gone with the exception of the architecturally safe station building, which became a restaurant, a disused tunnel and two goods buildings.

 We then made our way further through Heybridge, Millbeach, Goldhanger, Tolleshunt D'arcy, Salcott-cum-Virley and Great Wigborough villages and finally to Peldon where we joined the Colchester to Mersea main road after so many miles of a quiet rural road. We turned right onto the Mersea road to be confronted with a half-mile long traffic queue. It had clearly been there for some time as many of the car and bus occupants were enjoying the sun on the grass verges and greenswards. We slowly cycled to the front of this unexpected obstacle to find that the road ahead was extensively flooded. Flooded with salt-water to a rising depth of two feet or more, the tide was on the rise as it was a strood, Mersea Strood.

The floodwater was approaching a high tide, which occurs twice every twenty four hours or so and floods the half mile long strood. The Mersea Strood is the only approach road to the island and once the road starts to flood all traffic including buses in both directions, stop, much like Canvey Island in its earlier years before they built the Colvin Bridge. Depending on the strength and range of the tide, traffic can be bought to a standstill for several hours. Obviously there are some people who take a chance and cross too soon and get water terminally into their engines, and those with 4x4 vehicles that know what the depth limits are but then create long term rust problems as the salt water spray penetrates everywhere underneath their tall vehicles even at 5 mph.

We waited with so many others in the sun for an hour or so before wading through the slowly lowering water to the island and then headed to our campsite destination a couple of miles along the northern road towards the eastern point.

The campsite was much better than we had hoped for with a clean shower and toilet block and a small path to the waterside. The camping field faced southeast and had a gentle slope, which meant that it was well drained and being at one extreme of the sunshine coast, attracted a lot of sunshine. We made camp and an evening stove meal and hit the pillow after such a long ride with laden bikes and a late start.

The next day we ventured down to the natural beach. There were a couple of clinker built, green sailing dinghies for campers to use, a pretty beach with overhanging trees giving shade from the three feet high cliffs and the water was warm, pleasantly warm. The reason for this unexpected warmth was that the beach was just a mile or so opposite the Bradwell Nuclear Power Station that pumped out hundreds of thousands of gallons of heated water every hour of every day and night into the River Blackwater and its estuary. There is always a down side to good events, and this was the water's warmth encouraging the breeding of jellyfish that moved very much with the tides.

Jellyfish are not strong swimmers and so drift slowly with the tide out to sea and back, some-times in small swarms. Very unwelcome they are, but rarely sting and if so it is rarely serious, similar to a wasp sting that can be treated with anti-histamine cream or vinegar.

When the jellyfish were in any number we would avoid them by using the time to learn by trial and error how to sail one of the dinghies, especially the art of tacking. All in all we had a very pleasant time there and after a couple of days we planned to leave the tent there and make a long day of cycling to Walton- on-the-Naze and back, around eighty miles return but with a few hours spare to enjoy Walton's prime beach.

Obviously we timed the journey to avoid wasted time at the Strood awaiting the tide to drop, but it was still a longish journey going inland to Colchester to cross the River Colne at the first bridge and then, after finding our way through Colchester's busy streets taking the A120 to Weeley and then the B1033 to Walton-on-the-Naze. To cut down the time and mileage we thought that we would take advantage of a listed foot ferry to Wivenhoe from a landing place (hard) opposite near the bucolic Fingrinhoe crossing of the River Colne. The ferry was shown on the Ordnance Survey Map that it existed, but there were no details or contact numbers to confirm if it was still in service. We naturally assumed that as it was August, that it would still be in use and so we went out of our way a few miles in the hope of a successful and time saving crossing.

After eight miles of cycling we arrived at the sunny but seemingly abandoned riverbank hard and started looking for evidence of the ferry. Often in circumstances like this there would be a chalked blackboard with a timetable or a bench with a bell attached that you would ring for the ferryman's attention. No such luck, and after scanning both riverbanks for a large open rowboat, we decided that we were out of luck and would wait forty minutes and if still unsuccessful we would make our way to Colchester and distant Walton-on-the-Naze.

WALKING BACK TO HAPPINESS

An hour later we are cycling towards Colchester, disappointed of the no show of the ferryboat but looking forward by the mile to enjoying Walton-on-the- Naze. As we rode through the streets of Colchester it seemed that it was a dream of a summer with the sun, smiling faces and a background music that sometimes would become apparent from the houses with their windows wide open because of the warmth of the sun. It was 1961 and in particular was the music emanating from one terraced house that was Helen Shapiro singing her new and eventual top ten release of 'Walking Back to Happiness' which was happily booming out and really catching the happy mood of the time, almost a good-bye to the post-war healing period of the fifties and hello to the future and the sunny sixties. That song was truly inspirational and left us feeling very good. After passing through Colchester we were soon on the long but final leg to Walton with its pier, entertainments, beaches, ice creams and sunshine. After what seemed a very long ride, and with a very tall radio mast a mile to the north of us near the Bromleys that never seemed to vanish nor reduce in size until we got to beyond the village of Weeley, we arrived at Walton-on-the-Naze, parked our bikes near to the pier and enjoyed the vista, totally ignoring our saddle soreness, we had arrived at the sunshine coast and were very pleased to lay in the sun for a while.

After a few hours of fun we decided to make headway to our tent home, before it got dark, albeit due to the long summer days that wasn't until after ten o'clock in the evening. The miles passed surprisingly quickly, it seemed very odd, but always seems to be the way on the return leg of a journey. Maybe it feels that way because on the way out, you have not only the distance to your destination on your mind but subconsciously also the return journey which together can seem ominous, whereas on the way home you just tick away the miles with a mental satisfaction. We skipped chancing the Wivenhoe to Fingringhoe 'ghost' ferry, and arrived at the strood when tide was out and the road was dry other than a dusting of sea salt, and arrived at the tent at East Mersea and soon had the primus stove going and again, hit the pillow. After a day's break with a bit more sailing we made our way back to Wickford, home, a comfortable bed and decent meals again. I had accomplished much including the sworn oath to get motorised transport as soon as my provisional driving licence arrived in the post.

A DRIVING LICENCE AT LAST, 1962

At the age of sixteen I reluctantly laid my pedal bikes with which I shared so many happy miles and memories, in the corner of the garden shed and bought a second hand Douglas-Vespa 125 cc scooter. I was still in my final year at school at the time and was looking forward to an exciting life in the free world outside of school. It wasn't long before I discovered the shortcomings of the scooter's diminutive eight inch wheels on the average second class poorly lit Essex road, when at night time with little lighting on a newly completed road, and poor scooter lights I struck a seven inch kerb stone. With a small eight- inch front wheel it was like hitting a brick wall and it promptly threw me off. I counted the Moon twice so it was clear that I had done a double somersault, which badly sprained my right ankle when I landed and did a little damage to the scooter. Besides the poor lights and little wheels I got fed up with some lorries pushing to overtake my top speed of 42 mph which I found rather hazardous, it was just too slow on the main roads and it had to go.

Time for bigger wheels I thought and I bought a totally dead ten year old BSA 250cc C10 motor cycle that I paid just a few pounds for from a chap in Nevendon Road, at the other side of Wickford. There was no alternative but to push it home and learn something about the bike's dead magneto as I was still at school and needed to know more. The engine didn't run but I took a chance on it whilst still having the Vespa for normal use.

Two and a half miles of pushing a heavy old bike especially on a summer's day needed some serious thinking about, let alone my concern that it wasn't taxed nor insured yet. I figured that as it was totally dead and with an empty petrol tank the local police would treat it as nothing more than a trailer if they did confront me. After all I was doing no harm, and could not do any harm with an absolutely dead bike and as such I wouldn't have any trouble with the local police, most of whom knew us boys and we always gave them due respect.

To avoid any unwanted confrontation I chose a route that didn't use Wickford High Street but instead was three miles longer by going through the countryside and the village of Downham but unfortunately involving a long and very steep hill in Castledon Road Wickford. I asked my brother Alan if he would volunteer for the five-mile push, and brothers being brothers he was more than happy to oblige.

We collected the old BSA and started the arduous trek home. Pushing the dead BSA was not too difficult for the two of us, until we arrived at the bottom of the Church Hill in Castledon Road, boy was that hill tough. It seemed to go on and on and just as we appeared to breast it on a right hand bend, it climbed even steeper. Did we hate that hill and vowed never to tackle it again. After cresting the hill and pushing the bike along its crown we reached the top of Brock Hill, just a very scenic mile to the bottom and we were then home.

But hang-on, gravity had made the journey so tough so far but it was now payback time. A slight push from the top of the hill and we both leapt aboard and had a thoroughly exhilarating one mile free wheel ride to the bottom without any mechanical assistance at all and the speedometer reaching 32 mph, and just the rush of air passing our ears. This is really terrific I thought, it will be even better if and when I can get the engine running. At the foot of the hill the bike freewheeled to a stop and we dismounted and pushed it up a small rise and then we could see the last one hundred yards to our home, the feeling of elation was high after the two hour and five mile push, and then surprisingly around the corner from the opposite direction came a Police Car, just fifty yards from home, Bugger! it stopped and the two uniformed officers came over to us and asked what on earth we were doing. I tried to argue that as it was totally dead and with no fuel and no hope of running without major work that surely it came under the same trailer category as a dead car at the end of a towrope. They would have non of it and gave me a formal caution, ho hum.

What this event did prove to me is that,

1.There is definitely such a thing as bad luck

and   2. Murphy's Law always applies, what can happen, will happen.

After failing to get the BSA's faulty ignition sorted without a high cost, I bought a Triumph 150 Terrier motorcycle, a sprightly little bike that could take on most obstacles with excitement. I then achieved my first job and once graduating by age to a car licence I then alternated from a motorbike in the summers to a car in the winters.

My first car at seventeen was a 1946 Hillman Minx saloon with no heater, a slow side valve engine, awful brakes when going down a ramp backwards, but it did have a sunroof, lovely leather seats an opening windscreen and would touch 62 mph Wow! I owned it for one winter, sold it in the summer and replaced it with a Ford Consul that did have a heater, or maybe I should call it a warmer as it was never much good. When the heater-less Hillman's windscreen froze over inside with condensation from our breathing in the winter, you simply opened the windscreen fully on its top hinges and froze from the 40 mph sub zero gale! The only fun us lads had with that car was one day in 1963 we were fruitlessly chasing my brothers Alan's (Gogsy) faster Ariel motorcycle along the A127 Southend Arterial Road, when my front passenger, Micky Craven, opened the sunroof roof, whilst we were approaching sixty, stood up through the roof and whilst in a mad avant-garde moment with the effect of alcohol, he produced a sawn-off shot gun from his winter coat and let off two noisy cartridges at the distant Ariel Leader. I was livid, but as Mick said, the sawn off shotgun had a very limited range, couldn't harm a rabbit at one hundred feet, let alone a fleeing motor-bike and he had no spare cartridges, it didn't happen again, a lot of noise and a lot of worry. After that incident we frisked Mick every time before he came in the car again. I expected a lot better of him and marked his card. The Hillman Minx was replaced by a very green 1936 Vauxhall 14/6 Coupe that was bought as a joint venture for £8.00 which was typically two weeks wages for a teenage trainee or apprentice at the time.

TROUBLED GRAHAM

A group of us being Gogsy, myself, Graham and a Rettendon friend Colin Selvage, bought the Vauxhall between us donating two pounds each and consequently had great fun in it. As old as it was, it was ahead of its time with a four speed synchromesh gearbox, twelve-volt electrics, a decent heater, independent front suspension and a six-cylinder overhead valve engine. It could fly and made a mockery of any pre-war and most post war Fords. It had similarities to a Chicago hood's mobile, which unfortunately Graham could not ignore. Graham would drive the car most of the time, as his Dad would not let him have a motorcycle as being too dangerous for his chaotic behaviour. Graham's Dad Jasper seemed to be a nineteen fifties petrol head, always talking about Colin Chapman, Stirling Moss, Jack Brabham and Fangio. He modelled his moustache on that of Graham Hill and drove a lovely grey MG ZB Magnette Consort which he spent a lot of time and money on to give it a suitable image with raised rear suspension and a noisy exhaust. I got to know Graham when he was nine and I was eight and we lived opposite each other and went to the same school. As we grew older Graham followed in the slipstream of the time and drove any old car that he could get his hands on around his Dad's mostly overgrown four-acre poultry farm, apeing Broderick Crawford from TV's Highway Patrol, or a mysterious individual he called Crash Kavanagh. I often thought that he read too many comics and when too young to drive a car he rode his chainless tricycle in a crazy devil-may-care fashion in the road outside of his parent's house. Once Graham had gained a full car licence he daubed 'Christine Keeler slept here' on the boot-lid of the Vauxhall and soon was planning a fake bank raid with the Vauxhall on Barclays at Wickford High Street just for the hell of it, he was bursting with car licence testosterone, none of us wanted to take part in his stupid prank, all that is but Colin, who followed Graham wherever he went. I told Graham that he was heading for a short and long-term disaster and to totally drop the idea, but he thought he knew best and was determined to be a high-speed getaway driver albeit in a fake robbery. After the pretentious theatre in the bank with Colin, an alarming police chase followed including two dramatically driven police cars in pursuit of the manic Graham, who promptly hid the Vauxhall in his Dad's six feet high sedge grass field. Graham then sat in the Vauxhall with Colin, Gogsy and Mickey Craven, windows open and ears straining as one police car circled the closest roads to the poultry farm including the very bendy and narrow Hoe Lane with its chrome bell frantically ringing, looking for a rear exit. The second police car actually drove down the long poultry farm drive passing his family's bungalow and stopped at the field of sedge with the officers getting out of the car and studying and discussing whether to take a chance and drive into the six foot high grass knowing that like a theme park maze, they may indeed not manage to find their way out, or drive into a land drain or abandoned farm machinery. Graham said after the event that his senses were so accentuated with fear when hiding in that grass that he could not only feel but also hear his heart beating with a very heavy rhythm. He left the car hidden in the long grass for three months, and he lost a lot of sleep. His Dad, after seeing the police car dashing down the drive, guessed what was going on and was very angry, grounded Graham who had also just severely smashed his Dad's new Minivan, ending Graham in Hospital. Graham was severely rattled, with the police often watching his Dad's farm knowing that the culprit lived there. Soon afterwards he sold the Vauxhall under some very odd circumstances, we assumed it was now hot property for the Wickford Police and that Graham wanted 'out'. Graham changed remarkably after that event, no more Crash Kavanagh, dummy bank raids nor driving like a Chicago mobster. His Dad's reprimand had been most severe and had done its job.

When we used the Vauxhall it consumed a lot of oil and we took it in turns paying for the oil. It was a couple of years later that we discovered that when it was Graham's turn to top up the engine oil, he would simply withdraw the dipstick from the engine and momentarily hold the dipstick upside down to let the dirty black engine oil run towards the now upturned 'Full' mark and then show us proudly that it didn't need any oil, so he continually avoided buying any oil at all until he disposed of the car after that police chase, and we ceased trusting him. Age and the passing of time did not mature him and likeable as he was, financially he was kept at an arms-length. Graham became a used car dealer selling between dealers in Essex and the West Country but he was never any good with arithmetic and consequently in business he amassed a lot of debts amongst those dealers. His lack of reliable book keeping created a huge claimed threatened debt by the Inland Revenue, which he was unable to disprove without suitable books, and Graham was due for a very final and imminent court case for a lot of *assumed* tax. On the eve of the case Graham passed away. It seemed that he was hounded by the taxman to the very end.

His funeral at Burnham-on-Crouch was packed, mostly with Essex car dealers that liked him immensely as he was not actually totally dishonest, but was just incapable of making an annual profit and settling his bills. The dealers that attended, similar to the pallbearers who were joked to be revenue officers looking for familiar faces, were there on the very unlikely chance that his estate might have had a secret stash that could be big enough to settle his many many debts. One elderly dealer from the Wickford turned up in a wheelchair but found it too much to enter the church and returned home penniless like the taxman and everyone else.

An eulogy was read by one of the dealers who suggested that Graham, knowing his days were numbered, had a deal with the undertaker where a discount for his funeral was agreed with Graham for 'services rendered'..? services rendered? It was joked that the hearse driver noticed the mileometer going backwards on the slow drive to the church, services rendered indeed.

Graham had the last laugh, as always and even escaped the taxman, but he unfortunately left a very sad family and a disappointed group of friends.

Apparently, everyone likes a mischief-maker, just as every girl likes a rascal. Graham was indeed a mischief-maker of the highest order but never a villain, just a likeable rascal.

PART FOUR
MY FIRST EMPLOYMENT

MY FIRST JOB AS A HEAVY TRUCK MECHANIC, 1963

My first job after leaving school was as an apprentice heavy truck mechanic with C V Sales (AEC HGV) Basildon, after turning down a job opportunity with the Ford Motor Company. CV Sales (and repairs) was the main dealer in the South East for AEC heavy trucks. The dealership also carried out heavy repairs for Thornycroft, Scammel, Foden and Leyland trucks, the very heaviest and largest of trucks in the UK. Like many other lads at the time, my basic time was 57.5 hours per five and a half day week plus overtime as required at 1/3p (6P, new pence per hour) with 2 weeks annual holiday plus bank holidays.

Gross pay was £3/3/9p with a take home pay after tax of £3/1/3p (£3.06P). Amazingly at the end of each week, after paying Mum some housekeeping and running the bike, I still had some change left in my jeans pocket. To put this into perspective, petrol was 4/4 (22 new pence) per gallon, about 5P per litre. A bus driver earned £12 weekly and a conductor £9. A new minivan was £399.00 and a new Jaguar E Type was unbelievably less than £2000 excluding purchase taxes.

The work at the AEC/HGV dealership workshops was arduous, heavy and challenging, amongst a team of large, tough acting, tough talking but kindly and proud Yorkshire-men, mostly from the distant Heckmondwyke area of Yorkshire, who knew how to repeatedly and accurately swing a big fourteen-pound sledgehammer when needed. This was often when repairing the old twelve wheeled, four axle AEC Mammoth Major's rear balance beams when suffering seized or collapsed bearings, an art they taught me by issuing a stream of profanities and cursing at an imaginary individual that was taking advantage of ones grandmother as you swung that hammer, swinging it with relentless determination, gusto and hatred. In the workshop team besides the Yorkshire lads were a couple of Scots and two lads from Westmorland, and two large Essex lads, but an absolute absence of anyone from Lancashire. The War of the Roses still existed in the back of their minds and when test cricket was being played between Lancashire and Yorkshire. The updated scores were announced frequently on the extensive works public address system to great cheers or boo's as appropriate. Truth be known, theirs was like a dog and a cat relationship, they would often tease each other but were actually best friends. The Yorkies loved the Lancashire people as sparring partners that they could actually not cope without, remember, this was in 1963, many years ago, and the War of the Roses was five hundred years earlier than that. However the War of the Roses was still part of their loose banter.

The lads were all relocated from their Yorkshire homeland by a joint incentive between AEC of Southall who manufactured heavy trucks, buses and underground trains and particularly all of London's red buses and wanted an Essex centred dealership to take care of the increasing number of heavy trucks coming down from the North Country to Dover and London encouraged by the first new section of the M1. The newly formed Basildon New Town Council who needed new businesses as part of their economic plan offered new centrally heated houses to skilled staff from the North if such staff could find employment within the New Town's industrial estates, which was done by a tri-party arrangement. Typically AEC of Southall, Middlesex, would supply the stock and fittings of the new truck dealership whilst H.W.Wood of Heckmondwyke in Yorkshire who ran a fleet in excess of one thousand AEC heavy lorries would supply the trained staff, a national bank would supply the funding and Basildon Council would provide at favourable rates, the dealership land and building and housing accommodation for the new employees who had moved down from their colder but very proud Yorkshire.

The new houses were often still under construction when the Yorkshire mechanic was given his new job in distant Basildon. Each Monday morning many of the workshop staff would arrive at the Basildon dealership at 8.15 am after the long drive down the A1 and North Circular and A127, leaving their Yorkshire home soon after midnight. This situation might last no more than a very tiring six months until their new home in Basildon was ready to be moved into. They would move into local lodgings, or 'digs' as they were known, until returning to their distant families each Friday evening in Yorkshire. However, obviously, the six months were not always summer months, and not all cars back then had heaters, not only that but a few hardy souls came all the way down on open motorcycles, such was the toughness of a Yorkshire-man's spirit and the desire to live in a new modern house in warmer Basildon. With new furniture on the tick (Hire Purchase} and an escape from the Victorian cramped, unpleasant housing of the Yorkshire cities, the attraction was obvious. Such was the toughness of those no-nonsense Yorkshire lads that they repeatedly travelled so far overnight on a bike or in a car without a heater in the winter and put up with the hardships whilst looking forward to a better future.

THE BIG FREEZE WINTER OF 1963

That particular winter of 1963 was a Siberian winter and became known as The Big Freeze Winter. The snow fell in December to an average depth in southern England of twenty-four inches, which compacted and froze hard to a depth of a solid four inches on the roads that did not melt and could not be cleared until April, some four months later. It was harsh, very harsh indeed. In my mind I can still see a frozen mechanic, Dave Sulley arriving at work from Leeds that Monday morning at the dealership on his tired and well-worn snow encrusted Triumph 500 Speed Twin in the heavy snow, so cold that snow on the normally hot engine hadn't melted. He was numb and speechless and his now frozen and hence tiny piercing eyes asking for salvation. He was quickly given a continuous supply of coffee by the three sympathetic Yorkshire foremen, Ron Pye, Joe Connor and Ron Moorhouse, whilst he was allowed to very slowly thaw out and recover during the entire morning shift, hidden in the dark depths of the boiler-room.

NEW FROZEN ARRIVALS

At the dealership, the new heavy trucks continually arrived through that very bad winter as a 'chassis/toolbox 'unit from the manufacturer AEC (Associated Electrical Companies) in Southall, Middlesex (British West Southall as it was affectionately known). As most of the London Transport buses were built there it naturally became the settling point for the many coloured immigrants who by necessity immigrated from Jamaica to address the British manpower shortages caused by the war. The rolling 'chassis toolboxes' were known as such because that is exactly what they were. It was quite a sight to see one arrive at the Basildon dealership in the harsh winter of 1963. What arrived was a naked four axle, twelve wheeled HGV chassis and power unit with no body, no cab, no windscreen or wipers, no heater, no seats, just basic obligatory temporary sidelights, no mudguards nor wings on the front two axles, and red and white trade plates swinging in the biting breeze. During a typical cold, grey January day one arrived in the near blizzard. The driver sat perched and totally exposed and high in the open (no cab), doing motorbike style hand signals and heavily dressed in motorcycle clothing with goggles, leather hat and gauntlets added, and covered with thick frozen snow. He would be clutching between his legs, as a crude central heating aid, a large Thermos Flask, now full of icy slush. At the start of his journey at Southall the AEC factory canteen would have filled it with piping hot tea, by the time he crossed Chelsea

Bridge in London, he would have pulled up a couple of times and drunk the then tepid contents. A drive along The Embankment would lead him to the bus stop bay of Tower Hill tube station where he would again pull up, dash down the tube station steps and get his flask refilled with boiling water attempting to heat his body for the final two hours of the journey to Basildon. He was sitting on a four foot long wooden chest toolbox with a crude backrest, that chest was secured by two metal straps to the chassis. The only controls that he had were a steering wheel with a small instrument cluster attached to the exposed steering column, a gear lever and a handbrake and the normal three pedals. The delivery driver, after the four hour horrendous winter alfresco journey from Southall in the snow, was promptly lifted down rigger-mortis style, from his high perch by three burley Yorkshire-men, who promptly dispatched him to much cheer, to the sanctuary of the boiler room to slowly thaw out, poor sod. As he was carried past, he slowly held out his cold flask pleading for strong tea, strong *hot* tea! The rolling chassis would then enter the huge workshop where a cab and tanker body that had been hand built in anticipation, were attached over the next few days and the truck prepared for use. This became a regular event during that winter, but not usually in a full-blown blizzard.

M1 BREAKDOWN IN THE SNOW

At least once a week I would be told by one of the three foremen to use the office phone and phone home, and tell my Mum that at maybe 3.00 in the afternoon, I was about to go on an long distance overnight breakdown in the snow with a senior fitter, up North as they would say, and would not be back until the morning. On this particular day in the 1963 extreme winter, it was snowing heavily, but we had to do it, as we were the only ones in the south who had the equipment and know-how and could achieve a fix. Invariably there would be a heavily laden twelve wheel truck broken down on a major road up there or more often and even worse, in the centre lane of the newly opened first section of the new M1 Motorway near Rugby, a slow 180 miles away and we would have to travel up there, locate the victim without mobile phones, in the dark and sort the problem. More often than not it would be a seized back axle, the Achilles Heel of the HGV and a most difficult of jobs on a good day, let alone at night in atrocious winter weather with almost non-existent lighting and when you are very tired and cold. As some of the rear wheels of the failed truck were locked solid the very heavy locked up truck could not be towed to the hard shoulder or a service centre for repair, we would have to carry out the repair often in the middle lane of the motorway and remove the drive shafts and differential/s and drain the now ground metal contaminated heavy axle oil, rinse the casing and in the unpleasant virtual darkness. We then had to replace the differential/s rebuild the axle/s and replenish the oil in the axle/s depending if it was a double or single drive rear end and refit the propshaft/s which was a real chore as each axle needed more than two gallons of heavy viscosity 140 gear oil that was so thick with the cold that it was almost impossible to hand pump, so we took it in turn to slowly pump it, and with traffic flowing both sides of the stricken truck and without a national speed limit at that time, nor Police beacons, mobile lighting, high visibility yellow jackets, vehicle hazard lights and mobile phones were not yet available or even dreamed of. To protect the broken truck and the two of us in our dark blue overalls from a dangerous, if not lethal, collision from the approaching traffic, it was normal practice to remove the broken truck's driver's seat and place it in the centre of the carriageway at a distance of maybe one hundred feet behind the dead truck. It was then hoped that any approaching vehicle would spot the dark and unlit seat in the road, understand the predicament that we were in and avoid running into us, while we were underneath repairing the broken truck. During those cold bitter tiring nights, giving up was a forlorn dream, giving up was not an option we could never give up. As a matter of safety we would park the breakdown wagon with its sidelights on some fifty yard further along on the hard shoulder in the direction of the failed truck and would have to carry or drag the required replacement components to the victim in the centre carriageway as necessary. To our favour was that most traffic was much slower back then. To our disadvantage was that many vehicles had very poor 6 volt lighting and terribly unbalanced non-hydraulic and certainly no anti-lock brakes. Further, Jaguar, Aston Martin and AC from nearby Milton Keynes and Birmingham used that section of the MI as their test track for their new 150 mph sports cars, until that is, the government stepped in and stopped the practice. The relentless wind, whistling through and underneath the marooned truck, made matters rather unpleasant. With tyre splash from the rain, slush and melting snow soaking through you and the cold biting wind and numb fingers, it was no picnic and one could feel very alone in the friendless dark so far from home. We had no power tools on the wrecker, they were a luxury of the distant future or the main workshops. We were tired after the six or more hour journey from Basildon from a point where we had already been at work for seven hours before we left the depot on the way to the incident. We had started work at 8.15 am on that Tuesday morning, and had been working non-stop in the open with no heating and no evening meal nor hot drinks, and it is now 1.30am Wednesday morning, we have another six or more hour journey home in a thunderous old beast of a breakdown wagon with an ineffective heater and the snow has become a blizzard. My mind drifts . . . pray God, why did I not listen to my careers master at school and go and work in the bank? Once repaired and the failed lorry on its way again, it was time for the long journey back to Basildon in the ten wheeled breakdown wagon, which was built from a wartime RAF AEC aircraft tug. It was so slow that we only reached the dizzy heights of 42 mph on a few downhill stretches whilst coasting in neutral. This was done to give us a temporary respite from the unholy relentless and deafening racket from its large diesel engine that had absolutely no soundproofing. Conversation on the fourteen or more hour return journey was impossible unless we were coasting, it was like being in a steam locomotive cab at full tilt but without the luxury nor the abundance of heat from the loco's boiler.

You learnt to lip-read each other with little effect, physically and mentally it was very tiring and too noisy to fall asleep, but the coasting although illegal was less tiring and so maybe safer overall. It did however have its problems as when the ten-ton wrecker broached forty miles per hour it started to shake violently as it entered a speed range renown for rear wheel tramping and steering wheel oscillation (known as wheel shimmy to anyone who owned a Dagenham sixties built Ford saloon) but on a massive scale. The static and dynamic out of balance of its giant wheels and re-cut tyres came out of harmony and the entire thing shook until you slowed down to sub 40 mph again. Another major issue when coasting was the difficulty in getting the monster back into gear when travelling more than thirty miles an hour, as the huge six wheel drive transmission had no synchromesh action, just a so called 'crash' gear selection which took a lot of double de-clutching judgement, physical energy and luck to re-engage. So coasting was to be avoided but it was the only way to escape the many hours of incessant noise and down a hill might give us a much needed extra three or four miles per hour. Due to the blizzard we would not arrive back at Basildon until late next morning, deaf and hyper tired, where the thoughtful Yorkshire lads had got my snow covered Triumph Terrier motorbike somehow balanced in the rear of the Land-Rover 80 mule with it's welcoming very effective heater and a driver that would run me back to Wickford in the snow where Mum had breakfast and a bed waiting. As we left the depot for home, one of the foremen, Joe Connor, a jovial Yorkshire individual that liked winding apprentices up, called out to me, "Hey, Our Kid! get some sleep, we'll book you for another one if you don't mind, there will be at least two more this week Hah, Hah, Hah". Oh joy, oh joy!, oh joy! I would be well asleep before the Land-Rover had passed the first junction after being awake for the hectic twenty eight hour cold working day.

The relentless 'Big Freeze' winter of 1963 continued to stretch our resources at the AEC Depot. Again and again we would go out in the large AEC Matador wrecker or the small but gallant and capable Land Rover to help another distressed HGV, such as a Leyland Buffalo, a Diamond T, a Dodge, an AEC, Scammel or Albion.

During this extreme winter we had all sorts of calls for help from drivers of large trucks that had succumbed to the hard packed snow and ice, who just could not move their vehicles. Typically a heavy AEC or Thornycroft would just stand there on packed ice, all thirty or more tons of heavy truck with four axles, twelve wheels and eight of them driving wheels rotating but unable to get a grip and move an inch. The driver would have the engine running at high throttle with the eight wheels of the two rear driving axles rotating at thirty mph, trying to heat and melt the packed ice underneath the tyres without any success at all while the truck just sat there motionless. The ice was so cold and deep that the tyres just could not warm it up to melt that impenetrable ice. On one particular occasion, Tom Hardy (one of the older mechanics) and I travelled in the wrecker some twenty miles away to a stranded twelve wheel liquid lard tanker that had been stranded for twelve hours near Rainham, Essex. The driver had been stuck in a day long traffic jam on the icebound A13, but was less than a half mile away from his destination that was the Proctor and Gamble soap factory on Thameside. As with most drivers in that weather, he was long overdue at his destination and had been a long time since having the benefit of some sleep. He decided to take matters in hand and leave the A13 in his heavy truck and reach the factory that was already in sight, by driving over a perma-frosted fallow field to the Proctor and Gambles gate, after driving through and destroying the stout wooden fence that separated the field from the A13. Normally, no one in their right mind would drive a thirty-plus ton truck over a field, especially when it was formed of Essex clay of the Thames Basin variety. However, he took the only option available to him, reasoning that there was a perma-frost that froze any topsoil or other matter down to a depth of maybe twelve inches, he managed to get a hundred feet onto this eight acre field and got well and truly stuck, all wheels spinning but no forward motion. When we arrived it was now dark, but it was yet another crystal night with a full moon and the Thameside lights making it feel almost a though we had daylight. Our breath almost froze it was so cold but we were full of confidence, after all, our wrecker had initially been built as an RAF aircraft recovery unit for WW2, it was designed to pull a large damaged and loaded bomber without an undercarriage across a ploughed field to clear a runway. We entered the field through the same breech in the fencing that the victim had created. We did not worry about getting stuck as our wrecker had twelve forward and twelve reverse gears, and a four speed winch at both front and rear, it was possibly the very largest 10x6 (more commonly thought of as a 6x6) HGV on or off the road and just in case, we also had ground anchors front and rear, a heavy duty American crane and a built in workshop. This truck had been re-bodied and re-engined by us, and there was no way that we were going to get stuck, but we were equally confident that we could and would pull this loaded liquid lard tanker the last few hundred yards to its final destination in a trice, no sweat, there was no chance that we would give up or fail, or so we thought.

 Three freezing and exhausting hours later, after we had tried everything including deploying our ground anchors, we conceded defeat. The ground anchors were only ever needed as a last resort, and they had failed miserably, they just bounced and danced without penetrating into the pack ice and perma-frost and so gave us no anchorage whatsoever. The only course apparently left to us was to return to the dealership and fit snow chains that had never been used before, to the wrecker, which were in stock but meant returning in the morning and at that time the lard in the tanker would have chilled further or frozen into a non-transient and unusable state. However as a last resort Tom Said "Peter, pull the front winch cable out, and wrap it around that oak tree, we can't give up after all of this time, and using it as an anchor we'll engage the winch power take off, and with the little bit of help from the dancing ground anchors, we just might be lucky" The half inch diameter woven and spliced high tensile steel wire winch cable was so cold that it was hardly pliable, but with much difficulty I did as he asked. I could see that this grand old tree had been dead some years and I had little confidence that it would give us the anchorage that we so badly needed. Tom yelled 'Stand Clear' as he engaged the winch and gave the engine a few revs. The heavy woven steel cable took the strain and then the tree with a five foot diameter trunk, just snapped at the cable height just three feet of the ground. The roots were so frozen into the ground that they did not pull out and the trunk that was totally dead, frozen and brittle with the cold, just snapped and the tree came down, all thirty feet of it.

The wrecker returned to base with us and the next morning adorned with snow chains and with the extra and invaluable assistance of the incredible never give up Land Rover, the lard tanker complete with its frozen cargo, was finally pulled to its destination, but alas, we left a very difficult problem for someone else of melting the frozen solid lard to a fluid and pumpable state.

THE TAMING OF A RAGING BULL

Winter 1963

During another seized rear axle breakdown necessitating us to yet again fit a replacement rear axle differential in the centre lane of the M1, this time on a livestock carrier, we found the driver, was very concerned about the mood of the solitary bull that he was carrying. It had been trussed up for more than two days on its way down from Aberdeen and not surprisingly was getting a little fed up with his noisy, draughty, and diesel smelling confined environment. Not knowing that he was going to a happy holiday for a few months in the fields of Sussex with an attendant harem of lady cows, he was kicking off big time as though he maybe thought that he was going to an abattoir, maybe animals do talk among themselves. He was making the six wheeler too unstable for us to raise with the rather large manually operated side jacks with their five feet levers, which would give us enough clearance under the body to lift the huge steel differential out of its mother axle case. Fortunately, the driver was also a drover, a herdsman, and he said that without tranquilisers it would take many hours for the beast to tire and possibly, just possibly, make the vehicle safe to work on. With the January winter weather deteriorating and the shortening daylight we did not have the luxury of time. The driver suggested that with the help of a few other truckers, who were always ready to stop and help each other out, we could remove the bull from the truck to an adjacent field where he could go ballistic, burn of his excess energy whilst we changed the truck's differential, and then, later on with the help of another group of truckers, we hopefully would get the sufficiently tired beast back into the livestock carrier, or at least that was the plan. That was plan A, the truck had to be fixed, we were the only people south of Yorkshire who could do it, the day was late and the weather was getting worse, so that's what we did, there was no plan B. With the help of some passing truckers who we easily flagged down as most trucks maxed out back then at 40 mph, and if they were fully loaded, fighting an incline and driving into a head wind, they were maybe only hitting 30 mph and were easy to flag down. We briefly blocked the motorway's slow and middle lanes and moved the bull to an adjacent field after removing a fence section and hurriedly replaced the rear differential, which was nearly a two hundred pound mass of solid metal that took about five hours taking us into the evening. Now came the challenge of getting the huge bull back into the wagon. I had often seen this challenge of beast supremacy as a young teenager when working in the cattle-dock at Wickford Station's goods yard. The staff always won the battle with the beast as they had no alternative, again there was no Plan B, so I was ready for what was to come. The bull as matter of nature, would not want to re-enter the wagon as it appeared as a dark tunnel with no way out after a climb up the loading ramp, it seemed like a trap. It would therefore resist with great anger and power to avoid being cornered in there. The trick in a *horse*box was to have a small front door for the horse's attendant to safely and easily exit through once he/she had coaxed the horse fully into the box, that appeared with its crew door open to have an open end, and was often a box that the horse was familiar with. However, with a cow or more particularly a one-ton bull, it needed a totally different set of tactics with several noisy men, a course shrub to act as a whip, a choreography of precise timing and a lot of bravado of the men. The procedure was to walk the bull in a more relaxed manner to the bottom of the ramp with an apple, carrot or some grain as the first target, then swiftly whilst the bull was munching, a very strong, long length of rope, going through a double block and tackle that was already attached to an anchor ring on the wagon's bulkhead behind the driver's cab, was attached to the four inch bull-ring that went through the bull's nose. Then on the command of the leading herdsman and to the accompaniment of much shouting and swearing, the strongest and heaviest man would quickly take up the slack in the bull-ring rope and pull with all of his power and weight on the large rope with its' four to one advantage of the two blocks and cams serving that rope, at the same time the bull would be prompted up the ramp by a gentle or moderate if necessary thrashing of its' hind quarters by the whip-man using the shrub. Once the bull was into the wagon, there would be very quick and absolute action to raise the loading-ramp, shut the two upper-hinged rear doors and drop in the wedge shaped locking pegs into place. It rarely went as easy as that as the bull was not only a very large and stubborn animal but also an animal of great strength and weight and some intelligence, and seemed to know what was going on. The bull would often get to the head of the ramp with only its head in the wagon and being a canny Aberdeen Scot, refuse to move no matter how much shouting, swearing and lashing took part. When this impasse came about and it was obviously a stalemate it was time for stage three. The smallest and most agile of the herdsman was volunteered to be key to this final and rather dangerous tactic. Often there was a shortage of suitable slim and fit men and I would be given this final task. The key to it was using the bull's most tender parts to get it to move on and complete the final twenty or so feet into the wagon. The bull always had a huge pair of testicles, the size of small coconuts that hung down low and these were the target of stage three. At the critical moment when the lead herds-man had as much tension as he could muster through the nose rope and with a sharper lash with the shrub on the bull's buttocks, and a lot of very loud shouting of encouragement from all the men present the final persuasion was administered by the risk taking volunteer. The volunteer would simply give the bull's huge testicles a very, very hard grab and leap out of the way of the enraged beast that at that very moment of great pain and with a huge roar, would thrust forward with incredible energy into the wagon, and this is the procedure we used with me doing the squeezing. In very quick military precision, the rear doors and ramp were slammed shut and the drop pegs firmly put into place before the bull kicked them open or turned and charged. Job accomplished the bull could be heard inside the wagon going crazy, rearing up and kicking with much anger and really testing the strength of the wooden coachbuilders art, as he tried to destroy the wagon from within. All the men stood well back waiting the splintering of wood to herald yet another set of problems. Eventually the bull would tire and calm and then continue on his way in the wagon and in the snow to the Sussex barns and eventual lush spring pastures and his lady friends. All of that noise, violence and commotion was indeed for a good cause. If the bull knew why we did what we did he would probably have thanked us. Drama over! thanks were given all round to the truckers that had stopped to help, and get the wagon driver to sign our 'work done sheet'. We then climbed up and into the spacious but cold and noisy wrecker cab, but at least it was out of the awful weather and after a brief chat, a bit of hysteria and a post mortem of the job, we started the long unpleasant journey from the Midlands back down to Basildon. With the twin commercial sized but inadequate heaters on full demist trying to clear the large front windows and the large wipers trying to keep a pair of visibility slots in the heavily snowed windscreen our journey was going to be arduous. We just hoped that the transport café at South Mimms was still open twenty-four hours, we badly needed a pee, a large cup of Yorkshire tea, an egg or bacon sandwich, and a very well earned forty winks. After the long hours, extreme cold and physical exertion, we needed it. It was strange that we would normally awake after close on forty minutes on every occasion and we often wondered if a catnap like this acquired its name from its seemingly natural length of forty minutes, after all why not call it twenty, sixty or eighty winks, but forty it was called and after forty minutes I would normally wake and then disturb the noisily snoring overweight and usually past middle aged Yorkshire driver, much to his displeasure, and we would then journey on to our homes in Essex.

THE DEADLY A127

We obviously dealt with and attended a lot more local breakdowns and recoveries, some easy, some terribly difficult and some sadly involving a fatality.

One breakdown that I remember well was just two miles from our depot where an eight wheel Atkinson truck with a large Gardner 160 engine had failed on the westbound A127 Southend dual carriageway Arterial Road with a seized dynamo in December 1963. The driver found it too difficult to continue as the dynamo's triple drive belts also drove other essential electrical items on the refrigerated truck, like the wipers, lights and a heater. It was not long before we arrived at the scene during lunchtime, being a refrigerated truck it received instant attention and so we worked through our lunch. It was stationary in the slow lane, and only having the Land Rover at our disposal at that time we had to carry out a repair on the roadside. We quickly had the large high output dynamo disconnected, removed, and in the Land Rover together with the victims large discharged batteries and returned to the depot pronto to give the batteries a heavy boost charge for two hours whilst the electricians overhauled the seized dynamo. Due to recent total over-use the twenty-four volt batteries now had heavily sulphated cells and were therefore sluggish to respond to the charging. So two hours passed and that soon became three hours whilst we were trying to recover the batteries to a reasonable state of health. We re-loaded the Land Rover with the rebuilt dynamo, new belts and partly recharged batteries and returned to the dead Atkinson that was still sitting in the slow lane and lifeless. It was late December, so in our absence both twilight and then darkness had unfortunately descended onto the scene. Traffic was light and as we finally pulled up behind and to protect the failed truck, we realised that there was no street lighting on nor available and saw in the poor light something that we had wished not to, in the gloom and drizzle it seemed there were two very dim red lights in the blackness of the dead trucks rear. It was the rear end and tail lights of an ubiquitous black 'sit up and beg' Ford Popular that had driven into the rear of the failed truck, assumedly within the last half hour or so as darkness had fallen and its low powered and dim six volt tail lights with dirty lenses were still on. With our hand torches we could see that the driver was unfortunately dead, having gone partly through the shattered windscreen when his car, seemingly without braking, as there were no skid marks, had impacted the rear of the Atkinson. A passing Police Car pulled up and we had a very long late afternoon answering the Police with the truck driver and putting the Atkinson back into use, whilst crews from the local Ford dealer's recovery truck and an ambulance had the grim task of removing the Ford and its deceased driver for further investigation and attention.

  Of course we felt some guilt for not foreseeing the effect of the coming of darkness so early in the afternoon of very nearly the shortest day of the year. We also felt annoyed that accident warning aids such as traffic cones, illuminations and beacons were not yet designed nor available as well as being annoyed that the filthy weather tyre spray had obscured the Atkinson's few mandatory reflectors as well as that we were still living in a world where many cars, in particular the Ford Popular E93A had dull headlights from their pre-war and hopeless six volt electrical systems, and lousy non-hydraulic brakes with vacuum powered wipers that actually slowed down when you accelerated, non of which would help in poor weather of that day or an emergency. Let alone the need for adequate street lighting on a well used arterial road. Fifty or more years later I still feel remorseful when remembering the event. A man had died unnecessarily due to very poor street and vehicle lighting

ON WITH THE NEXT

The work at the dealership was varied but was always on heavy goods vehicles of seven tons and upwards, to more than thirty tons or so, almost always with slow speed diesel engines of between seven and fifteen litres with a maximum of engine speed of just 1400 rpm and maximum road speed of a very noisy 42 miles per hour (usually downhill) and slower when loaded or travelling uphill. There was always general servicing going on as well as major overhauls or building and fitting drivers cabs to a new 'rolling chassis' that had been driven down from various manufacturers as already described. One of the more memorable events was during the spring of 1963 when a large Bedford steel transporter carrying twenty four tons of steel lost its brakes on the North Circular some thirty five miles away. A mechanic (Dave Sulley) and an assistant were dispatched but had to use our small petrol powered Land Rover 80 and take a set of tools and hope that they could affect a repair. Normally the big AEC wrecker would have been used due to the size of the failed vehicle, but alas, the wrecker was on one of the many duties some distance away and the steel transporter was not to be left in its rather dangerous position blocking traffic lights. The Land Rover was one of the first models built and was rather diminutive in size compared with articulated steel transporter that needed help. It was hoped that Dave the mechanic could create a fix to avoid waiting many hours for the wrecker's return. We waited for Dave to return with whatever news he had.

Mobile phones didn't exist back then and many roadside phone boxes were unserviceable for one reason or another, so contact is lost. Some seven hours later and much to our astonishment, Dave arrived back and unceremoniously walked into the canteen and politely asked if a few cars could be moved out of the approach road to give him access. When we walked out of the building to help we were surprised to find that he had towed the laden steel transporter back to the dealership with absolutely no brakes other than those on the small Land Rover. The Land Rover had pulled the heavily loaded articulated truck back to the dealership in low ratio first gear, at a maximum of 12 mph on a fixed tow bar. It took over four hours to complete this very delicate thirty-mile and assumedly impossible towing mission.

From that moment on, we all had great respect for the game and relatively small Land Rover that continuously punched well above its weight in an arena of giant trucks, and Dave Sulley the mechanic for his driving skill and courage. Towing an un-braked trailer of any size is a nightmare, but when it weighs twelve times more than your tow wagon and is six times longer and it is thirty miles to base on a trunk road, then it enters into the land of the crazy and highly skilled madmen with nerves of steel.

Breakdowns and recoveries were always enjoyed even when suffering the over-long days that were involved, the wrecker's poor heating, mind numbing noise, and the hours of working on a cold windswept carriageway, but we always enjoyed the individual challenges of each job.

The insane noise created in the workshop by the power tools, compressors, revving lorry engines and neighbouring Bonnalack's bodyworks by the hand panel beating to create the cabs and five thousand gallon tanker bodies, could only be matched by Dante's Inferno.

OUT OF THE FRYING PAN

One day in the summer some months later, the noise was so intense to complete a fleet order of some AEC aggregate tippers on time that it was as noisy as a shipyard and I just walked out early in the afternoon without warning, out of the frying pan, but with a throbbing head. This maybe partly brought on by my ruptured eardrum that was caused by the ATC rifle practice with Lee Enfield 303s a few years earlier and the eternal noise of the wrecker. As an escape I found my way to the local Rootes Group (Hillman, Humber, Singer, Sunbeam cars and Commer and Karrier trucks) Dealership in Wickford, Fuller and Gadsdon Ltd. They were also agents for BSA and Francis Barnet motorcycles and JAP and Villiers plant engines and all manner of plant machinery as well as the Rootes Group vehicles. A busy and varied community firm that I thought would be very interesting to work for. They had been asking after me for a little while, so I walked in unannounced and I accepted their job offer. It was nearer to home, slightly more money and considerably less mayhem. Happy days at last and Fuller and Gadsdon used micrometers with delicacy as often as CV (Sales and Repairs) the AEC Dealership, used fourteen-pound sledgehammers in full flight. I did however miss the comradeship of the larger than life Yorkshiremen and the mighty beasts that we repaired, but there was great pleasure in tuning twin carburettors, reboring engines and overhauling transmissions and leading the repairs on the Rootes Group commercial and Commer's unusual two stroke diesel TS3 trucks.

THE SUMMER WEEKENDS

 Understandably I looked forward to my summer weekend breaks with my mates on the motorbikes and away from the intensity of a busy garage workshop. A pleasant saloon car with a heater, quiet engine and a smiling character-less blonde listening to a dull Home Service dominated car radio didn't quite give the right release to my gruelling work regime. Like so many other lads of the time, whether working on the dreadful North Sea trawlers in winter storms, down those awful coal mines, in the infernal North Country steelworks, Satanic Mills' and shipyards, or experiencing the noise and dehydration of driving steam trains, the out in any weather building yards, or unloading ships before the introduction of containers, many lads toiled very hard, very hard indeed for their £3.00 or maybe £5.00 per week. I needed the excitement of a reasonably powerful bike and a challenging brunette girlfriend to balance out the physical work of repairing vehicles. The redheads that I knew were a step too far even for me. I didn't want a Boadicea nor a Maggie Thatcher (a no-nonsense and unknown war-lady of the future, then), such ladies are best left to defending our country and causing grief to others. Even Enzo Ferrari knew this when he named his hairiest car the Testa-Rossa (translates from Italian to Red Head!) and Barbarossa, albeit a man, was the name given to at least two red bearded warriors in history, a Roman Emperor and a Pirate or Corsair of The Ottoman Empire. Maybe it's a nod of acknowledgment from Enzo to the red headed woman from Britannia, named Boadicea, the only warlord, male or female, to put the Romans, his country, to flight, and that was out of their most northerly outpost, Britannicus, some two thousand years ago and she made them flee twice! The Romans also failed to control the very difficult Scots, many of them being red headed, by building a wall, Hadrian's Wall, and then another wall fifty years later, Antonine's Wall, after Hadrian's Wall was not effective enough. However, they could not control *this* lady, Boadicea, her tale is legendary and is worth following. There is a most dramatic statue of her and her abused and distressed daughters aboard her terrifying chariot adorned with wheel mounted sabres, chasing the fleeing Romans, on a plinth at the north end of Westminster Bridge in London, overlooking a statue of Churchill and The Houses of Parliament. Even Maggie Thatcher, also a redhead, can't claim such an impressive podium. Give me a homely lively honey blonde or brunette any day, a powerful redhead is great, but not for me. Did someone say it is an excess of iron in their blood, hence Maggie's title, "The Iron Lady" I am a realist, not a defeatist.

The world was quickly moving on, yet mobile phones, computers, Face-Book, Skype, credit cards, the contraceptive pill and easy obtainable drugs, colour TV, portable power tools, a 40 hour weeks and 5 weeks annual leave and the internet were still an unbelievable forty or fifty years away into an unknown future, and soon, men were no longer dying of old age at fifty five years, just think about that for a moment.

Slide Rules, physically tough jobs, long hours, and early retirement or death through ill health were the standards of the time, yet our well respected Tory Prime Minister Harold Macmillan (SuperMac) proclaimed that "we've never had it so good" maybe he was right, but in hindsight that statement would hardly reflect the future. His statement was followed by the Duke of Edinburgh saying that the British worker "Should get his finger out" maybe he was more concerned for the future than Harold MacMillan was, and not being a diplomat was a little more outspoken. Macmillan then had the night of the long knives when he sacked seven of his ministers due to the state of the economy. The swinging sixties and its music made sure that the country recovered until the industrial unrest of the seventies had passed and the *magic* Mini and its' replacement, the *tragic* Allegro as our latest all British new car, were replaced by Japanese Hondas and Nissans built at our previously proud and busy factories in the north and the midlands that had been closed by industrial disputes and were now empty and hence strike free.

Maggie Thatcher, our then Prime Minister, had made it clear that you can argue with bosses and union leaders until the cows come home, but you will never, ever win against a determined woman, especially a redhead.

However, maybe our deep but positive experiences and the moving background music, is why the Swinging Sixties are so fondly remembered by those of us that were lucky enough to have been there.

A CRICKET MATCH with The Rettendon Rabbits

In the pretty village of Runwell, whose ancient church is also known as 'Our Lady of the Running Well' and out of sight to the world at large in the valley between Runwell and Rettendon, was the rather extensive Runwell Mental Hospital. It was built in the nineteen thirties much like a small garden city and to an attractive colony plan. Access was strictly limited to relations, appointments, staff and necessary trades. The imposing iron security gates stood some twelve feet high as was the perimeter fencing and a well-staffed guardhouse protected the gates and the grounds. The company that I worked for as a mechanic in nearby Wickford, Fuller and Gadsdons Ltd, often sent me there with the transporter and a second-man for security to collect one or two of their vehicles to bring back to the workshops for servicing. Some of their vehicles stayed in the hospital grounds for all of their life and we serviced them there, and they were never registered or taxed for the road and never achieved a mileage in excess of a thousand miles each year or a speed over 25 mph or used higher than second gear. Unregistered was a small fleet of Morrison electric floats for use as dustcarts, laundry vehicles, internal ambulances and general-purpose use. All of these vehicles needed our Ford Thames Trader transporter to get them to our service workshops. Also unregistered was a museum piece of a Fordson 7V, V8, open cab fire engine, New York style from 1936, complete with a windscreen and chrome bell and always looking immaculate in bright red, that had never been used in anger, which we periodically serviced or repaired on site. It had only been used for exercises and grass or out of control bonfires. Previous to this they had an adapted large pre-war Vauxhall saloon with all four doors permanently removed towing a water-pump trailer, and a roof ladder-rack was added for the same purpose. Registered for road use however, were two Bedford coaches, one was of the popular and delightful twenty-nine seat OB model which acted as a staff or visitor's coach and doubled up as a laundry collection and delivery vehicle to local hospitals. The other was a modern sixty seat basic utility bodied military style transport personnel carrier that was used as a regular passenger coach connecting the hospital to the nearby town-centre of Wickford and its station. There was also an immaculate black Riley 2.6 litre Pathfinder saloon for chauffer use to convey the management when needed. The hospital was laid out like a country park and the well spaced out-buildings, be they the St Luke's Chapel, wards, theatres or administration block, boiler house or entertainment hall, gymnasium, dentist, hair parlour, and labs were architecturally attractive. It was clear that at *this* hospital, the aim was to cure peoples' problems by pleasantness rather than dictate or firm control. Although it had some high security wards, people with lesser problems such as moderate fits were more normally helped. Only at a much later period of time and with the advent of effective passive drugs did they remove the high perimeter fencing and the forbidding gates.

 Once a year however, the hospital was open to the public for a day as a summer fete atmosphere and cricket matches were laid on between the staff, the patients and the local cricket team in their fully equipped cricket ground complete with a pavilion and a movable sun blocking wall. Some of the cricket balls flew with very high velocity, so care was needed. Whenever you viewed the hospital from the surrounding fields, the mobile sun wall and pavilion reminded you of the cheerful mid-summer fete and the cricket matches. During that period, my brother Alan had just had his shotgun licence renewed by Sergeant Pepper at the nearby

Rettendon village Police Station and asked me if I would like to go shooting with him. When I avoidably said that I haven't got the time nor interest to shoot ducks, rabbits and pheasants, he replied, Rats! No, not game, but rats! Why not come shooting rats in a tree, it's great fun.

He then explained that near the Rettendon Church and in the adjacent land of the Runwell Mental Hospital was a tree plagued with rats that were playing havoc with the local farmers' small livestock and his general livestock's food store, and that the farmer had asked for help. Ah, that sounds a bit more interesting I replied, as I loathe rats. It wasn't very far and we were walking the lane towards the fine Anglo Saxon Church and after skirting the church there was the attractive panorama of the Runwell Valley, a view of the mental hospital and the farmer's fields, hedgerows and trees. Alan had already passed me a gun, a twelve bore pump action three shot Cooey Canadian shotgun and I loaded it with a couple of cartridges in the magazine and one in the breach. Alan soon pointed out a well balanced medium sized Oak tree that was maybe three hundred years old and said focus on that Oak which was two hundred feet away. Sure enough it was alive with rats, and tally-ho, the hunt was on. We took a few more steps and noticed there were a couple of rabbits, which were foraging in the field margin of long grass nearer to us. 'Go on' said Alan there's a chance for you to have a pop at one. I automatically raised the gun and took aim. I took one look at the rabbit nearest and he sat up, ears erect and took a long look at me. I thought, hang on, I haven't come here to shoot you. After re-aiming fifty feet in front of him, I gently squeezed the trigger,

> . . . . *Run rabbit, run rabbit, run, run, run, don't let the farmer have his fun, fun, fun. He'll get by without his rabbit pie, so run rabbit, run rabbit, run,* Bwammm! *Run-run!.*(5)

...the shotgun shouted whilst giving me the expected heavy nudge to my right shoulder. Bwammm it went, not like the sharp crack of an

125

RAF Lee Enfield 303 rifle, nor the absolute BANG! of a Remington double barrel shotgun, nor the sudden loud snap and hand singeing flash of a revolver or the spite of a pistol, but Bwammm bloody Bwammm, Ouch! A moment or so later once the ringing in my ear and the temporary numbness to my senses had cleared, I took a look at the result of my chivalry and to my surprise the rabbit was still looking at me. I wondered is it shell shocked, have I hit him, is it rigor mortis or even worse, have I winged him I pondered, then, like a dog asking for a favour the rabbit lifted a front leg and like a cricket umpire declaring an 'out' and at the same time using an index finger/paw as an insult, promptly hopped haphazardly as rabbits do, into the hedgerow and was gone.

 Alan suggested that there was a misfire because the cartridge shot stirred up the dust where they landed well short of Bugs Bunny, maybe because the cartridges had been stored in a damp place with recent heavy rain. Only when he reads this book will he discover that I deliberately mis-aimed.

    Judging by the 'Umpires' gestures we conceded,

        Rettendon Rabbits   1

        Wickford   Rockers   0

We then continued as planned and partly culled the rat population of rural Rettendon, helping the farmer and giving us temporary but annoying tinnitus that returned in later years as a punishment for our bit of fun.

PART FIVE
TALES OF THE TURNPIKE
Events that occurred within fifteen miles of the Rettendon Turnpike, an ancient Essex crossroads.

The Wickford lads, most of whom I went to school with were an active and fun loving lot. There was Ray Nash, Ray was a great guy in every sense of the word and was big and very strongly built with huge hands and without an ounce of fat on him. In the evenings he was a bouncer at the very lively and sometimes riotous Locarno Ballroom in nearby Basildon. His tales of the other bouncers and him, barricading the double entrance doors with furniture to protect the ballroom and staff from drink inspired mobs as there were virtually no knives, drugs and hand guns then, leaving you almost agape in disbelief. During the day he was a service mechanic at the nearby Rootes Group Dealership, Holmes and Smith Ltd, which was previously Fuller and Gadsdon were I also had worked. Ray had a great sense of humour that did not diminish even after he drove his beautiful blue and yellow Cadillac Bel Air into the rear of a parked lorry on his way to work one morning, badly smashing his car and putting Ray in hospital with really nasty face wound. The lorry was badly parked on the brow of a hill. Ray pulled out to overtake it and had the disadvantage of the restricted view that one gets from a left hand driving position and the low morning sun in his eyes. When an oncoming car appeared over the brow of the hill, Ray had no option but to brake hard and steer left, straight into the back of the badly parked lorry. The front of the Cadillac's long bonnet hit the back axle of the truck at the same moment as the trucks chassis went through the Cadillac's windscreen and as cars did not have seatbelts nor airbags back then, Ray head-butted the chassis and left his rugged face even more rugged with a terrible long scar. Only the excessive length of the Cadillac's bonnet possibly saved Ray's life. If the bonnet had been any shorter even by just two inches Ray would probably have been killed. No thanks to Cadillac though as American cars did not have the sharper brakes and handling of British cars back then and better brakes would no doubt have saved him head-butting the truck's chassis. Ray's mischievous, fun loving nature seemed to be enhanced by his accident battle-scar as he eventually married the Wickford Carnival Queen, Jackie, who besides being very good looking with an exciting personality, had the most stunning Sapphire Blue eyes you could ever imagine. When in her presence you could not help but look into and study the depths of her beautiful blue eyes, yes, totally unreal, no wonder she became Wickford's Queen. Ray always had a stonking great Cadillac or a Chevrolet Impala, complete with left hand drive to cruise around in, it suited his image well. Ray always managed to raise a genuine big smile, a true character of the sixties and still alive and kicking many years later.

Another character was popular Crazy Peter Bird, who mostly rode around on a large, noisy BSA side-valve motorcycle with an open sidecar. The motorcycle combination, or combo' as we nicknamed bike and sidecar outfits, was old, tatty, noisy, oil leaking and frighteningly fast. Only Micky Craven, who was often bike-less due to his drinking costs, would dare to ride with Crazy Pete, a mad pair together indeed. Micky travelled well with Pete at great speed, not because of the engine power but by the way Pete threw it about either on full throttle or very heavy braking.

WELCOME TO THE HOUSE OF FUN

The Night of the Ice Crystals, 1963

In the New Year's eve' 1963/64, deep in the unusually cold 'Siberian' winter, many of us attended a mad new-year party at Micky Craven's parents' bungalow in Swan Lane Wickford. Micky and Crazy Pete got very drunk and in their delirious state and after Micky put his fist through the back of his guitar because it wouldn't play 'Do you love me, now that I can dance' they thought it would be fun to go for a six mile ride, at midnight with snow hard packed on the road. Everything was lit up by a very bright moon lighting up with brilliance all of the large frost crystals created by the Hoar Frost, that had been spectacularly created by the airborne frost on everything that you looked at in the bright moonlight. During that cloudless black but star-filled freezing night, a night of ice crystals it certainly was. They shot off on the BSA (commonly known as a Big Beeza) and sidecar combination, bare-chested and with no head gear, coat, shirt nor gloves, and it was the Big Freeze Winter with an air temperature of just eight degrees Fahrenheit which is a very cold minus thirteen degrees Centigrade before you considered the considerable chill factor. Many of us tried to stop them in their madness, others thought it was such a daft idea that they wouldn't go further than a hundred yards before returning and seek the unheated but relative warmth of the bungalow, and so ignored them. Off they went in that stunningly beautiful but unbearably cold night and when they didn't return for forty minutes or so, we thought that they had crashed on the ice and we started de-icing one of the unheated cars to go looking for a catastrophe. At that moment in the crystal night's magical but strange silence, and to a roar of a thrashed large Beeza, they returned in a flurry of snow with a big sliding three-wheel skid. They were still waist up naked and full of loud exclamations and bravado. They dismounted the poor overworked bike and amazingly were not only now totally sober, but seemed no worse for their ridiculous ordeal, no frost bite, no numb fingers and no shirts, no blue skin, and no sense-no feeling as they say and continued madly partying complete with a broken guitar.

> *Welcome to the house of fun, Now we've come of age,*
> *Welcome to the house of fun, and the Lion's Cage,*
> *Welcome to the house of fun, Temptation's on its way,*
> *Welcome to the House of Fun (6)*

Another of the lads, Micky J. (Mad Mick- not Micky Craven) however, was a rather different kettle of fish if not a little mad and worrying to be within a hundred yards off. To many, he was truly obnoxious as he was always cussing, whistling high pitched shrieks between his teeth, spitting at the slightest provocation and acting with total disregard to the law and common decency. Mad Mick was the only one of us who would regularly ride his motorbike on pub runs, get drunk, fall of his bike and be a danger to us all, so we avoided him like the plague. Mad Mick (Micky J.) worked at English, the towns' butchers shop. He was well paid for this horrendous job and bought a new Norton Jubilee motorbike and leatherwear with his earnings. Unfortunately the Norton soon lost its sheen as he kept falling off it, drunk. When not merrily cutting and chopping up meat of all types in the shop he worked in the abattoir (slaughter house)which he thoroughly enjoyed. He normally proudly and noisily rode around the town calling out the odd obscenity to other lads from the saddle of the butcher's trade pedal bicycle that he was riding. The trade bike was an odd thing with a back end of an adult's ladies bike with the traders name and message on a metal panel fixed between the two diagonal and parallel frame tubes. This rear part of the bike was very much attached to the front forks of a child's bike, which meant a small front wheel above which was a metal box frame that could accommodate the trader's wares, in this case meat and its by-products.

He never seemed to have a decent relationship or any time with the fairer sex. On the odd occasion that he did it would be with Ginger Sue, a fiery petite redhead that had a ravenous appetite for a biker, almost any biker that he often shared with the BSA Bantam thrasher, Speedy Reedy (John Reed). Ginger Sue was an explosive time bomb and having had a liaison with almost every biker except me she was seriously shop soiled and not my kettle of fish. She often could be found at her pleasure residence, which was a field of very long coarse grass alongside the junction of Swan Lane and Richmond Road in Wickford. We went looking for Mick one

Sunday as he had planned a bike ride for all of us to Castle Hedingham in North Essex, where he madly suggested we stormed the seventy foot high walls of this Norman Castle, he was always an idiot and this suggestion proved it. He hadn't arrived at the pre-planned rendezvous at the Castle pub in Wickford's Broadway, and only he knew the route, so we went looking for him. Our first and successful search was at the long grass field in Swan Lane. We pulled up and could see the long grass swaying on a wind free morning. We cut the engines and immediately could hear the high pitched ranting of Ginger Sue as she verbally protested and lashed into him for being too drunk from the previous pub crawl to please her.

> *I know I can see you as there's magic in my eyes, I can hear you in the long grass now there's a surprise, I can hear you for miles and miles, I can hear you for miles and miles, I can hear you for miles and miles and miles and miles and miles. . .oh yeah ! (7)*

The sound of our bikes when started up and threatened to leave him there at the mercy of Sue, was enough for him to burst out of the long grass, hotly pursued by the profanity-belching redhead and leap onto the pillion seat of the nearest bike, Speedy Ready's BSA Bantam 175, and take flight whilst still buttoning up his shirt. I can still see Sue in my mirror now as we hurriedly pulled away, one hand re-clipping her bra and the other gesticulating with much anger at Mad Mick for displeasing her, and above the noise of the accelerating bikes, did I hear her repeatedly call to him" You Banker, you Bloody Banker"? There was far too much bike noise for me to be sure of exactly what she yelled. He certainly was a bloody butcher, but banker, the mind wonders. One thing was confirmed that day and that was that hell hath no fury like a woman scorned.

However, Mad Mick's day of reckoning was to come in the hands of Micky Craven. English the Butcher's small Ford delivery van that

Mad Mick frequently drove had a rear access arrangement that was by upper and lower tailgates. The lower one dropped down until it was horizontal and restrained by two chains and acted as a load platform, whereas the upper tailgate lifted up to horizontal and was held there with two side supports where it acted as a weather canopy, an easy and practical arrangement. Mad Mick had a repulsive habit whilst driving the van, he would often reach into the rear of the van and grab a piece of raw meat from the deliveries and eat it with relish as he was driving along. He was oddball, very oddball indeed.

Once or twice a week Mad Mick would carry out the delivery round to South Hanningfield and the surrounding villages in the butcher's van, a Ford 5cwt 100E van with a lethargic but indestructible 1147 cc side valve engine that wheezed desperately when it was cold and running on choke, together with its overstretched three speed gearbox where the driver was always looking for a fourth gear that just didn't exist. Sometimes he would take Micky Craven not just for kicks but to get the round done quicker so that they could enjoy the odd pint later on. One of his rounds was delivering and selling meat in the village of South Hanningfield, where there is a long medium grade hill with detached bungalows spaced every 50 metres or so on either side of the road.

To cut down time on this section of the round their method was for Mad Mick to leave the van at top of the hill whilst carrying his large wicker delivery and sales basket by foot, which was full of poultry, meat and game and walk down the hill going door to door. At that time Micky Craven did not have a car license and therefore not being legally able to drive the van down the hill, would sit in the passenger seat and without the engine running would frequently release the handbrake and let the van freewheel under gravity alone down the hill a short distance, whilst steering the van from the passenger's seat and controlling its speed and stopping at a suitable spot for Mad Mick to refill his basket, by the rather powerful handbrake. On this occasion, Micky Craven as normal awaited Mad Mick to arrive back at the van to replenish his basket at the back of the van, and at a very precise prejudged moment Micky Craven released the handbrake and let the van roll further down the hill. Mad Mick a little annoyed ran downhill basket in hand, after the van, shouting his usual obscenities and caught up with the vans rear tailgates, again at a critical moment after partial reloading, Micky Craven released the handbrake again for another twenty foot of catch me if you can, again with Mad Mick in hot pursuit whilst shouting his usual obscenities. On the third attempt, Micky Craven applies the handbrake a little further on and pulls it up very, very sharp and the van virtually stops dead. This time Mad Mick misjudges and could not stop himself from running down the hill at full gallop complete with the now reloaded basket after the runaway van.

He ran straight into the back of the van colliding his forehead with the van's open upper tailgate and knocked himself out with his deliveries of poultry, meat and game, sausages, bacon and ham, scattered all over the road. Mad Mick recovered to a drop of whisky that he kept in a hipflask in the van, administered by a grinning Micky Craven, and a piece of customer's steak to hide his now blackened eye. This was possibly the final episode in Mad Mick's way of life before we virtually sent him to Coventry and saw very little more of him, which was just as well, as he was a liability and an embarrassment.

I could see that the attitudes of some of the Wickford lads were slowly taking the direction of nearby Basildon lads and with some of the crazy Basildon girls were heading for trouble with the authorities, as purple heart drugs smuggled out of the American airbases in Essex such as Wethersfield, were becoming available in the active new town, so I started to study my options.

By chance I met up with some old school pals who lived in the villages of Woodham Ferrers, Battlesbridge, Rettendon and Rawreth within five miles east of Wickford and were less main town oriented. They often gathered at the rather less than salubrious Four Aces

Café on the Burnham-on-Crouch Road, Battlesbridge. We met there during the week and it was suggested that on the coming Friday evening we would meet at the White Swan Petrol Station in Wickford and then ride on as a group to lively Basildon. It was late September so the evenings were getting darker.

THE ARRIVAL OF NIPPER

An inventor of perpetual-motion ?

I arrived there as planned at seven thirty in the Friday evening and was soon followed by Brinnie (or Brian) on his immaculate and well-engineered Velocette Valiant. A 200cc masterpiece that was too expensive to be built in mass production to be successful. Brinnie was closely followed by a few lads riding a mixture of cheap, aged and smoky, two stroke bikes, but one was well late. It was tall Adrian Emberson, all 2044 cms of him (or Nipper as he was strangely nicknamed as he came from a family of very tall people but was always his Mum's *nipper*). Laid back Nipper was one of the most likeable and amusing of the lads but was always the one who was late, often *very* late, it was sometimes jested that as he was so very tall his head lived in a different time zone. He was a full three hours late without passing any messages to a first date with Debbie. *I'm so tired, tired of waiting, tired of waiting for youuu, I'm so tired, tired of waiting, tired of waiting for youu. I was a lonely soul I had nobody 'til I met you, but you keepa' me waiting all of the time what should I do?* (8) for heavens sake marry him Debbie! (which she eventually did) and then we won't have to wait for him any more with his slow smoky BSA C10 and eventual slow Harley Davidson. He must have met the only truly extra tolerant girl in the county. Brinnie said that Nipper was on the way but would be rather late as he had run out of petrol near his home in South Woodham Ferrers. He had then gone home and had borrowed some paraffin out of his family's room heater and after putting the paraffin into his rather tired BSA 250 side-valve C10 he had managed with difficulty to bump start it, but it was suffering a huge loss of power and was now very slow and grossly overheating, so can we wait for him.

 Suddenly in the distance we saw what appeared as two very dull lights and as they got closer they were accompanied not by the sharp rapping of a motorbike engine at a pace but a noise more akin to a steam roller with low boiler pressure, issuing a struggling 'wooff wooff wooff'. Soon we can make out in the darkness a relatively slow moving motorcycle struggling to make 30 mph, with an outsize rider with a big smile from a large set of teeth with a dull headlamp that had long lost its silver and an engine that was running so hot that it glowed orange in the darkness like another dull headlight. It was Nipper on his old side-valve BSA running on paraffin and it really stank as only partly burnt paraffin can smell, with a grin on his face that a Cheshire cat couldn't hope to imitate. When ingenious Nipper reached us the engine was so hot that it wouldn't switch off and continued in perpetual motion, running without fuel nor sparks. Eventually Nipper stalled the engine to stop it, and it died. He said that the bike got slower and slower on the five mile journey from South Woodham Ferrers and he needed to fill the petrol tank with low grade petrol for his side-valve engine so that he could journey the further five miles with us to Basildon. The engine was so hot that it was still glowing a rather dull orange even though it was now no longer running. Nipper tried re-starting it but with no avail as the compression had vanished with the huge temporary heat expansion of the engine. He pushed it over to the petrol station so as to fill the tank whilst the engine was cooling down, but the pump attendant would have none of it until the engine had lost its colour and no longer presented a fire risk. Half an hour or so later and we were on our way with the old BSA sounding particularly unwell and stinking and smoking the road out until the unused paraffin/petrol mix in the fuel tank had been used up and the unburned paraffin in the exhaust system had evaporated away. Welcome to the gang Nipper. Nipper later bought a more suitable AJS 500 Spring-twin which was also too small for his six feet eight inch height even though he rode it from the rear of the dual-seat, and he replaced the AJS soon after with a 750 flat head (side-valve) Harley Davidson which had great street cred' but as far as braking, acceleration and top speed were concerned with its very low compression ratio, three speed gearbox and tiny brakes, it was totally disappointing and dynamically as good as an erectile dysfunction, until he re-engined it. As for handling and braking, well, there was a long corner that it failed to negotiate at a moderate speed on the A130 at Great Baddow, and Nipper and the lazy bike left the road and destroyed a large farm gate, ending up broken in a field, it just didn't handle like his AJS or even his ancient paraffin burning BSA C10. It was a ponderous craft . . . . but hey, who cares, it was a Harley, and was the only bike that could take his towering height. It had running boards, Buffalo horn size handlebars, a foot clutch, a hand gear-change on the side of the petrol tank and a huge leather Cowboy style saddle that was sprung loaded to compensate for the lack of any rear suspension. The huge saddle would come up and *spank* Nipper's backside with vengeance when he was reunited mid-air with it after being momentarily airborne when he and the bike leapt over a hump back bridge and became momentarily separated from each other. You could see that it was designed for the Desperate Dans or Boss Hogs of this world who seemed to thrive on cow pie that contained a cattle-stock growth hormone in its ingredients. The engine, being a side valve was indestructible if you over-revved it between gears. If you went too high in the revs, the engine would suffer with asphyxia, run out of power and start gasping at 4500 rpm. Whereas some of the British overhead valve engines would rev up to maybe 7000 rpm before tiring. This made a significant impact on performance.

Slow, outrageous, and only suitable for over-sized people, best sums up this Harley Davidson but it is still a talking point some fifty years later whilst so many of the other bikes are long gone and best forgotten. It became the centre of attraction wherever we went and also when Nipper, Brinnie and I rode to the 1965 Motor Cycle Show at Brighton with the Vincent and Venom they always attracted a small crowd when parked up. After the farm gate incident Nipper had no option than to rebuild the Harley into a quasi-chopper and replaced the engine with a reconditioned unit from Frank Warr the Harley Davidson dealer in Fulham, London. Due to the lack of suitable transport Nipper physically carried the very heavy engine on British Rail and then the underground trains and continued to carry it through the streets to an astonished reception at Warr's. He then carried the large replacement engine back all the way to South Woodham Ferrers. Nipper was very tall, very strong and often strangely crazy.

BRINNIE'S STORY

A sailor's son

Brinnie (Brian Woodman) was always one of the South Woodham Ferrers lads and his only interests were his mates, his pretty blonde girlfriend Jenny, and his Velocette Venom motorbike. Before he had a motorbike he was in the church choir and regularly rang the church bell. His skills were very evident as he certainly rang the bell with his pretty girl friend and superb Velocette motor bike. He would never let any one of the three down. Never a bore, always smartly turned out and forever looking for the next stage of adventure and excitement, especially burn ups on the bikes where he was a safe but very fast rider. I often met his sociable Dad when calling round to his house in Mount Pleasant Road, South Woodham Ferrers who would welcome me into his mesmerising radio shack that was a large garden shed full of electrical radio apparatus and gadgets with a plethora of external wires, and very tall aerials. He could, and regularly did talk to people in the evenings on the other side of the world from this shed by bouncing his radio signals off the upper atmosphere, which was a black science back then. Brinnie's Dad acquired his skill, ability and dedication to his hobby from the fact that he had been the Radio Officer aboard the famous ocean going, state of the art, four thousand horsepower military rescue tug, 'HM Rescue Tug Turmoil'. 'Tug Turmoil' was stationed at Falmouth in Cornwall near Lands End for the rescue or general help of large ships and warships crossing the Atlantic Ocean or elsewhere. It was the Tug Turmoil with Brinnie's Dad as the senior Radio Officer aboard, that went to the epic rescue of the freighter 'The Flying Enterprise' on it's journey from Europe to The United States that slowly started sinking in a furious Atlantic storm more than three hundred miles from Land's End in the winter of 1952 after a crack appeared in the floor of the bridge and wheelhouse. For several days the ex American Liberty ship, 'S.S. Flying Enterprise' stayed afloat but listing at 45 degrees or more with the crew sealing shut the watertight bulkheads before the storm was at full fury and jumping into the sea with its ten passengers and being rescued all but one, by an American destroyer and British rescue ships. It had a general cargo on its manifest including many tons of pig iron bars. *It is said* that they were actually bars of gold and Zirconium for the building of the world's (American) first nuclear submarine, the USS Nautilus. The loss of the Zirconium put back the building of USS Nautilus by more than a year. At a time when there was no GPS, deep ocean radar, nor highly reliable and accurate RDF pinpointing over long distances, somehow, like finding a needle in a haystack, Tug Turmoil located the stricken Flying Enterprise that was without power far into the Atlantic Ocean and with great difficulty probably using radio triangulation and dead reckoning. The tug's temporary first mate Kenneth Dancy, without a life jacket, jumped ship from The Turmoil to The Enterprise to secure a tow rope lead line and then The Turmoil started towing The Enterprise the three hundred nautical miles (345 land miles) back to Plymouth in the worst Atlantic storm for thirty five years. With the World's media watching all of the drama on daily TV news reports, the evocatively named thirty seven year old Danish captain of the Flying Enterprise, Captain Kurt Calsen, like a true traditional sailor, would not abandon his ship until it went totally below the waves. For two weeks he stayed on the slowly sinking and heavily listing ship with no power, to protect the owner's rights against several salvage ships that after reading the ships manifest, realised the potential value of its cargo was likely to be considerably more than the $7 Million stated, and were ready to pounce and claim salvage the moment the ship was abandoned. There were pictures in the press of Captain Calsen, the only remaining crew member left onboard, hanging on to the highly exposed rear rails of the Flying Enterprise like a crazed yacht racer in a storm, with the propeller in the air and the side of the ship now underwater whilst under tow by Tug Turmoil and rolling wildly in an Atlantic storm, so far out into the storm lashed ocean. After the dramatic rescue and salvage attempt by Her Majesty's Rescue Tug 'Turmoil', to a point where the sinking Flying Enterprise at the end of Tug Turmoil's huge five inch diameter tow rope and Turmoil were just twenty miles or so away from Lands End which would have been visible on a clear day. Such an incredible achievement, when the storm returned and the Enterprise took on more water through the heavily tilting funnel and was therefore doomed, the tow rope broke and The Flying Enterprise vanished below the waves with Captain Kurt Calsen and the tugs first mate that had bravely taken the tow rope's lead line to the Enterprise, running along the now laid flat and submerging funnel of the sinking ship and making a swim for it in the cold January North Atlantic and they were rescued by Tug Turmoil, as The Flying Enterprise finally slipped forever below the ocean, stern first to a salute of ships whistles, horns and sirens from the escorting flotilla and their crews removing their hats in respectful sadness.

A sad and dramatic end to an epic struggle that held the World's breath for two weeks

Brinnie, like so many of us born just after the war, and the son of the Radio Officer whose skill found the disaster struck "Flying Enterprise" in that storm-lashed ocean, came from a tough generation.

THE NIGHT RUN TO BOURNEMOUTH

*CRASH, KERUMP, CRUNCH, and OUCH, BLOODY OUCH. ? What the F? . . . . .*I am laying in a bus lay-by, dazed, motorbike laying on top of me, with its' warm exhaust on my leg, and a slight but worrying smell of petrol, looking up at a nearby town clock, and the clock is telling me that it's nearly half past eleven at night and asking, what am I up to? For a few moments, I asked myself the very same question. Furthermore there is this stone faced chap on a horseback looking down at me contemptuously, wake up I say to myself, and get a grip of things. After clearing my thoughts I realise that the arrogant man on a horse is nothing more than a large statue of William of Orange, King William III, well dead and nearly forgotten, frozen in stone for any misdeeds he was guilty of. I muse to myself that when I die I'd rather be buried in an Essex churchyard in a worm proof and cosy coffin and the mental comfort of a dead ringer bell, than to be frozen in stone.

Time to get back on my bike and restart my journey came to my mind, but where am I?

The previous summer, my best schoolmate, Peter Andrews (Andy) had moved away from Wickford to Bournemouth with his parents, who were decent church people. During the first summer's evening of moving in to Bournemouth, Andy took the new neighbour's (also good church people), bubbly, buxom and forward thinking sixteen year old daughter, Jackie, to the local park and throwing his family morals to the wind, made her pregnant. He never did anything by halves. Randy Andy indeed, but then, Jackie was no prude Ruby either. Jackie was an attractive, 5ft 7" bubbly bespectacled honey blonde that mother-nature had adorned with a splendid 42 inch pleasure chest that she unsuccessfully tried to hide behind a fishnet top. Jackie, nor anyone near her was able to ignore this asset, and other teenage girls were always green with envy to the point of being totally cattish. Oh how ones memory occasionally sharpens.

Jointly, the decent parents gave them a homely house, they married, the child was born and fortunately they became a happy family. Twice a year they would invite me down for a weekend, occasionally with a friend and usually on my bike to share their company for a few days.

The journey from Wickford to Bournemouth was always done after my work as a vehicle mechanic during a Friday evening, leaving Wickford around 7 pm and arriving in Bournemouth about 11.30, four and a half hours riding a bike fast for the 160 miles. There were no motorways back then, hardly any dual carriageway sections, plenty of moderate speed main-roads, too many 30 mph speed limits, South London to avoid or suffer, plenty of unfamiliar bends and junctions, poorly or non-lit roads and worst of all, tiredness and uncertainty.

Top speed of the bike made little difference, it mattered how swift it was and how good the lights, brakes and handling were, I never got the journey down to less than three hours and forty minutes, which was on a Vincent. No matter how hard I rode the bike, nor which bike. It was just a long and very intensive ride.

Tiredness was always a problem on a late night long run, one would think that with a constant sixty or seventy mph gale in your face with the open face crash helmets that we used for decades, and a busy engine and like being in a steam train's cab, that you could not possibly get tired on a pleasant summer's evening run, even if it was after a physical and busy day at work, . . . not so.

On this particular occasion, I was delayed getting away from work by necessary overtime attending to a broken supercharger driveshaft on a Commer TS3 refrigerated truck, It had to be fixed to prevent the frozen contents from melting. The truck failed late in the day and came in late and I'd already put a clutch and head-gasket in a Hillman Imp and then put a new drive chain and gears in a Benford cement mixer and missed lunch. Consequently I left Wickford nearer to eight o'clock, more than a little hungry and unfortunately did not have a pillion passenger to keep me company. So I popped a Mars bar in my mouth and put an apple and another Mars in my jacket pocket and opened up the Greeves Sports-Twin motorbike, an astonishingly rapid and smooth 250 that was based on a competition scrambler whose road-holding was just unbelievable, and made a dash for it. A127, A128, A13, Dartford Tunnel, Sevenoaks, Otford, A25, Reigate, Hogs Back, Guildford, and the A31 to Winchester, it's time to pull up because I'm getting a little tired and it's gone ten. I remember wishing the bike was noisier and rougher to help me keep awake but alas it was just a very rapid smoothy, I pulled up at a junction on the A31 and whilst eating my apple and second Mars bar I waited for a motor bike or sporting car to pass and act as a challenger, a sparring partner, a pace car even, I needed a burn up badly to keep me awake. But all that came along were Fords, mostly 3 speed and slow, or Austins and Hillmans being driven at a genteel Sussex pace. What I needed was a Manic Mini, a Triumph Vitesse, an egoistically driven Jaguar, or . . and then it happened, into the junction at high speed came a nearly new Dragoon Red Ford Cortina Mk1 GT. The race was on and I could now stay awake a little longer, twenty or so fast miles later the Cortina screeched into an industrial estate, dust flying, and he was gone! in the middle of nowhere. I assumed that either he was involved in a robbery and was trying to outrun me thinking that I was a Police Bike, or that he was a shift worker and was running very late on timekeeping. Either way he was gone, and unfortunately I did not see him re-appear in my mirror, drat! I had lost my fast ride challenger and it was now return to the awful quiet darkness and sixty more tired and lonely miles to go.

  Shortly after this escapade and after regaining some speed and after singing loudly to myself to keep awake and slapping my own face as best as one can when wearing a crash helmet, I succumbed to the reality of it all, and pulled up in the first town that I could find without taking a note of its name, and being too tired to shut the engine down properly nor turn off the petrol, I put the bike on to its centre stand, climbed back on, quickly rested my helmeted head on to the handlebars and headlamp and fell into a deep sleep cosily inside the crash helmet, with the engines heat giving me some comfort. . . .Some time later . . .CRASH KERUMP AND OUCH, . . BLOODY OUCH. . .*What the F*. . .the bike and I are strange bedfellows and on our sides on the pavement edge. I assumed that I had moved in my sleep astride the bike and losing balance, toppled over, I guessed that more than half an hour had passed since I had stopped as the exhaust now resting on my trapped leg was not hot enough to burn through my jeans, so I quickly picked the bike up and after plenty of lusty kicks of the kick-starter with the petrol temporarily turned off, the choke off and the throttle wide, to clear the now flooded carburettor, induction system and fouled sparking plugs, it sprang into erratic life in a cloud of crazy blue two-stroke smoke, and after deciding 'Where am I ?' or were I was. After studying the phone numbers painted above a few shops it was clear that I was at the square at Petersfield, Hampshire. After circling the deserted square and finding a road-sign to the A31, and with a handful of throttle to clear the bike's throat of the accumulated petrol in its crankcase and the fuel now turned on again, I shot off into the night on my bike like a startled cat leaving William of Orange forever frozen in time sitting on his horse and surrounded by billowing smoke as in a battlefield, excepting that it was of a blue pollution variety from a twentieth century steed. I headed towards The New Forest, Ringwood, and Kinson to complete the night run to Bournemouth soon after midnight, and a happy few days enjoyable break before returning to Essex a little more awake.

  Bournemouth as always is a lovely town to visit with its avenues of pine trees, and its chines adorned with rhododendrons. The views from the many cliff-tops of Poole Bay with the Old Harry Rocks off Swanage to the right and The Isle of Wright with the Needles Rocks guarding the Solent to the left, with many white yacht sails, give it an unmatched panorama. A bike ride to from Bournemouth to sunny Swanage, considered by many to be the jewel of the South Coast, is fascinating with the journey through the fast running waters to Poole Harbour on the popular chain ferry from Sandbanks to Studland Bay making a good day of it. Car parking in Bournemouth, as always, is both difficult due to the lack of adequate car parks, and very expensive. A motorcycle or the Yellow Buses, make most sense. Slow moving traffic makes matters worse. It is a high quality town that is the victim of its own success. Bournemouth has a beautiful Central Gardens and fine golden sand beaches, a far cry from the cobbles of Brighton or the miles of mud at Southend-on-Sea. The frustration of its traffic can be avoided with a visit to the National Motor Museum at Beaulieu or to the quaint waterside and ancient warship building, road-less village of Bucklers Hard which are not too far away.

The following year I did the same journey a little less tired on the noisier Royal Enfield Bullet in the spring and the Vincent that I had then just bought, in the summer and I stayed awake, wide-awake throughout the journey, lesson learnt.

JUST FOR KICKS

Summer evenings and weekends in the sixties were wonderful, especially if you had a decent bike and mixed with a decent bunch of like-minded lads, and a few fun-loving but daring and obedient teenage girls. The girls had to be obedient or they were not allowed on the back seat of the bike where it was, hang on tight dear, hold very tight,

> *Hold tight on the count of three, you've got to stay close to me, Hold tight to my belt, this bike really goes like hell, Don't shut your eyes nor wiggle and shout, here comes another roundabout, You'll never fall, each time I call Hold Tight, Hold Tight, Hold Tiyiyiyiyiyight . . .(8)*

145

. . . and do exactly as I say, this is going to be very fast fun, . . . Have you got strong nerves? No room for dizzy bimbos here. The truth was that rarely did any of us lads take a strange girl for more than a hundred yard experience down the road, as we rarely carried a spare crash helmet and we were very aware of the risks, especially with some of the air headed young girls. Often when returning to a parked bike, there would be a small group of giggling young girls daring each other to ask for a quick thrill. We so often disappointed them and said sorry but no, because a ride *without* their slowing down influence, was much more fun than to enjoy the slack suggestive promises of the "Kiss Me Quick" hats of the Southend-on-Sea tarts.

Friday evenings throughout the county would usually be spent in the local village hall youth clubs. For decades this had been the routine with the local village girls turning up dressed to attract but in defensive groups, giggling and teasing the local bike lads who wanted an evening's fun. Because they didn't want to kill themselves being drunk on their bikes, these lads did not want to spend the evening in the pub. They would however go to the local village hall with its young girls. With the 78 or the more modern 33 and 45 rpm records being played on a Dansette record player, or in a corner there would invariably be a few others who would be excitingly chasing through the wavelengths on an Ekco or Pye radio trying to tune in and refine the poor reception of the apparently law avoiding music coming in across the nearby North Sea from Radio Luxemburg, on 208 metres. Pirate Radio was on the way. BBC, being the boring 'Auntie BBC', only transmitted pop music for an hour each day and all of the teenagers searched out the few alternative pirate stations to enjoy the evenings, listening to The Beatles, Elvis, The Who, and Cliff Richard.

Saturday mornings mostly meant the lads went to work on the building sites or in the garages and shops as part of a five and a half day, fifty two and a half hour week which was normal back then. Saturday afternoons usually involved cleaning and tuning the bike ready for the morrow. Sundays were usually spent with the boys on the bikes on a trip to Brands Hatch, a burn up to the coast, a visit to a local hill-climb, scramble or grass-track event, or an afternoon at the notorious Blinking Owl Café on the nearby A127. Sunday and the Owl was just for kicks.

> *Just for kicks we ride all through the night, my bird hangs on in fright as we do the ton for Kicks, we meet the other ton up boys at Teds caf' every night, we just pop in to see the birds and sometimes have a bite, we spend a couple of hours tuning our machines with our black leather jackets and our oily greasy jeans, Now the M1's not much fun, 'til you try to do a ton, a burn up on my bike, that's what I like.(9)*

With the background music industry of Elvis, The Rolling Stones, The Beatles and The Who, Big Bopper and Acker Bilk, the sixties had arrived with a bang. Adding to the dynamics of the time, the fabulous and stunning Jaguar E Type was introduced at a speed, price and styling that left Ferrari agog.

THE NOTORIOUS BLINKING OWL 1964

The Blinking Owl Café was strategically placed at the bottom of a long hill (Rayleigh Cutting) alongside the London bound side of the A127 Arterial Road dual carriageway near Rayleigh in Essex. Within easy reach of the East London and without a speed limit for most of its life, it was a very popular visiting destination for bikers wanting a burn up from London and central Essex as well as the Southend-on-Sea lads, and Londoners returning home on their bikes after a day on the seafront. It was the scene of much activity with upwards of a hundred bikes filling its large car park on a sunny summer's day. During the 1960's the Owl was managed by Len, an unsmiling middle-aged portly bushy-moustached individual and his raven-haired wife, who had an unfortunate and coincidental twitch to her face. I'd hate to think the place was named after her. At times it was a busy place with its fast road position but also as it had a rare condom machine in the gents that attracted the lads from afar.

NO CONDOMS? No, oh well, cough sweets will do!

In the sixties, long before the contraceptive pill was available, let alone the morning after pill, it was usually left to the lads to obtain a small supply of condoms. You could of course, go to the local chemists, where once plucking up enough bravado, you would approach the counter where invariably an unsmiling and authoritative looking woman wearing drop dead awful Dame Edna Everage glasses, would offer to serve you with an eagle eye, maybe she was an unhappy middle age virgin who disapproved or was jealous of your planned use for her goods. She would suggest with her assertive eyes and without passing a word that she knew you or your girlfriend's mother and would blow cover. At which point you would ask for some unwanted cough-sweets and beat a hasty retreat. Dam, DAM! . Alternatively you could go to the local barber, even if long hair was the trend so you didn't want his scissors in full flight, but he would cough to the back of his hand and quietly ask, 'anything for the weekend Sir?' Again, he might know your girlfriend's Dad. Either way he would certainly know all of the local lads and may expose you in his eternal small talk to his clients. So the few known places in South Essex that had a secluded condom machine enjoyed good business. Condom machines didn't ask questions. You just hoped that if you travelled some distance to the Owl or elsewhere to operate the said machine that it was not empty nor defunct on your arrival which would thwart your best laid plans for the next few days or week.

Being in the country, the Owl was a place of many fragrances. Often when you neared it on your bike during the evening, you might define the various odours wafting in on the summer breeze. One might ask oneself, is that the fragrance of the oft overfull cesspit, nay, maybe 'tis the glorious smell of Castrol 'R' emitting from a BSA

Gold Star or other sports-bike exhaust. (Castrol 'R' is an expensive vegetable based engine oil that was marketed for racing motorcycles by Castrol and has a smell similar to burnt or rotten cabbage, namely carbon tetrachloride), and is actually quiet addictive to many. Nay, I say, 'tis non of these. So what on this pleasant Earth is it that hides the pleasurable aroma of the sweet Essex countryside's summer evening flora?

ARSON of THE VENDING MACHINE

Arrive at the Owl, park bike, kill engine, deeply inhale, no, no, no, . . .gently and cautiously inhale, after all, the Owl's smelly air on a bad day could be cut with a knife, it is dark, the nights are coming forward, hence the need for this journey. In the pitch dark, all inquisitive noses point in the direction of this strangely aromatic event, emitting from the gents toilet block in thorough and total darkness, in the centre of the rear car park. An unloved building, whose cheap un-tiled but white-washed breeze-block walls retain the awful smell of so many decades of much discharged and unwanted urine. Do I have to go in there? I ask myself. Do I really have to go in there? there was no option. The next few days are dependent on this visit. Into the deepest pit of smells and darkness that stand guardian around the money grabbing condom machine I venture, slowly forward into this wretched place, the solitary light bulb dangles hopelessly as it is emitting virtually no light from the ceiling. Almost totally covered with the fried bodies of dozens of blinded and inquisitive but now dead flies, Oh Joy. Oh Joy! I borrow a cigarette lighter from one of the lads and flick it into life, and there in the flickering abysmal gloom is partly the source of so much foul air, there, looking as though it has been born in a prehistoric cave of stalactites, is the grotesque looking remains of the condom machine that has been the victim of a revengeful arson attack. It has suffered an unexpected thermal torture typified by a user seeking retribution after risking making his girlfriend pregnant when one of this machine's products split in action. The machine is now burnt and blistered, the plastic operating handle has melted. Molten latex that had earlier oozed from the machine's bowels during the awful inferno, hangs like dried candle wax snots from its various machine joints where the condom stock has been set alight by some angry lad, who dowsing the machine in lighter fluid, and then in an act of machine phobia and hatred, set it alight. The sad machine appeared to have been crying. Bah !

This was such a common occurrence that the machine's owner, The London Rubber Company was reluctant to promptly replace it. Understandably many bikers were asking, who ruined the machine this time? The ruinous person had spoilt so much entertainment for so many lads (and girls) for up to a month, whilst awaiting a replacement machine. If the arsonist could be found he would almost certainly have been lynched or castrated, slowly, due to his selfish revenge. Whoever he was, he had a price on his head.

Sadly there were no letters from France on that day, just an arrogant Frenchman by the name of Charles De-Gaulle in the news saying *Non-Cordial, Non Cordial*, as he didn't want us to join the Common Market where our products might damage his industries'. Maybe the condom would soon be replaced by the not yet available contraceptive pill, and the 'French Letter' would be consigned to history, *Non-Cordial, Non Cordial, Non Entente Cordiale! O'u sont mes produits?* from the land of 2CVs, snails and frog legs, I can hear him cry. A bit rich for someone that we saved from drowning in the English Channel, and then gave him his country back. Maybe Brexit will have the last laugh after all. *Non Cordial indeed.*

RECYCLED DOUGHNUTS

In the roadside cafés it was not unknown for uneaten doughnuts or rum ba-bas to be seen being placed back into the glass display cabinet for re-selling, and the Owl was no exception. No doubt this happens elsewhere throughout the food world. What was hideous about the Owl was that it was not unknown for one of the bikers who disapproved of this recycling and was hell-bent on a bit of fun, to deliberately leave an uneaten jam doughnut on his table. He would not ride off on his bike before posting a awful nicotine stained dog-end from a nasty ashtray, deep into the doughnut's jam orifice and then scram. When the café' owner later cleared the tables, the uneaten doughnuts and Rum Ba-Bas were often recycled to the next hungry biker or trucker. Yuk!

Eventually the café owner was seen religiously emptying the ashtrays and not recycling jam doughnuts any more, maybe he ate a 'recycled' one himself, and after sinking his teeth in, stopped the penny-pinching practice. Ugh, a self-inflicted justice, a just dessert indeed . . . if there ever was such a thing.

Beware of the jam doughnut !

One of the spectacles at the Owl was the Jukebox Record Race where a brave challenger would put a nickel (silver sixpence) in the jukebox (Nickel Odeon) and dash out to the car park, start his bike and ride like a scalded cat to the first London bound intersection on the A127, turn and then shoot off in the reverse direction to the next Southend bound intersection, turn and then accelerate like fury and with very heavy braking back and finish the lap at the Owl, dismount and return to the Jukebox before the record ended.

Few but the mad tried it more than once as it needed a very quick bike and a very quick rider to achieve it. Most would choose the music that maybe lasted twenty seconds more than the norm' and would have a helper holding the bike at the ready with the engine running for the off and taking the bike from the rider at the end of the madness while he ran to the jukebox. The very craziest would race against a piece of music taken at random and have to start his bike at the start of the race and at end of the race, put it on it's stand, an extreme challenge. Only the likes of hell-for-leather Clyde Cardy with his sharp turning and lightning quick Triumph Bonneville could do it.

Not many would attempt it, and those that did risked a blown engine, a broken chain or a pile up. But then, few were as quick as Clyde.

Canvey Beach Bus

The Canvey Island horse-drawn beach bus. Summer 1946.

The Grace Darling Bus

Nearly one-hundred years ago and with an epic story to tell.

Queue for the Canvey Island Ferry

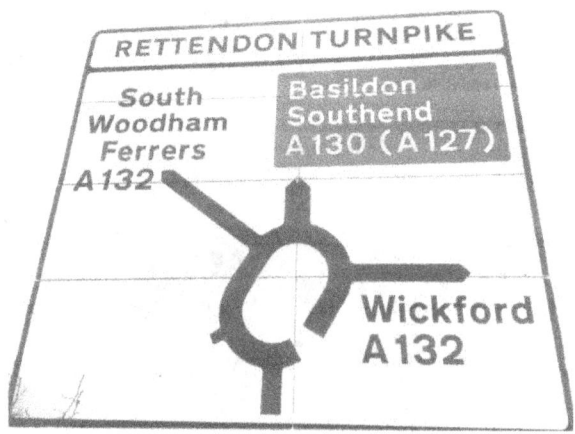

The Turnpike Road Sign

The area from which much of the fun started.

Bikes and Lads at Jaywick, 1964.

L to R: Malcolm 650 (BSA Road Rocket). Brinnie (500 Velocette Venom). Myself (Royal Enfield Bullet). Easy Dick (Norton Jubilee). Jed (Greeves 250 Sportstwin) and Nipper (AJS 500 Spring Twin).

Bikes and Lads at Jaywick, 1965.

Another Jaywick shot, this time in the summer of 1965. L to R: Brinnie (Velocette). Myself (Vincent). The Bear (BSA Golden Flash). Malcolm (BSA Road Rocket) and Nipper (AJS 500).

Keeping the Saddles Warm

These Nottingham barmaids took no prisoners.

Author, Easy Dick and Vincent.

Easy Dick and I at Brands Hatch after a fast ride down from Essex.

Brighton, 1965.

Myself, all 6ft 8inches of Nipper, and Brinnie.

The Rebuilt Harley Davidson

Rebuilt after the farm gate incident. The monstrous Harley was the only bike eventually big enough for Nipper's size.

The Harley Davidson

The bike before the altercation with the farm gate.

Vincent and Velocette.

The very likeable Bear at Essex Avenue, Jaywick, with two very rapid bikes. The Vincent and the Velocette.

The Thunderous Vincent

Engineering Magnificence.

Fifty Years Later

Myself astride my 1959 Velocette Viper, some fifty years after the Mods and Rockers riots of Clacton and elsewhere.

PART SIX
Three Wheeled Chaos.

AN EPITAPH TO THE SIDECAR WORLD

In the late fifties and early sixties many families travelled by motorcycle and sidecar combinations. Typically Dad would do the riding and Mum would either be pillion or travel out of the wind and rain in the relative but noisy comfort of the sidecar that may have one or two extra seats for children or adults, with a squeeze. Families would travel hundreds of miles happily on holiday in the UK or even Europe in this manner, and it was seen as a bit of an adventure. It was a lot more affordable than a second hand or new car, which still commanded high prices due to the post war shortages that still prevailed. During the few years after the war some dealers would not sell you a car unless you had a car to part exchange for them to earn tomorrows living. The sidecar outfits were a lot cheaper to buy than a used, often pre-war car as you could buy an unused ex-army large engined BSA M20 or Norton 16H from Pride and Clarke in London for just £29. 10 shillings and then attach a second hand or new sidecar to it and suddenly you had dependable family transport, great in the summer as many had cheap canvas sunroofs, but wrap up very warm in the winter was the routine. Before too many years passed, in 1959, the British car industry reacted against the older models of the pre and post-war years and refreshed the market with attractive and economical small family cars. With such tempting models being offered on easy terms (hire purchase) such as the stylish Triumph Herald and Ford 105E Anglia, the exciting Mini, the rapid Hillman Imp and the endearing Morris Minor Traveller. Sidecar owners went in droves to active car dealers and updated their family transport to a stylish out of-the-weather four-seater, with a heater and no kick-starter. So many a sidecar chassis was either buried in a back garden after the burning of the plywood body on the fortnightly bonfires, or were sold cheap as chips to sixteen year old first time bikers. Very soon the government tightened up the motor cycle laws to prevent incapable and inexperienced learners buying large engined and high powered ninety miles per hour solo motor cycles by limiting the size of learner motor cycles to 250 cc which at that time often had a top speed often no more than seventy miles per hour, until the Japanese motorcycle invasion of the mid sixties made a mockery of the relationship between engine size and top speed. As the government did not extend the engine size limits to sidecar outfits, many lads got hold of an old 500 or 600 cc motorbike and sidecar outfit and after discarding the plywood sidecar bodies and tying on L plates, drove them round with a lot of noisy drama and looking and sounding rather cool, with maybe a few planks or an old door lashed to the bare sidecar chassis. They felt more like a Rocker than those who rode around on L-plates on a smoky, sluggish, two stroke James, Francis Barnet or Excelsior. There were a few exciting exceptions from Norton (the Jubilee), Royal Enfield (the Crusader) or BSA (the C15 Sports) with a proper four-stroke engine with a more rapid performance, and a fast and very attractive two stroke, the Ariel Golden Arrow. But alas, they were new to the market and could not be bought at the knock down prices that many learners could afford. The insurance on the sidecar outfits with a big banger engine was very low due to the historic low accident rate of the big engine Panther, BSA or other outfits. With the cloth capped Dad and his family on board, they were statistically the safest vehicles on the road. Eventually, with adventure seeking sixteen year olds changing the accident statistics, insurance premiums would raise, but not before most of these outfits had been thrashed, trashed and the owner had then bought a faster solo or a car. Few of the sidecars lasted into the future as their bodies were laughed at with the exception of products from Steib and Garrard that were open torpedo styled and looked totally terrific when attached to a Vincent Rapide, or an Ariel Square Four or BSA 650. Amongst every group of lads there would be at least one lad who rode a sidecar outfit, or 'Chair' as they were humorously known.

A RETURN TRIP TO THE ISLE OF MAN

Many motorbike conversations were overheard and discussed at The Blinking Owl every time that we visited and we would often be involved in their planning, if not the eventual and sometimes crazy outcome.

A typical plot that was not too long in the planning but was well thought out and executed with the exception of one *critical 'what if' scenario,* was set up by three of the well known Southend bikers led by Gary, if I remember rightly of Leigh-on-Sea, who decided to visit the annual TT Races of the Isle of Man in June of 1965 using a BSA 650 A10 Gold Flash and a sidecar.

The plan was for them to leave their solo motorcycles behind at their homes in the Southend area and then all three to travel up to Liverpool, itself quite a long two hundred and sixty mile and six or seven hour journey on a motorcycle, before taking the motorcycle and sidecar combination, a 'Combo', on to the Isle of Man Steam Packet ferry to Douglas on the Isle of Man in the middle of the Irish Sea. The holiday period short stay accommodation on the Island during TT week was always fully booked, and so the ingenious plan of the lads was to find a convenient field and set up camp, possibly free of charge in the tent and camping apparatus that they would stow in the boot and deep foot-well of the sidecar. So far, so good. It was to be a wet week but they were prepared for a hardy existence just to enjoy the TT experience. The bike racing was thrilling with several lap records being smashed on the long Snaefell (Snowfall) Mountain Circuit despite the wet weather and foggy sections, cross winds up the higher part of the mountain especially on the Senior TT Race due to the increasing invasion of very high revving multi-cylinder machines from Italy, and Japan. Simply, higher revs equal higher horse-power (BHP), as BHP is the direct resultant of RPM multiplied by torque. However, higher RPM and multi cylinder construction is often combined with unreliability and unaffordability, especially to the privateer riders who form the majority of the racers.

The circuit is almost thirty-eight miles of terror and with the many rider fatalities it is known as the most dangerous race in the world.

The Senior TT races for 500 cc machines are six laps and two hundred and thirty six miles and more than two hours long, climbing and descending a mountain, traversing tram tracks, going through villages and country lanes and over the notorious hump back bridge, Ballaughs Bridge. With maximum average lap speeds in 1965 averaging round 100 mph, with some speeding down the mountain at 150 mph, this not a race for the faint hearted. There are races for smaller engine size with even the tiny 50 cc class averaging more than 80 mph and motorbike and sidecar racing not far behind the tremendous speeds of the Senior Class, because with a sidecar they can skid around corners like a racing car. Gary and the lads went there to witness the races and the dicing between multi champion Mike Hailwood and the young Italian Giacomo Agostini, both competing for the World Championship on the very high speed Italian MV Augusta four cylinder racing bikes. Giacomo slid off at speed in the wet at Sarah's Cottage and retired unhurt. On the very next lap, Mike Hailwood crashed at the very same spot on a sister bike, an MV Augusta and damaged the bike and ended up with a bloody nose and torn leathers. Mike would *not* give up, he remounted his messed up bike, and after kicking it rideable, he rode it to the pits, twice, for accident repairs. Not only did he complete the race but won it an average speed of 91.69 mph including the crash and extra pit stops for first aid to his nose and emergency repairs to his bike. This was the slowest speed for six years due to the appalling rainstorm and very high winds, but Mike beat Joe Dunphy on a Norton and Mike Duff on a Matchless to second and third places. Mike Hailwood (Mike the Bike) doesn't give up, even in the face of disaster, *He wins.*

At the end of the week is the traditional 'Mad Sunday' where all and sundry motorcyclists and sidecar jockeys are allowed to try the circuit out on their own road bikes, both an invitation and a recipe for a disaster.

Not surprising Gary and his crew decided to try their skill and luck, or lack of it, on the powerful BSA 650 combination that had brought them all the way from Southend-on-Sea a week earlier and raced round the thirty six mile circuit at a thrilling pace until after seventeen miles they approached Ballaughs Bridge at a speed where their luck ran out.

They became victims of the hump back of Ballaughs Bridge where most bikes at racing speeds become airborne for a noticeable distance and if they don't land in a straight line then a crash is a certainty and sometimes fatal. Regular three wheeled combinations rarely landed square and in the impending crash Gary broke a leg, the bike was bent and the sidecar body destroyed. The *critical 'what if' scenario* had now played its trump card.

How do three lads get home, nearly three hundred miles in the rain, with a badly damaged bike, no sidecar to ride in and the rider/owner Gary with a broken leg, they thought that they had found a way.

Gary didn't give up. A local garage with a welding kit straightened his BSA and sidecar chassis, a local timber yard sold him an old house door, which the lads lashed to the now exposed sidecar chassis, and they embarked on to the ferry back to Liverpool and prepared for their long journey back from Liverpool down to Southend-on-Sea in distant Essex.

Once they had disembarked at Liverpool it didn't take more than a couple of miles of riding to realise that whilst two of the lads on the motorcycle were practical, Gary the hapless owner of the motorcycle and sidecar could not possibly endure the long journey back to Southend-on-Sea sitting amongst the camping gear that was acting as cushions strapped to the household door that was lashed to the now exposed sidecar frame and chassis. Not only was it very uncomfortable but he was also in pain and the wet weather on the A5 down to London would just saturate and destroy the plaster encasing his broken leg. So the plan changed again, but with a surprising outcome.

The new plan was for the two lads in good health to indeed travel down to Southend on the remains of the combination that was now bereft of its body but to let Gary basically hitch-hike down to Southend with his leg in plaster.

It seems like a mad and selfish act, but they made the plan whilst sitting in a Liverpool transport café where a trucker offered to take Gary down to South Mimms in North London to another transport café, where he was due to make a break in the journey and hope that Gary would find another sympathetic trucker there to take him the final fifty miles to Southend, and so he did. However Gary's first thoughts of travelling by a lorry were not very happy as he thought that with a broken leg, how could he possibly climb up into the high cab let alone put up with the hard uncomfortable ride that was the reputation of goods vehicles of the time. The trucker replies "eyup lud" in the typical Lancastrian accent (eyes up lad), "not t' worry 'bout them there concerns, my truck is one of them thar new Bedford TKs, itsa flier with a bench seat to rest your broken leg on and a low floor givin' it easy access, not like one of them Yorkshire juggernauts, you'll be awlrite with me lud" and the plan went ahead and he got to South Mimms before getting another ride in a Ford Transit also with easy access and a bench seat from South Mimms to Southend. Not only did Gary get to Southend warm and dry but the lads on the bike got a thorough dowsing in the rain in the wet seven hour journey, and Gary arrived in Southend before his mates on the remains of the combination, as they had to keep stopping to dry out. Where there's a will, there's a way.

MORE SIDECAR MADNESS

In the very early sixties the demise of the traditional family type of sidecar came very quickly as learners ripped off the ugly utilitarian bodies to make them go faster and not look like their Dad or great uncle minus a cloth cap. More vanished as the not very substantially built plywood bodies were being destroyed in relatively minor collisions.

There was one almost laughable incident on the eastbound A127 near Upminster on a sunny Saturday afternoon when a sidecar outfit laden with four Romford Rockers, two in the sidecar, was knocked for six by a van exiting Childerditch Lane at too great a speed and going into the path of the happy rockermobile that was on its way to the Golden Mile at Southend-on-Sea. The sidecar jockey tried to avoid the oncoming collision by whacking his brakes on and swerving into the fast lane of the A127, but to no avail. The sidecar was heavily clipped by the van and with so much inertia and impact its body broke free from its chassis and carried on to Southend with no wheels and now separated from the bike and with two Rockers still aboard until skidding eventually to a halt to much amusement of the Romford Lads who saw it as part of a 'good day out' The Romford lads were very much like the East Enders and could always see the funny side of things, whether trivial or more dramatic, it seemed as though their view was the bigger the drama the bigger the laugh. At least they didn't have to scrap nor bury the sidecar body, it was just dumped on the roadside and eventually rotted away.

Another event that convinced lads not to buy an outfit was one autumn evening in Wickford where many of us gathered each evening at the 251 bus-stop with its double length bus bay. Crazy Pete on his fire breathing Big Beeza M20 outfit saw fit to let Colin Selvage, a likeable 'I can do anything' Jack-the-Lad have a ride of his outfit. Colin, having ridden many miles without too much incident on his Triumph Tiger Cub, wouldn't listen to a brief piece of advice from Peter and gave the bike a hand full of throttle, dropped the clutch and with much noise, smoke and dust, pillion and all, vanished under the railway bridge towards Basildon . . . but didn't exit the other side on the left hand bend and things went worryingly rather quiet. We waited with baited breath for a few moments and then dashed under the railway bridge to see Colin laying on the right hand pavement, rousing from being knocked semi-conscious, his pillion passenger leaning against a lamp-post repeatedly saying "what the hell happened" "what the hell happened" and the BSA big banger side valve outfit going round in circles without a rider, on the triangular pavement outside the greengrocers and the electrical store, handlebars on full right lock and managing to continue going round in circles whilst its unstoppable low RPM engine kept going Chuff De Chuff De Chuff until someone leapt forward and raised the valve lifter and stopped the mayhem. It was a comical scene but totally brought about by Colin refusing a few words of wisdom from the outfits owner about a torque steer similarity, especially when there is no passenger in the sidecar and therefore no weight in the sidecar, and especially when your only passenger is riding pillion and even more so if you are accelerating hard. After the event Colin stuck to his Tiger Cub until he had a slow speed head on crash with a fibreglass milk-float in Basildon, with me as pillion which damaged his pride more than the bike or the milk-float and then decided to get a car, a tidy but totally unlikeable 1948 Morris Ten.

Being a passenger on a sidecar outfit was pretty uneventful if not very noisy if travelling in the sidecar body with the big bike engine working hard to maintain momentum whilst next to your right ear. It was often more enjoyable to ride on the pillion of the bike behind the rider or Jockey and leave the sidecar empty if there were just two of you.

EASY DICK

Dick Schmeig was a likeable and stout fun loving mate from Brentwood. I got to know him at Southend Technical College where we were both technical students, he being a trainee mechanic at a historic country garage at Rettendon Common. The garage owner gave him an old motorcycle and sidecar outfit to use for his daily commute as there was no cross-country bus route from his home in Brentwood to work at Rettendon Common. The bike was an old and far less than elaborate AJS 500 cc single cylinder bike that always refused to start due to a weak magneto unless intoxicated with a large gulp of easy start (an ether aerosol) and two quick and mighty prods of the kick- starter. The first hefty prod usually created a tremendous bang with a violent backfire of flames through the carburettor which had to be promptly followed by a second kick for the engine to consume the flames that danced around the carburettor from the vaporizing easy start vapour and spilt petrol from the flooding and backfire, *or* we had an unwanted bike fire from the backfire. It was always a terrific experience to stand back and watch Dick as the bike shook on the first backfire dropping a mixture of oily mud and rust onto the parking spot followed by a lions roar when it actually started on the rapidly following second attempt. He always carried an aerosol can of easy start but never a fire extinguisher in his coat pocket, in the same style of instant availability as Popeye's mate Wimpy who had a ready-to-eat BBQ hot-dog in his top hat. Hence we nicknamed him Easy (Easy Start) Dick, a name that very much suited his easy going and likeable character.

Dick would often pop over to visit me at Wickford on this Goliath of a bike and I introduced him to the Four Aces lads where he was much accepted. On one occasion whilst we were taking a ride around the scenic and local Hanningfield Reservoir back-roads, we entered a bend a little too fast. It was a very acute and green-leaf hairpin bend without any helpful camber. It was a narrow but reasonably busy lane that was impossible to navigate through this bend's inner and tighter radius at more than an ambitious 20 mph, regardless how good your tyres were or how many wheels your vehicle was built with. A lowly 15 mph was really its safe maximum. On this occasion the dynamics of the sidecar outfit were not at their best as I was on the pillion seat of the bike and the old family sidecar body was empty. Dick misjudged this tight left hand bend and under-braked entering at a very critical 22 mph, just too fast and the sidecar lifted, wheel in the air, the bike and the two of us started leaning wrongly to the right and with a panicky shout of "Oh S**t!" from Dick, I climbed onto the roof of the air-born sidecar and brought it down so that the sidecar wheel was back in touch with the road again. It was as exciting as dinghy racing without getting wet but far more dangerous. Fortunately we stayed on the road albeit on the wrong side and fortunately there was no oncoming traffic.

Some weeks later Dick came over again to Wickford and being a fine day we decided to leave his sidecar outfit at my home and go to Brands Hatch on my Royal Enfield Bullet to watch some racing. We had a little bit of time on our side which was just as well as I found that during that night my Royal Enfield had suffered a puncture in its back tyre. Rather than travel to Brands Hatch in the noisy and slow through traffic sidecar outfit, we elected to remove the back wheel of the Bullet, repair the puncture in the inner-tube and then take the wheel and tyre in the sidecar outfit down to a local garage in Wickford where we could over-inflate it to centralise the tyre on the rim and then deflate it to it's correct pressure before putting everything back together and making our way to Brands Hatch which was just over an hour and a half away.

All went well and I climbed into the back seat of the sidecar and with its front folding seat folded down and with the folding canvas sunroof fully open Dick dropped the now re-assembled but still deflated Bullet wheel slowly into my lap. It was a bit of a snug fit with the back of the wheel and tyre nudging into my chest and the front of the wheel and tyre neatly trapped against the sidecars scuttle just below its windscreen. Nice tight and cosy I thought. With the usual dramatic backfiring performance Dick got his old AJS going and off we went with a slight joggling ride to the local garage in Wickford just two miles away. We arrived at the garage and Dick said if we can do this quickly then the bike engine will probably keep running and he won't have to suffer the nonsense of getting it going again. Stay in the chair he said and I'll inflate the tyre whilst it's still in your lap. It seemed a fine suggestion to me and so he connected the 200 pounds per square inch airline to the tyre and before you could say 'Jack Robinson is a figment of some-ones imagination' the tyre inflated with a slight winding of my chest followed by a short but strange screech of tortured plywood followed by a bonk. Hmm, I think Hmm! What's all that about, did you hear that Dick? I asked, and with a bemused look on his face he walked curiously around the outfit before bursting into a hearty laughter and telling me to sit tight. The tyre even though now inflated was now oddly loose against me, so Dick removed it through the roof and said that I best get out of the sidecar and have a look, which I inquisitively did.

 The sidecar body was wrecked, when the bike wheel and tyre were inflated on my lap, they rapidly increased in diameter by maybe as much as six inches. That six inches had to go somewhere and as the tyres was already jammed tight between my chest and the sidecar scuttle, the sidecar surrendered and its plywood body was suddenly pushed upwards and parted from its plywood floor along with the noise of hundreds of one inch nails being extracted like teeth on a dentists chair, from their job of holding the body to the floor.

 There was nothing for it than to ride back to my home, Dick being the jockey on the AJS and me sitting in the sidecar holding the Bullet wheel with one hand and holding the sidecar body down with the other. We arrived at my home, put the wheel back into the Royal Enfield, had a laugh, then a good day on the Royal Enfield to Brands Hatch and later that evening Dick rode his sidecar outfit back to Brentwood after lashing the body down with some rope and promptly showed his contempt for the old thing by disposing of it and replacing it with a surprisingly good used Norton 250 Jubilee solo motor cycle. This set of stories are so typical of the death knell of so many sidecars in the UK, it is no wonder they are virtually extinct now, almost nobody loved them, liked them or wanted them after the affordable Austin Mini hit the roads.

CLYDE CARDY

Some years after the madness of the sixties and when most of us had become married and started our own families we all continued having a hankering for a bike in our new so called settled lifestyles worlds. Clyde, Clyde Cardy, our fastest rider was no exception to this refusal to let the past be the past and created a very successful name for himself in International grass-track sidecar racing winning many trophies and he also became The British Champion in 1979/81 with some of his achievements now being in the public domain.

He took his rather quick Godden 500 outfit around the European seasonal events calendar in the seemingly impossible back of his Mini Pick-up. This was followed by a Ford Zodiac engined LWB Transit and eventually a Duple Coach, complete with an onboard workshop with living accommodation for four. Just as Russian Dolls, they may well have parked inside each other, but make no mistake, there was no room for toy dolls, only adult dolls in Clyde's rough and tumble red blooded world.

During a 1982 event at Kampen in Northern Holland, Clyde suffered a rather bad accident when leaving the start line and at the first bend when the preceding outfit skidded broadside, in the ensuing collision, Clyde, his passenger Allan Stone and the outfit became airborne. With the outfit landing back onto Clyde, his spine was broken and Clyde ended up in much pain in an Amsterdam hospital and obviously without the advantage of an in-the-future mobile phone to explain to his wife Grace.

Frustrated Clyde eventually self discharged himself against all and best advice, and with the discomfort of being strapped to a wayward domestic door in the back of a Transit van, he was bought back to his wife in Maldon, England for a further six weeks total rest much to the despair, anger and hidden delight of his worried wife.

You can imagine how she must have felt when she answered the door-bell and then understandingly raising the roof to seeing Clyde, who she hadn't heard from, being carried into the house by his mates, tied to a door! It would seem that this event and following the return from the Isle of Man of Southend Gary also tied to a door, earlier in this book, suggests that in every sidecar rider's toolkit, a door should be included.

No doubt Clyde being Clyde made some whimsical remark to his wife that would have not have helped matters at the time. All successful men need an understanding wife and certainly on this occasion Clyde proved just that.

PART SEVEN
ICONS OF THE SWINGING SIXTIES

RADIO CAROLINE and The Mods, 1964.

During 1964 trends changed, some people misguidedly thought for the worst. Radio Caroline came on the air, brushing aside unpopular legislation, transmitting from an old ship the 'Mi Amigo' that was swinging at anchor in The Black Deep, in the North Sea, amidst the troublesome sandbanks some three and a half miles from Frinton-on-Sea, off the Essex Coast. Suddenly, everybody wanted to listen to Caroline on 199 metres, as everyone loves a pirate and you could receive its 'outlawed' music seven days a week rather than the BBC's unimaginative one hour per day. Besides filling the country with enjoyable popular music Radio Caroline was instrumental in making The Sixties Swing.

> *When I was young I'd listen to the radio waiting for my favourite songs, when they played I'd sing along it made me smile, Those were such happy times and not so long ago how I wondered where they'd gone, but they're back again like a long lost friend, all the songs I loved so well. Every shing-a-ling-ling ling, every wo—o-oh still shine, All my best memories came back clearly to me, some can even make you cry, just like before, its yesterday once more, its yesterday once more. .(11)*

> *I'd sit alone and watch your light, my only friend through teenage nights, and everything I had to know, I heard it on the radio, So don't become a background noise, a backdrop for the girls and boys who just don't know and just don't care, and just complain when your not there, You've had your time and had your power, You've yet to have your finest hour, Radio, Radio. . . .(12)*

Radio Caroline kept in the limelight by the 'Mi Amigo' losing its anchor and running aground in a snow storm onto Holland Haven beach near Frinton-on-Sea in January 1966 and the DJs being rescued by a rarely used but essential Breeches Buoy. After the rescue the 'Mia Amigo' was re-floated and immediately restarted transmissions but after further anchorage problems and some fourteen years later it dragged its anchor again, chains and all, in a violent storm and got blown some miles south until it crashed into the Long Sand sandbank and sank after a heroic rescue of the DJs and Wilson the canary, seemingly named after the Prime Minister, by the Sheerness lifeboat and its crew. The storm had unfortunately blown the 'Mi Amigo' inside of the British Territorial Waters Limit, so when the DJs were taken to Sheerness in the lifeboat, they were accommodated in the Police Station and promptly charged with operating a pirate radio within British Territorial Waters. Even though it was now a wreck, it was deemed still able of transmitting, and so an offence was plausible, if totally unfair and senseless.

Mia Amigo was then replaced by much larger 'Ross Revenge' which also broke loose at a later date unknowingly to its crew and then drifted for many further miles onto the fearful Goodwin Sands in the English Channel near Dover where the odds against being lost forever into the absorbing sands are said to be no better then two hundred and fifty to one. With such a calamity of disasters, Radio Caroline certainly knew how to get maximum publicity and keep the Sheerness and Harwich lifeboat crews busy. Ross Revenge was recovered with difficulty and still exists (2019) albeit mothballed, near Bradwell-on-Sea. Essex.

It is said that Radio Caroline was named after Caroline Kennedy, the daughter of John F Kennedy the then American President. The Caroline's on air presenters became known as Disc Jockeys and became household names, such as Dave Lee Travis, David Hamilton, John Peel, Tony Blackburn and others. They would come ashore at Harwich on a weekly alternating rota and travel by train down to Liverpool Street Station in London where they would be mobbed by the media and love-struck young females. It seemed that they loved themselves too and were loved by the girl audiences but not by so many boys. There was resentment from the Essex boys because the disc jockeys who were seen as self-appointed soft heroes, would replace the dynamic and rather motivating local rock and roll bands in the small dance halls at weekends. These household names introduced a new type of entertainment to the village halls called a 'Disco'. The sensual and sometimes dramatic live music band, usually of five lads, was being replaced by a single stranger sitting at a desk, who many saw as an overpaid smiling publicity seeker with the gift of the gab, no particular skill, just flashing lights. Many young girls were most excited by these DJ's visiting their village halls, and started flirting with them. The bike boys then found the London Mod culture was also starting to infringe the Village Hall dances. Tensions in the motorbike boys were already high and the Essex motorbike boys (Rockers) were now losing their girlfriends to smartly dressed and softer attitude lads (Mods) on slow, over adorned scooters as well as the highly egoistic DJ's

THE MAKING OF THE MODS

In the late fifties and early sixties the rag shops in London set the clothing market and trends alight with bright coloured, imaginary styled but cheaply made dresses, coats, boots, trousers, and the forever stunner, the miniskirt. The resourceful East London tailors in a successful attempt to get their businesses profitable again after the post war drabness and poverty, ingeniously attracted the lads to their outfitters to buy smart clothing on the American drip payment method. The marketing method was to take a small percentage of their weekly wage and the switched-on tailor would keep the lads adorned in the latest cool fashions from Italy, made in the swet shops of Whitechapel or Poplar. The idea spread to the motorcycle dealers too, who were not to be outdone and were on a run with the increased motorbike sales cause by the effects of the 1959 super-summer, a summer of so many long sunny days and record temperatures that gave a big boost to any seasonal businesses. The bike dealers decided to offer cheap Italian scooters, designed in Italy but built in Bristol by Douglas Motorcycles (The Douglas Vespa) or the Italian built Lambretta to the lads, again taking a small percentage of their wages. The method was known as Hire Purchase, the dramatic appearance of Italian scooters and Italian styled and inspired clothing and shoes creating the 'Mod Look'. This helped in no small way to drag London out of its Blitz bomb damaged eyesores and the depressing sight of so many classic and ordinary buildings that were caked in soot from more than 700 years of coal fires and steam locomotive smoke. The toxic mix of coal smoke, river fog and motor vehicle exhausts caused the lethal yellow 'smog' that blanketed London and forced the government to act with the 1956 Clean Air Act and Smokeless Fuel Zones. Further, this country had lost so many young men in the two wars that there was a shortage of lads to employ to drive the buses and tube trains, hence the many Jamaicans migrating here on the SS Empire Windrush to populate Southall and to fill the vacancies. The English London lads could now pick up a well-paid job easily and then afford the Mod clothing and scooters. For city lads, the sixties styling revolution had started.

 Not so however for the lads living in the countryside of Essex and elsewhere, where well paid jobs were not so available and the farming market not very profitable, which meant low pay for farm labourers. Labouring was often the only employment available beyond twenty-five miles from London to unskilled lads unless living in the industrial Midlands or North Country. The closing of many railway branch lines and poorly used stations by ICI's (Imperial Chemical Industries) notorious Doctor Beeching, who was employed by the Government to turn the railways into a profitable enterprise while it was facing heavy competition from the effects of the motorway building programme, made commuting from some villages a no go once their branch line had been closed. Long distances often exceeding twenty-five return miles to work or entertainment and pot holed roads and many unlit country lanes meant the slower small wheeled scooters were just not suitable in such a rural environment. So the country lads found that the only acceptable mode of transport was a motorbike with the benefit of a thrilling but possibly dangerous riding experience. As the bike was essential to get daily to work in all weathers including winter rain and snow, and fibre glass fairings were in their infancy and very scarce, the biker had to wear heavy leather protective wear.

The fact that most scooters could hardly reach 50 mph, even without a passenger, which many motorbikes would easily pass in second gear, did not remove the contempt that each group had for each other. The low speed of the scooter was of little relevance in London due to congestion even in the fifties and sixties, however the scooter did give some weather protection for the Mod's fancy clothing and shoes during evening and weekend town cruising. In comparison to this, the bikers target was the magic ton, 100 mph, in an evening or weekend. Many sporting 500cc bikes could brush it and the 650's would chase nearer 115 mph, 120 for the very fastest. One brand, Vincent, built bikes that could truly achieve 125 mph, the Black Shadow or the aptly named 'widow-maker' as it was sometimes called. Vincent even built a bike that would brush 150 mph without a streamline fairing or supercharger, the Vincent Black Lightning. .

THE SCENE IS SET FOR TROUBLE, 1964

Spring Bank Holiday weekends would always see a large number of London visitors travel to the coast in cars and on motorbikes. This particular year (1964) was much different to previous years as there was an extra surge in car and bike licence holders as it was nineteen years after the war end, eighteen years after many more boys than normal were born in London and now had their own two wheeled transport. Most of them came on scooters, as they were the ideal London transport.

They were then confronted at the seaside by the visiting bikers (Rockers) from outer London, typically Romford and the countryside, much fewer in number on their roaring and much faster exciting motorbikes. These lads were mostly blue-collar workers or labourers and trainee tradesmen and engineers.

Flashy but slow scooters adorned with too many mirrors and spotlights for the smart and well off town lads with their tent like Parkas hiding expensive modern Italian clothing, or fast and exciting powerful bikes for the rough and ready fun loving country lads who spent most of their spare time and money keeping their bikes necessarily reliable and safe for the fast and long countryside commutes or burn ups, eyeing up girls and ignoring Mods.

Most of the Mods were white collar workers and during the working week they would hop on the bus, trolleybus or tube in bad weather, as work was often less than a couple of miles away and keep dry, keeping their prized scooters out of the elements.

The only common denominators between the two types of lads was that neither where high society, they all had high egos, adored the mini skirt and swung to the rhythm of The Who, The Rolling Stones or The Beatles, and everything else was based on selfishness and bravado.

So the scene is set with two groups of lads with conflicting ideologies, different disposable incomes, and vastly different transport styles and needs, but all adoring pretty girls and the sixties music.

We then had the Mods and Rockers riots of Clacton, Southend-on-Sea, Margate and Brighton that are now Legendary. Whilst there was the inevitable summer weekend clashes sometimes funded by reporters from the tabloids who would give ten pounds to anyone who would start a fight, ten pounds was equal to two weeks wages to many and was obviously influential to the fights.

We would have small skirmishes in the villages and smaller towns where the Mods, encouraged by their larger numbers would take on smaller groups of Rockers, bur rarely on a one to one basis. One Basildon Mod, full of bravado approached me one winter morning at work at the HGV depot where we both worked. After following me into the gents where both of us would hang up our scooter or motorbike kit, he passed a typical sarcastic remark about us Rockers wearing unglamorous storm proof kit and before too long we were fighting on the toilet floor over such a trivial matter, I suddenly found that the fight had turned and it was now going in my favour. I was now on the offensive. I was now seeing very red and he was like a failing prey seeking mercy as I lashed back at him. I felt all-powerful and mighty, but strangely very wrong and sorry for him. With my adrenalin flowing with gusto it was a job to stop, but stop I did, much to his surprise, and I let him go and swore never to get into a fight again. It was a most frightening experience as I was totally on the edge of losing all control. If I had not managed to stop my arm muscles in their full flight of fury then the consequences could have been absolutely awful, a brief and worrying trip into the animal world, which still lingers within us. Sadly, animals can't divert their frustration on dustbins or pianos, but *we* have brains and compassion to tell us when to stop, enough is enough, just stop, and walk away, tomorrow is another day, and turn to the piano or drum kit, or crappy dustbin if need be, for retribution. To continue the fight and become the proud victor would have cost both of us our jobs and me to receive an assault charge. My first job that morning was to replace an AEC Mammoth Major's seized rear spring shackles on a heavy lorry which took the full force of a fourteen pound sledge hammer in furious flight as I let off steam and de-stressed.

Contrary to the tabloid press, the motor cycle lads or so called Rockers, did not go looking for trouble with the Mods, we had no time for them and their slow buzzy scooters that were not exciting to ride and didn't see them as a problem, we were almost arrogant of them. We spent most of our time and money riding our motorbikes, and visiting biker cafés. We were happy to let the Mods go in their own world, matters only got troublesome when the London Mods invaded the seaside towns in vast numbers at weekends and started the troubles. The first was at Clacton where a thousand scooterists where said to have invaded the town in the Spring Bank Holiday weekend of 1964. The tabloid press, always in search for sensationalism, fired matters up and after Clacton there were copycat troubles at Margate, Hastings and Brighton. Any Rockers just got in the way and nearly always tried to stand their ground albeit mostly outnumbered. At Margate on Sunday May 17th 1964 was the biggest reported battle where one hundred Rockers were reportedly attacked by five hundred Mods and were embarrassingly escorted off the beach by a Police cordon. However there were some London Rocker gangs that would go to the seafronts just looking for a fight but they were in the minority. The Police often arrived secretly at the scene of the seafront disturbances in ambulances acting as Trojan horses that they commandeered from the health authorities and arrived by shock force into the mayhem. Unfortunately a bad reputation that was set by the press and the Rockers were always portrayed as the aggressors when in fact they rarely were. The hoards of Mods were the problem, displaying power in numbers.

During the weekdays we rarely saw a mod in the countryside, or at the seafronts as they seemed to stay in London or the larger towns and we continued with our normal happy and exciting motorbike lifestyle.

We had the odd conflict with other lads that were up to no-good, typical of this was an event one evening after the four of us were driving away from The Royal Oak public house in Danbury after a drinking session. We were travelling in a spacious Morris Oxford that I had and the engine failed. After a quick assessment it was obvious that the camshaft fibre drive gear had shed its teeth and would need attention the next day.

We pushed it into a lay-by and decided to sleep the night out in the car until daylight. The lads, Nipper, Brinnie, The Bear and I had drunk plenty and soon got into a relaxed snore which unfortunately kept me a little awake as I, being the driver, was not so drunk.

After an hour or so I was aware of a car passing slowly and then soon returning and parking on the opposite side of the now quiet road, followed by the soft slamming of it's doors. In the pitch dark I raised myself from my sleepy position and could just make out some lads with lowered voices at the open boot of their car and then leaving their engine running, no doubt for the benefit of its heater, they approached our car that we were sleeping in and obviously thought that it had been left unattended. They started jacking it up after releasing the wheel nuts, no doubt to steal the wheels. It was all happening very quickly but I thought this could be some fun as I tried very hard to waken the lads quietly so as to spring a surprise like a multi Jack-in-the-Box.

After a lot of drowsy mumbling, the four of us were primed, albeit sluggish from drink and ready for action, bursting our car doors open with a sudden and loud 'gotcha you buggers' Quicker than Jumping Jack Flash they sprinted to their car and were gone . . .leaving behind a Ford Zephyr jack and wheel-brace.

I soon sold the jack and brace into the local community, no doubt to the rascal that left it behind, and with the proceeds bought a new camshaft drive gear for the Oxford. One can imagine the sudden laxative fear that the thieves suffered when in the midst of the darkness they were disturbed by four semi drunk rockers including the huge silhouettes of the bear and all of 6ft 8 inch Nipper.

PART EIGHT
THE THRILL OF THE BIKES

AND POLICE CHASES OF SOUTH EAST ESSEX

The policing of the roads was undertaking a certain amount of change in the sixties with the opening of the Motorways and the wealthy who could buy off-the-shelf 125 mph motorbikes and 150 mph sports cars. The new line up of police cars were called Panda Cars, usually 75 mph Morris Minors and Ford Anglias, then there was the General Purpose Police Cars that were typically spacious but without glamour the 80 mph Austin Cambridges, and finally Z Cars that were usually spacious 90 mph six cylinder and six seated Ford Zephyrs. These were the cars often chosen by the Essex Constabulary and Southend Provincial Police. Other counties chose similar cars but the London Metropolitan Police often had the tough and more powerful Wolseley 6/90 as a general-purpose car. As a publicity drive and to deter speedsters the London Met' had a fleet of superb high speed V8 Daimler Dart sports cars that were initially driven by a squad of WPC's and upgraded their General Purpose cars to the Wolseley 6/110 while the Flying Squad got the extremely quick and beautiful Jaguar Mk 2 saloons. Meanwhile, Southend had a small number of Farina Grey Austin 6 cylinder Supercharged Westminsters, large and fast in a straight line but a bit ponderous and scary on fast bends. The Westminsters were however able to catch two memorable local speedsters, Tornado Smith and Derry Compton Smith, more of which is written later. The police cars all had a chrome bell on the front bumper that rang frantically but could hardly be heard by most motor cyclists at speed and when wearing a crash helmet, they also had on the rear shelf (there were no hatchbacks then) a large roller blind that when unrolled proclaimed in very large print 'POLICE-STOP' which was operated by the driver pulling a bathroom type light control-string that ended above his door, this only had an effect once the police car had got in front of the speedster, a sometimes impossible if not highly dangerous manoeuvre in the floppy handling overloaded police cars. In the early sixties the only popular saloon cars that handled well were the MG Magnettes, Jaguars and most Italian cars like the Alfa Romeo, some Fiats and the rather exclusive Lancias. Once the Motorways were in use matters changed, The Mini Cooper and then the Ford Cortina GT showed that motoring could be fun. With the advent of radial ply tyres, disc brakes, visco-static oils and seat belts, ordinary saloon cars and subsequently police cars, got a lot faster and safer at speed or in a chase, especially round the bends. The Blues and Twos that we know off today replaced the inadequate chrome bell and the newly introduced electronic speed traps really did spoil the fun. The motorcycle cops either had the rather slow small and silent, 'Noddy-Bike' a 200cc Velocette LE or the much faster Triumph Speed Twins (London Met and Essex Police) or Norton Dominators or 650 SS (Southend Police). The Southend Police Officers had a minimum height requirement of 6 feet for the men or 5ft 10 inches for the Women Police Officers. Size mattered in the Southend area due to the troublesome drunken East-end Londoners that visited the resort every weekend and most summer evenings creating frequent violent brawls outside the riotous seafront pubs, clubs, strip joints, casinos and dens of iniquity. Southend, being a provincial authority and on the coast issued all Officers with white helmets, this was very helpful on the occasions when there was joint crime control actions between the Essex and Southend Constabularies.

One evening, I was returning from the Southend College on my sprightly Greeves 250 Sports-Twin, where I attended a motor vehicle construction course on a day release basis from work, and I soon followed a gently travelling Morris Oxford along the London Road that exited out of Rayleigh and its 30mph limits. I decided to overtake it and as it was a reasonably well-lit street, I could see that just fifty yards ahead we would both be going through the speed de-restriction signs. So I gave the bike the gun thinking that it was safe to do so and that I would offend no-body. The wonderful howl of the bike's twin cylinder Villiers two stroke engine with a Siamese exhaust at full throttle was suddenly put into a strange chorus, sounding much of an unpleasant musical percussion and woodwind harmony, a quick glance in the mirror gave me the answer . . . a black Austin A55 police car was trying to take the pair of us, bell ringing frantically. I continued the overtaking procedure and promptly turned first left out of harm's way, or so I thought, but no, the police car was following me. Oh heck! I thought, and rightly or wrongly continued trying to avoid a collision with the pursuing police car by riding the bike on its limits. It was within a housing estate that was now outside the thirty speed limit, which was hypothetical in this case, as the tight and frequent junctions were extremely difficult to take at 30 mph let alone any faster. It was dark, the streets were empty and there was no speed limit, so why was I being chased, was it because for the last fifty yards or so of the limited section I had accelerated from the thirty to maybe forty-five mph to overtake the ambling Morris Oxford? I don't know, we bikers were often the target of the police. However the Greeves' superb handling and road holding kept the following police car at bay, I could see my silhouette projected by the police cars lights on the houses at T-Junctions in front of me, and those silhouettes danced up and down and at weird angles as the Austin's overloaded and crude suspension created an unstable chase for the violently driven police car. Eventually the police car's headlights seemed to fade as it became more and more distant behind me and then, as fast as the pursuit had started, it was no more. I continue to ride home, alone, heart thumping and expecting a police car to confront me at every junction. In those far off days before computers existed and gave instant information access, it could take the police many months to trace the current owner of a particular vehicle as each vehicle's log book's information was kept on manual record at each County Hall of each County Council where the vehicle sequentially was or had been taxed. The enquiring police would have to write to each and every Council in sequence to establish who and where the vehicle had been kept and may well run out of the statutory time limit allowed to commence proceedings after an alleged event. This however did not do my nerves any good, as during the assumed three month time limit I was conscious of every knock on the door, approaching police car or police visit to my place of work, expecting big trouble due to my seemingly avoided capture or for avoiding arrest for a reason I could still not be sure off, worrying times. I decided that in the future that I would stop at the slightest suggestion from the police to avoid a repeat of the uncomfortable three-month suspense that otherwise would follow.

BUILT LIKE A GUN, GOES LIKE A BULLET

Was the punch line of the Royal Enfield Motor Cycle Company, only in this case it was a speeding Bullet motorcycle being chased by a police car that itself committed Hara-Kari in the failed pursuit. After riding the delightful and super smooth Greeves to Bournemouth a few times, I decided to trade it for a bike that was more lusty to keep me awake on those long late evening runs and ended up with a stunning 350 Royal Enfield Bullet. The maker's legend was 'Built Like a Gun, Goes Like a Bullet' and so it seemed. A proper bike with sporty good looks, very sure footed, good brakes and with a punchy exhaust beat. It was not a very fast bike and certainly not a high velocity bullet but it went where you aimed it, quickly, made its' mark, and was reassuringly safe, it was comfortable to ride on long distances and a very likeable bike in it's bright chrome and metallic red finish. The best that I could coax out of it on the level and without a very long run up was seventy-five mph.

THE CHASE

However, in the spring of 1964 I met up with a few of the lads on their bikes at our usual haunt, the Four Aces Café on the Burnham Road near Battlesbidge. We decided, that being a sunny Sunday afternoon that a few hours at the Blinking Owl Café some seven miles away on the London bound A127 Arterial Road dual carriageway would be a bit of a hoot. There was leader of the pack Clyde Cardy, on his lightened, tuned and bereft of silencers, rather rapid Triumph 650 Bonneville, also was Brian Woodman (Brinnie) on his equally tuned and lightened Velocette Venom 500 with a very loud and totally open eight inch megaphone exhaust and myself with an old pal, James Anthony Jay (JJ) as a pillion. It was an easy ride along the old A130 to Rayleigh, then a very noisy climb from the ensemble up the steep Crown Hill, from where the noisy bikes tried to tip-toe up the further rise past the Rayleigh copshop (police station) then down to the Rayleigh Weir roundabout on the A127, and then a final magnificent blast down the A127 to the fabled Blinking Owl Café, one and a half miles on. And that is exactly what had happened, with the exception that my Royal Enfield Bullet was the slowest by some 25 mph or more and I unknowingly had a desperate police car on my tail. The police car had been sitting in the Weir car park awaiting an offender to chase and suddenly it hears the thunderous approach of the open exhausts of the Bonneville and Venom with me being the unlucky tail end Charlie. Without us knowing, it gave chase. The black Austin A55 Mk 2 Cambridge police car complete with sloppy suspension, chrome bell, large overloaded boot and an occasional 80 mph top speed, was now in hot pursuit. Totally unaware of his proximity to us, and travelling in excess of 80mph down the hill for the first time in its life chasing me and a pillion, and the Bonneville and Venom disappearing into the roaring distance, I felt the normally very steady Bullet wobble very heavily for more than a hundred yards. I raised my gloved hand over my mouth and yelled to JJ, "Puncture?" *"We wobbled?"*, JJ shouts back, with no crash-hat, (as they weren't mandatory then) and his long golden flaxen hair flowing in the 80 mph gale and transistor radio in his ear) he shouts back, "No Puncture!" I was jiving to the Dave Clark Five who were on the trannie singing (the totally electrifying) *'Do you love me, now that I can dance '* not knowing that we have a Police Car watching his wild jiving whilst close up our bum, with his bell ringing furiously. The police car wasn't going to catch the Bonneville and Venom travelling in excess of 100mph in his asthmatic Austin, but he sure hell was going to catch me, or so he thought.

> *Do you Love me, now I can really move, Do you love me, now I'm in the groove , Do you love me, do you really love me, now that I can dance . .watch me now. .shake, shake, well you're drivin' me crazy. (13).*

The bike wobbles but suddenly, and still unaware of the Police Cars existence behind me I arrived at the Owl with much drama. Decelerating rapidly through the gears with much style from 80 odd mph down to virtually zero with wheels locked and smoking tyres, with an unexpected Crummmp!!! and a glimpse of a black car to my left and an unbelievable amount of flying shingle everywhere and dozens of bikers looking agog at the event unfolding alongside the A127. I think 'My God' as I carefully traverse the loose roadside stones and cycle track and enter the Cafés car park, My God, I think, that was some entrance, and where did all that loose shingle come from? and that black car...

I dismounted, and JJ was gone, Oh yes, he was very much gone, so I heaved the bike onto its stand and glanced round at the entrance, from where so much shingle dramatically had become airborne, and there to my utter astonishment on the cycle track that runs continuously between the road and the car park, was a Black Police Car, looking as though it had suffered a hernia of the highest order or worse. Its nose was down with blown front tyres, dented wheel rims and what suspiciously looked like a collapsed front suspension. Steam was gushing out from the radiator where it had burst or the head gasket had blown, as the engine had suffered the ultimate sacrifice under some supreme effort. GOLLY, I thought, what the? There were mocking chants from four-dozen or more bikers, who knew this officer well, as he was a persistent speeding bike chaser from the nearby Laindon Police Garage, who had lost his Southend based Supercharged Austin Westminster A127 Police Chase Car for the day and ended up with the much lesser Cambridge. The officer now outside his sad Austin Cambridge with a furious expression on his face, so furious that his sudden high blood pressure had turned his face red with rage, he beckoned me down from the Owl car park to the front of his rather busted car. At this point, I was still unaware that he had been chasing me, nor what had happened. Says I to him, looking at his gushing radiator and quickly recapping that my bike had indeed suffered an unusually heavy wobble

Says I to he...

"What's happened, has something fallen off my bike officer and gone through your radiator?

Says he to me...

" Fallen off your bike, my article (or similar such words) says he to me, fallen off your bike?

"No, you were travelling at excess speed down that hill so fast that I couldn't catch you, 83mph to be precise.' 83 mph and there is a 50 mph limit. Didn't you hear my bell!!! I'm getting a little fed up with chasing you Jack the Lads"* said the rather irate officer as he got his notebook out, *"and what have you got to say for yourself."*

Again I said to him, with his Austin letting off steam in the background, *"Did something fall off my bike?"*

"Now listen here Jack the Lad, don't give me any lip, you'll be prosecuted for excessive speed, Full name?"

 I nearly said Jack, but thought better of it, but still didn't know the order of preceding events and exactly what had happened until being told later by Len the cafés owner, then it became clear how close to a severe accident I was and that I was indeed breaking the new summer speed restrictions, in style.

192

I was at that moment, being embarrassed in front of the large crowd of Rockers who were watching events unfold during that warm sunny afternoon, and being called Jack as well as facing a large fine left me stunned.

> *Hit the road Jack and don't you come back no more, no more no more, no more, Hit the road Jack and don't you come back no more, what'd you say(14)*

Has something fallen off my bike officer and gone through your radiator? Bah Humbug!. At least it was a good downhill blast to music and sunshine and a rapturous and unexpected welcome at the Owl and applause when I left, by some appreciative bikers who had enjoyed the afternoon's impromptu and unusual entertainment.

Did I hear his bell, with a Royal Enfield and the Dave Clark Five at full chat and the distant Venom's open megaphone's 150 decibels, let alone the Triumph Bonneville's open rifle style exhausts still ringing staccato in my head at another 150 decibels, the answer was No! I *did not* hear his bell! JJ on the back might have heard it as he wasn't wearing a crash-helmet, but alas, he was listening to The Dave Clark Five at full volume on his tiny transistor radio (trannie) screeching in one ear and eighty or more miles an hour of slipstream in the other ear, and was also, like me, suffering from 'megaphonitis' or similar from the Venom's large megaphone. Enduring much humiliation the officer had to stay with his car close to the baying crowd of insulting leather clad bikers for a long period, until a crew could be raised on a Sunday afternoon to man the Police recovery truck and attend to his exhausted Austin Cambridge. So sad, I hilariously thought. When it was transported away again I was applauded. So touching.

It transpired that his Austin A55 Cambridge made a gallant effort to catch me down that hill, but seeing that he was about to lose the chase and with his engine overheating and the radiator blowing off, he made a foolhardy last minute attempt to stop me leaving the highway and entering private property by mounting the kerb at speed and entering the cycle track to cut off my access to the private car park and freedom. The plot failed when the old Austin Cambridge blew its tyres on the sharp six inch high York-Stone kerbstones. Idiot, he could have killed me, however, the results of this race were Cambridge cop car-Nil (Dead) and Me-Minus £5.00 (speeding fine). Ouch, as an apprentice I was earning £4.10P per week, and a bus driver £12.00 that resulted in an expensive £5.00 fine, more than a weeks wages indeed, being the cost of this epic tale. But now I am part of The Owl's legend, so maybe it was money well spent.

  I blamed Harold Wilson, our Prime Minister at the time because in an attempt to cut down on the accidents by old cars and motorbikes on the new Motorways, he had introduced a national 50 mph speed limit on all UK dual carriageways in the summer months only, and this chase happened during the second weekend of that summer speed control period. In my defence the advisory signs were inadequate as the only one en-route being obscured by a truck I was overtaking, I just did not see the solitary sign between the Weir and the Blinking Owl, let alone realise that we were in the second weekend of the speed control. The only dates that I cared to remember were with girls.

JACK THE LAD

  When the dealership where I worked (then changed hands to Toomey Motors a Vauxhall and Bedford dealership) heard the story, the service manager laughed and said "that sorts a lot of problems out, you'll now be known as Jack" He had been trying to figure out an answer to an unusual problem as we were obviously pre-computer then and we had five mechanics, of which I was one of two with the same Christian name which was causing confusion in the administration office with all the paperwork created on every vehicle repair, as a trial they had named us clock numbers 4 and 5, which still led to admin' confusion, so now I was simply Jack, as in the Police Officers jibe of Jack the Lad, I was not amused.

THE ARRIVAL OF THE THUNDEROUS VINCENT

I soon realised that a really fast and good looking bike was essential to keep up with the faster bikes and retain ones Blinking Owl's reputation with the spectacular ending to the Police chase on my Royal Enfield Bullet that sunny summer afternoon, it was also clear that a motorbike that could not exceed 83 mph, and at that, downhill, left you vulnerable as a tail-end Charlie to any Police car or indeed Police motor cyclist. We bikers were unfairly and heavily targeted by the traffic police no matter which county we were in. Sure, like most motorists, we sometimes broke the 30 mph speed limit, but the only time that this was done with any significance was when the roads were relatively empty, or in the late evenings. It could be said, and with some accuracy that most of the time we were only a danger to ourselves. Motorcyclists, unlike most scooterists and normal motorists, were mostly very mechanically minded, often with an engineering knowledge, and by necessity kept their powerful bikes in safe and fine fettle. We knew the potential risks and the bikes were kept in good order to reduce those risks. We would spend more money on improving our bikes than probably anything else after Mums housekeeping, even girlfriends came lower, much lower in priority, and we certainly didn't go for glamour accessories as the scooter lads did. We had great fun going fast round corners and going fast in top gear on the few dual carriageways that were long enough to let you comfortably exceed 80 mph. There were no open road speed limits back then so if you were pulled up by the police, that was often once a week or more, you did not get a speeding ticket, just a time consuming lecture on the danger of excessive speed. This seemed a bit rich to us as all of the Essex Police cars were lazy hard working Austins that could carry two officers with a load of kit in the boot and two suspects in the back, but when the cars were middle aged they were almost dangerously unstable when chasing even the slowest of motorbikes. I started looking for a bike that would not attract a chase by an Austin Cambridge as the officers would hear its exhaust and smell the Castrol R in the air and assuming it was a rapid bike, not bother to get involved with a futile chase. Then I found it, advertised in the South Woodham village shop window, a previously unheard of 1954 Vincent Grey Flash replica in road trim and finished in stunning black, which was nearing completion of a stem to stern major refurbishment and overhaul. A brief phone call followed a visit to a Terry Pain, a meticulous engineer at his parent's house in South Woodham Ferrers where the advertiser, Terry, led me to a shed in the bottom of his garden. The sight that greeted me when he opened the shed door was just breathtaking. There, standing on its own front and rear high lift stands was this magnificent machine in an almost complete condition. It was truly stunning, with new tyres, new alloy wheel rims, four brakes all with duralumin back-plates and air scoops on the fronts, electron engine plates, Marchal Headlight, Albion TT4 close ratio racing gearbox, an Amal 10 TT9 open mouth racing carburettor, a Lightning 2 high-lift camshaft, an Alpha big-end, a re-balanced crank, twin rear sprockets, ten stud wheels and every nut and bolt individually and freshly hand lathe made in duralumin with all of the nuts being domed to an eighty three per cent thread depth, and a no baffle exhaust, even the handlebar had been reduced by four inches in length, giving it a mean look. I could wax lyrical thinking and talking about this engineering masterpiece, but the finishing touch was that the entire bike including the power unit, but excepting only the bronze finished carburettor and alloy wheel rims, had been lightened and beautifully stove enamelled in black, with a gold pin-line on the tank. Wow, I thought, Bloody wow, can this be true, can this really be mine. It was either an absolute magnificent replica or the original model nicely upgraded. Either way it was a pure pedigree Vincent in a wow factor condition and of engineering magnificence and a mean look with it's shortened handlebars. He said that it had been a no expense spared stem to stern rebuild that had gone well over budget until his future wife had put the brakes on him putting it on the road and maybe being killed or badly injured. I had no future wife at the time, so there was no contest. We happily agreed a price on completion of the rebuild of £90.00. This may seem ridiculously cheap from five decades later, but it was a lot of money then, six weeks wages in fact, but it was worth it. A totally wonderful bike . . . and it ran on Castrol R which gave off a deliciously arrogant aroma to anyone that dared to chase it, including the asthmatic Austin Police Cars of The Essex Constabulary. Only the Sunbeam Tigers, Daimler Dart V8s and the Jaguars of London's Met' and Flying Squad might need respecting. Four weeks later, I collected the Vincent and entered a very different motor cycling arena, remembering that the rebuilder had warned to take care as the bike was a tough ride with its shortened handlebars and uprated rear springs, "On a poor road you need to keep the rear dampers slack or have a pillion passenger he said" how right he was. This bike rode high and mighty with a total indignity leaving a trail of noise from its baffle-less exhaust, close ratio gearbox and the smell of carbon tetrachloride (Castrol R) to anything else on the road behind. When I first pulled away from Slater's Garage just along from The Whalebone public house in South Woodham Ferrers, the first sensation of the bike was indeed sensational, with its narrow handlebars making it feel very solid and purposeful and the very high first gear I soon found that I hadn't fully let the clutch out until approaching 35 mph, and that was in first gear, I eventually found that it could approach 60 mph in first gear, 80 mph in second gear and close on 95 mph in third before heading to the heavens in top. There was so much mid-range torque that coupled with the close ratio gearbox it was a very rapid bike without even trying. It had a deep, sharp and loud baritone exhaust rumble combined with a very healthy induction roar unlike any other motorcycle that I had come across. This bike had thunder, Thunder by the bucket-load, and I quickly discovered that it was like an attractive but adventure seeking girl, noisy, exciting and on occasions you would have to hang on tight, very tight and hold your nerve. It had so much torque (low down power) that I only ever needed to push the revs high in each gear if I was chasing Brinnie's Velocette or Clyde's Bonneville, both very fast bikes. The superb Vincent's brakes, being from a heavier model could stop it inside twenty feet from 30 mph, nothing else stopped that quick. The clutch however could not cope with the very high torque that the engine was creating at low RPM. The engineer that built the bike initially fitted a high compression ratio piston that did not help matters, especially with pre-ignition, detonation and localised overheating of the combustion chamber that one experiences with a high performance large air-cooled cylinder. At a much later date electronic ignition and detonation detectors were invented and overcame much of the problems. To lower the BMEP (brake mean effective pressure) and hence torque an original compression ratio piston was fitted taking it down to 7.3 to 1, which allowed for the lower grade fuels that were the only available fuels in the early fifties when the bike was built. With such uncontrollable power still remaining at pull away the only steps that I could use was to strengthen the clutch spring pressure action by adding a second set of clutch springs from a 700cc Royal Enfield Super Meteor and increasing the gauge of the clutch release cable. The clutch handlebar lever became very heavy, but due to my occupation as a HGV repair mechanic I had strong hands and could cope with it. The result was no more unwanted clutch slip above two thousand rpm and before the bike got into its stride, and by using not too much throttle at pull away.

Riding the mighty Vincent was an acquired art, unlike any other bike that I had ridden before or since. It was in many ways a strange ride like riding a very fit horse, maybe this was the thinking from its designer Phil Vincent. When you rode it you sat high and aloof, leaning slightly forward to counter-act wind pressure on your body at very high speed. With the handlebars shortened by four inches, a critical two inches each side, ones hands are only fifteen inches or so apart, just as reins control on a horse. The shortened handlebars did not help to avoid a very frightening rider induced tank-slapping at speed caused by an initial bias on one hand when being lifted off the saddle momentarily on large bumps or airborne landings over hump-back bridges, being over-compensated by the other hand and commencing the frightening 'tank slapper' which is where the handlebars and entire front suspension viciously oscillate from left to right and back, out of control and hitting the fuel tank stops on each extreme. A good cure for a hangover or a cure for constipation, either way a tank slapper was a must to avoid. My first and only experience of one of these frightening and uncontrollable tank slappers was briefly outside Butlin's Holiday Camp at Clacton whilst hitting a road undulation at just 50mph. The problem was that the Vincent, being of an older design had a steering damper, which I unwittingly had left slightly loose, after that event I always left it nipped up under tension, making the bike's steering rather rigid and an absolute physical fight on a fast chase along any bendy country lanes or second class roads. Returning to the riding position of the bike, next are your knees which are further apart than your hands at maybe eighteen inches as they grip the fuel tank, as opposed to the horses body, next are your ankles which are set even further apart, maybe twenty four inches apart on the footrests that hang from above the engine like a horse stirrups, but to avoid the rather wide Vincent crankcase rather than the horses widening body. The horse similarity does not end there though. To add to the excitement, the rear suspension is unlike other bikes of the era that had plungers, swinging arms, sprung hubs or solid rear ends. The Vincent rear suspension was of a novel cantilever type that was most comfortable as the dual-seat was hinged at its front behind the petrol-tank, a sign of the eventual future, the seat rear was supported by styled alloy friction dampers, to the live rear cantilever frame. This had the rather pleasing effect of gently raising and falling the rider over road undulations. So there you are, sitting high on a thoroughbred that can kick before the off, having a fast exhilarating ride with your steed below you giving you a gentle rising/falling galloping motion while your hands are steady on the controls, steady also are your ankles set high off the ground, but your knees and elbows are actively working as friction hinges while gripping the beast to keep you aboard. Again just like riding a thoroughbred horse, a superb experience. I eventually found that the best way of riding the Vincent fast was to leave a little more than a pinch of friction on the steering damper control knob and hold the handlebars loosely in my hands, and the bike built with the rigidity of a section of RSJ steel girder, would steer itself at any speed with a little bit of my input from my backside through the seat. This method worked very well on dual carriageways and most sinuous second class Essex roads. The exception was the B1010, the road to Burnham-on-Crouch, for the final three miles to Burnham was a series of ninety degree, thirty five miles per hour bends round ancient field boundaries, here 'bend swinging' was a joy and of a tremendous and extreme nature. The rigidly built Vincent was too long and heavy to take tight bends at speed in the normal manner as say on a Greeves and so the best line of attack on this section of road was to leave the steering damper a little loose and both *lean and steer* the bike round the bends. However, you had to remember to nip up the damper on the return journey once exiting the bends and entering Althorne or the bike would delight in reminding you who was boss with a hint of a tank slapper on the delightfully serpentine route back to Rettendon. The road-holding of the Vincent when bend swinging, was of the highest order, more secure but unlike the delightfully nimble Greeves, that I had earlier owned. Both of the bikes had very high footrests, which allowed extremely high angles of lean and the Greeves with its lower centre of gravity would lean to such an alarming degree that I unintentionally over a period of time, scrubbed the legend 'Avon Speedmaster Mk 11' off the front tyre's sidewalls. This was done by almost laying the bike flat through bends, an astonishing statement but that is how superb the bike was. I never saw this effect *on any* other bike, other than on a hard ridden and thoroughly enjoyed Greeves.

But the Vincent was in a different league when it came to street credibility, or should I say 'Blinking Owl cred'. It was a mechanical beauty, which followed a huge heritage, a wonderful roaring exhaust, an addictive smell of Castrol 'R', and a challenge to the reputation of any bike that tried to out-pace it. There seemed nothing that it was not capable of. It was rock solid, very fast, would stop on a dime as the Americans would say and drew attraction wherever it went. I always rode it very hard with the twist-grip wide open and hard against the stop wherever the roads would allow it, which caused much strain on the engine and transmission, so hard did I ride it that it suffered a broken gearbox bearing, being a mechanic I relatively easily fixed it. The noise the baffle-less Vincent created when climbing a long fast hill and with the extra weight of a pillion passenger or when in the company and varying sonic harmony of a big single megaphoned Velocette was remarkable, and music to a biker's ear.

Kick starting a Vincent was an acquired art that was only really matched by the Velocette Venom big singles. After flooding the carb' if the engine was not hot, and deciding on the right amount of choke or magneto advance if one was fitted as on a Velocette, it was a matter by practice and experience of easing the engine to the right static position past top dead centre using the kick-starter and the valve lifter together, and giving one almighty heave onto the kick-starter at the same time as being instantly ready to very rapidly lift your right leg, foot and knee well clear in less than a split second should the engine not fire up normally, but fire backwoods and with its heavy flywheel throw you over the handlebars and possibly breaking your leg or ankle if you were not quick enough to take the avoiding action. This happened to a previous owner to the Vincent after rebuilding the engine and getting the ignition timing a tooth out of alignment on the magneto drive gears, the bike kicked back on starting and after a somersault he broke his collar bone. It always took me around twenty five seconds longer to start the Vincent than a twin cylinder bike as I had to take time getting it right. Doing a somersault over the handlebars, often in front of a crowd, would not be cool.

The Vincent was so fast that Brinnie was soon modifying his already fast Velocette Venom to keep up. The Vincent and Brinnie's particularly now faster Velocette Venom, were acknowledged to be the quickest bikes in the area besides Clyde Cardy's astonishingly quick revving 650 Triumph Bonneville. Not only was Clyde able to put the best modifications on it but he also had a unique ability to go round corners at speeds that normally had a Triumph snaking and the rider easing off. It is no wonder that he became a British Motor Cycle and Sidecar grass track race champion on more than one occasion.

BIRDS BIKES AND BURN-UPS
And, THUNDERBIRD JOHN (BIG JOHN)

The following week-end we again meet at the Four Aces and this time some extra bikers joined us, including Ray White, Barry Hathaway, Ted Harris with his permanent and easy going girlfriend Brenda and Gogsy on his Ariel Leader with Trevor as a pillion and another old friend joined us was Big John, (Johny Dones) the Triumph Thunderbird rider, amongst several others.

Big John was a gentle giant who had his own undisputable opinion how to take a big Triumph round a challenging fast bend. Triumphs of the time were very rapid, partly due to their quick revving Edward Turner twin cylinder engine and partly due to their lightweight frames that would flex if you didn't keep a steady but gently positive throttle when bend-swinging. Big John's method was to declutch on the over-run and late brake when entering a bend, drift through the bend declutched, and then releasing the clutch and open up again whilst still navigating the bend's exit. This dangerous tactic would induce some horrendous snaking that he claimed to control but at the expense of the nervous constitution of anyone riding alongside or close behind him. He had recently progressed from a sprung Hub Triumph Speed Twin 500 to a more modern Triumph Thunderbird 650 and had not yet mastered the extra power and was going into bends too fast. As there was a reasonable group of us, including my brother with Afro Trevor wearing his huge new sheepskin jacket as pillion, we decided to go and see Gerry and the Pacemakers who were due to perform at the Locarno Ballroom at Basildon where my good friend Ray Nash was a Doorman and was sure to let us in. It was a spectacular event as all music shows were in the sixties, and we came out with sore voices from singing and in high spirits, which showed in the exhilarating acceleration that we enjoyed on yet another warm summer evening. We charged along the almost deserted and newly built Basildon Upper Maine (A176) and then turned into the new Cranes Farm Road (A1235) dual carriageway to the Ford Tractor Factory roundabout and beyond. A quick glance around to make sure our exhaust noise hadn't attracted a Police Austin Cambridge, nor a dreaded supercharged Austin Westminster or Police Norton Atlas motor-cycle that would sometimes hide near the nearby Laindon Police Garage, and if all was clear then it was full throttle to the next roundabout a mile away outside and the new Ford Tractor Plant, where it was squealing brakes and tortured tyres to kill enough speed to safely get round the roundabout before another blast on the hill's other side on our way eventually towards Wickford another three miles further.

There were quite a few bikes on that evening ride, adrenaline was high and we unavoidably bunched a little too tightly as we entered the Ford Tractor Factory Roundabout at speed. Unluckily Gogsy on his Ariel Leader with Afro-Trevor as pillion was directly in front of Big John on his wobbly Thunderbird. The Ariel did not have the more powerful brakes of the bigger Thunderbird that came whooshing past the Ariel at the very last moment into the roundabout, and when Big John did his myopic anti wobble party trick on his Thunderbird and then stopped unexpectedly dead in the midst of the pack on the roundabouts circuit, Gogsy had nowhere to go to avoid disaster. Gogsy, always known for his very quick reaction, somehow at speed and leaning left into the roundabout, flipped the bike, his pillion and himself into the opposite stance and mounted the new roundabout's proud new kerbstones at right angles at 40 mph to the right, the impact launched the Ariel complete with crash helmet-less rider and pillion Trevor with his Afro hair in full flight into the air by some three feet, they landed separately, with the bike landing first and momentarily staying upright in the soft freshly harrowed soil of the roundabouts centre, followed very quickly in succession by both rider and pillion who both landed incredibly into their pre-impact riding position with the two stroke engine still revving wildly and in a moment they were gone. When the rest of us reached the far side of the large roundabout, Gogsy, bike and pillion were nowhere to be seen and initially we feared the worst. We quickly scanned the hedges and found nothing, so we slowly rode on, keeping eyes open for evidence of Gogsy and Trevor's aftermath. Eventually we found them, on the side of the road, two miles further on towards Wickford with an exploded front tyre. The violent impact with the roundabout kerbing had broken the front wheel axle spindle bolt and the now unstable wheel and tyre assembly carried on rotating by leaning heavily to one side and suffering heavy friction between the inside of the left hand front fork leg and the front tyre's left hand side wall. Eventually, after two miles, the tyre wall got so hot that it exploded and stopped the bike dead, next stop, a ride in the butchers van of Mad Mick. Eventually, everyone has their use, even distasteful Mad Mick.

Gogsy relented, realising that a 250 lightweight had no chance in the company of the bigger British bikes that most of us had, especially when carrying a passenger and so replaced his Ariel at Pride and Clarke in London with a magnificent nearly new, black Matchless G12 650. We all learnt a lesson to keep clear of Big John and his Thunderbird but it took one last near disaster between Thunderbird

John and this time Brinnie on his Velocette Venom at the Battlesbridge river bridge before we all made a determined effort to send him to Coventry, along with Mad Mick who kept falling off his rather nice Norton Jubilee when drunk, which he often was, and caused us similar problems to Thunderbird John, and also so nearly The Grudge, but Her Maj' got to him first.

My brother however, was a little unlucky with the Matchless G12 650 twin that he bought. Twice he had a wrecked engine from thrown connecting rods that were the result of careless servicing and a loose oil return pipe whilst it was being serviced for the previous owner. The first time was at a moderate speed as a solo just fifteen miles away on the A127 at Southend-on-Sea, whilst the second time was some eighty miles away whilst attached to a side-car along the MI in Buckinghamshire. The Southend failure was nearby so I towed his very dead Matchless home with the Vincent which had no problem cruising at eighty miles per hour to our destination with the Matchless on tow, although very great care was needed at a much slower pace around roundabouts. However, for the M1 failure, due to the distance and the partially loaded sidecar, we opted to use Mother's Wolseley 1500 as a towing vehicle which it coped with quiet well, to the surprise of many motorists that we passed who were cruising in the slow lane.

The local section of the A130 trunk road before it was upgraded with dual carriageway sections was a twisty road with short or very steep hills, road junctions, a crossroad, narrow river bridge, a low and narrow railway bridge, and an antiques village to pass through. It was a road like the not too distant but much longer Burnham-on-Crouch road that demanded full concentration to enjoy it to the full, no less so than when passing through the ancient riverside village of Battlesbridge, with its historic brick, cast iron and stone bridge over the River Crouch at its head of navigation. You approached the bridge from the Chelmsford direction full of gusto after quickly descending a one in twelve hill at high revs in third that terminated in a sweeping and moderately tight second gear left hand-bend after a sudden noisy drop down through the gears under a fabulous echo creating railway-bridge. You then opened up the throttle for a quick two hundred and fifty yard sprint to the old river over-bridge, which was taken flat out in first after taking the approach ramp that took the road through ninety degrees. With the bike trying to leap airborne off the exit ramp you continued the bend swinging past the Watery Lane junction situated on a very tight ninety degree blind bend through the exciting 'S 'bends through Goose Cottages and the more obstacles before you reached the small village of Rawreth and eventually the Carpenters Arms pub and junction. Few motorcyclists resisted the temptation to enjoy this section to the full. On one of the final rides before the road's re-alignments a small group of the South Woodham lads were enjoying this three mile section and they included Brinnie with his 500 Velocette Venom and Big John with his 650 Thunderbird who both came down the hill towards the railway overbridge at great velocity, Brinnie rounded the bottom bend first due to a more stable bike and rider. However, after this bend, John on his 650 Triumph twin wrongly decided to outpace the rapid and fine handling 500 Velocette on the two hundred and fifty yard sprint to the river overbridge tight ninety degree approach ramp and after taking the Velocette with very little braking distance left, John did one of his trade-mark de-clutching and extreme braking when entering a bend. The Triumph Thunderbird predictably wobbled and snaked after passing the Venom at the very last moment by John over-braking with his large, powerful but clumsy hands and John came off his Thunderbird and the too close for comfort Velocette Venom was knocked flat. Brinnie and the Venom parted company and skidded across the right angled northern approach ramp of the ancient bridge and were destined to going over the road edge and plummet to the River Crouch some twenty feet below or even worse fate would be to plummet into the vile riverbed mud should the tide be out. Either landing would be a disaster as recovery would be almost impossible especially as there was no lifeboat service available during the week and only a limited service given by local yacht clubs at the rare weekends when they are hosting a yacht or dinghy race turning at Battlesbridge. So as the bike and rider skidded to an almost certain dunking in the mud and salt water, fortune was on their side, as the wide Velocette's handlebars became snagged on the lower Safety Rail of the Bridge's ramp protection guard rails and the bike's passage under the rail and into the calamity below was arrested at the last moment when the handlebars snagged and stopped the bike and rider going through for a ruinous plunge.

I had already used up most of my nine lives and Brinnie was rapidly using up his, and after Big John dismounted both Brinnie on his Venom and Gogsy on his Ariel it was unilaterally decided that enough was enough and we politely distanced ourselves from Big John and 'sent him to Coventry' together with Mad Mick on his Norton and felt a whole lot safer without them when out riding fast.

THE EXCITING OPEN ROAD

Such is the sheer thrill of riding a powerful bike on good road and on a fine summer's day that it brushes the accusation of debauchery.

Motorbike or open car rides in the Dengie Peninsular were always scenic, interesting, fast and fun. A couple of miles east of Wickford is a junction, now an interchange, known as The Rettendon Turnpike. From here there are two good routes into the very attractive, indeed beautiful, Dengie Hundred Peninsula. It starts off as the B131 to Burnham-on-Crouch. At South Woodham Ferrers there is an attractive spur route (B1418) to the north to ancient and interesting Maldon, some seven miles away. A little way beyond South Woodham Ferrers to the east however, the road splits as the high road and the low road. The low road after re-alignment, is *now* the main road (B1010) to Burnham-on-Crouch and in spring and autumn, it apparently has the foggiest record in the UK as it runs parallel with the River Crouch and its salt laden marshes, with stunning river-views from Althorne, and then on to Burnham-on-

Crouch, some 15 miles away. It is a bikers dream with fast, slow, very sharp and blind bends, some with no camber, and some with positive and adverse cambers. There are also steep and short hills, humps, junctions, cross winds and some spectacular river views. It is not a high-speed road but an open road without pedestrians and had in the sixties little town traffic. It is full of challenges and it keeps you very active on the saddle unless you are riding on a slow bike, maybe a lightweight or veteran/vintage type. The dangers on this route are slow moving tractors, some with very high and *wide hay loads and some without effective mirrors or indicators,* jay walking pheasants, mud, cattle or horse dung on the road, horse riders and the odd herd of cattle on the road, blind hills and blind bends, no street lights and occasional fog. Some bikers see it wrongly as a mini Isle of Man route and travel too fast and risky, and there has been some fatal and near fatal accidents. There is much more traffic on it now than back then and to be candid, modern high performance superbikes are a danger on it, but in the sixties the route was more suitable for the Velocettes, Nortons and Speed Twins that could breast 100 mph only on a dual carriageway rather than the modern Kawasakis, Hondas and Yamahas and modern Triumphs that approach 200 mph. Because of this, Essex Police moved their motorcycle division to nearby South Woodham Ferrers and scout the route regularly with their bikes and helicopter, especially at weekends and they come down very heavily on speeders on this particular route. Having said that, to enjoy this area on a swift ride whilst riding safely, and within the limits is still a joy, just keep within the limits, both legal and sensible. If you come off your bike and vanish into one of the many roadside deep ditches *you may not be noticed until the next day's mid-day farm traffic if indeed then.* There is another route by travelling the old high road, through the villages of Stow-Maries with its World War 1 vintage airfield, Cold Norton and Latchingdon and then enjoying the main road through to Mayland and Steeple and Bradwell-on-Sea. This is historically not a very fast road and it has been de-graded between South Woodham Ferrers and Latchingdon, not only is it with speed limits but it also has, and for some time has had, some wide 50 mph bends that have no camber and have a very slippery pebble-dash stone road surfaces and speed humps in the villages. It was widened and strengthened beyond Latchingdon in the fifties to accommodate the large out of gauge Pickford's loads that helped build the Bradwell Nuclear Power Station rather than for speed. It has in places some spectacular views as it overlooks the Saint Lawrence Bay on the River Blackwater on the approach to Bradwell-on-Sea. The dangers are *no camber* bends that have little or no warning, tractors, mud and cows herds moving to pastures anew, cross winds *and very low friction and frightening pebble dash* road surfaces *especially in the rain*. However, on a summer's day it is very picturesque.

At the heel of the Dengie Hundred and just south of the Rettendon Turnpike are the villages of Battlesbridge and Rawreth. They are both placed on the A130 main road that connects Southend-on-Sea with the County Town of Essex, Chelmsford, and on to Cambridge. The A130 was a slow road due to its pre-Victorian narrow and winding history and was always overcrowded. Three new sections have been built, one at Bedloe's Corner in Rawreth with another section linking up across the fields with an underpass next to the Blinking Owl Café on the A127 and another section by-passing the weight and width restrictive old bridge at Battlesbridge connecting to the Rettendon Turnpike. For a while after their initial completion but before the formal opening, two of the sections were physically there, but were cordoned of by some temporary plastic fencing.

Whilst chatting one evening in the Four Aces Café on the Woodham Road in Battlesbridge, we noticed that we had a full compliment of our most powerful motorcycles and riders with us and so we decided to have an evening of scratch races on a newly completed but not yet opened one mile dual carriageway section of the nearby A130 at Rawreth, what was to become the Rawreth By-Pass on the way to The Blinking Owl. It was getting dark and it had been raining which kept us café bound for a while, but the rain had now stopped and the shiny black tarmac roads were soon drying in the warm summer night air, and so we deemed the roads soon to be safe for some thrilling burn-ups. The heavy cloud from the rainstorm obscured the Moon and made it very dark. We had a couple of pillions to bolster numbers for the occasion, one of them being the likeable but rather troubled lad we called The Grudge. In the total darkness but with our eyes slowly getting accustomed to the deepening darkness we parked the bikes on the large, rock hard, dry summer clay (even though it had been raining) grass verge alongside the unopened section. We parked the bikes in a circle to create a small cosy heat arena and two at a time of us would leave the circle and belt the living daylights out of our bikes in a two lap point to point race of about two miles per lap, with Bedloe's Corner being the start and finish but turning on the new and unopened roundabout at Carpenter's Arms. First it was the 500 Velocette and Vincent 500 big singles, a particularly noisy but fast pair of performance bikes. The two laps started with the riders hugging the fuel tanks to reduce wind drag and a full on start, and enough noise to wake the dead in the nearby Rawreth Churchyard. Holding the bikes' long stroke engines to well over six thousand revs per minute at a tremendous crescendo before changing up to the next gear made them fly. At the end of the downhill start and after passing the first half mile the two were cresting over 100 mph for a brief period before the riders slammed the brakes on and sat bolt upright for the wind resistance to help reduce the bikes speeds to 40 mph before circling the new camber-less roundabout for a return blast to the top of the not-so-distant small rise to the start line and another go. The Vincent was marginally faster than the Velocette on the downhill run and marginally slower than the hot Velocette on the returning uphill run. It was obvious that had I lowered the gearing on the Vincent where the clutch was not fully released until 32 mph in first gear, the Vincent was likely to have been faster than the very fast Velocette in both directions. Lowering the gearing was no more than turning around the twin sprocket rear wheel. But I didn't change the ratio because the sight, smell of Castrol R, and sound of the Vincent pulling away in such a high gear from the Blinking Owl was sacrosanct as it always attracted a biker audience when it pulled away, so I sacrificed some high-speed acceleration for some low speed drama. Next was the chance for the 650 twin-cylinder BSA, Triumphs and Matchless of The Bear, Big John and Gogsy, with their individually distinct exhaust notes echoing against the trees to try and show a clean pair of heels to each other. There was loads of lovely noise on the overrun from the big twins or from the big BSA's deep burble and sparks from the scraping centre stand when circling the roundabout positioned at one end, or the Matchless' Siamese exhaust when given the gun, or the quick revving of the Triumph Thunderbird with the sound of a dozen cracking rifles. With no traffic, and being dark, no wildlife nor pedestrians and only two of us at a time it was deemed totally safe and harmless besides one of the lads, out of the blue, or maybe black was more appropriate, got a couple of bee stings on the back of his neck, which struck us as a bit strange but for what reason we were later to find out.

It was a good evening, no booze, which was always too risky, and no girls to take home early, just a night of lads being lads, with the lads, and their bikes. As midnight came and went and with the smell of the lavender fields and the bikes' Castrol R hanging in the warm damp air, we all readied to leave with big smiles on our faces, but hang on, someone's crash helmet is missing. We rode our bikes round in circles in the long rye grass trying to find the crash hat in the total darkness, without success. Suddenly there is a call from the far side of the unopened dual carriageway, it was the Grudge, who had been missing for a while and hearing the bikes start up did not want get left behind. Not only that, but he was wearing the missing helmet which he had quietly borrowed earlier in the evening. Apparently, when he borrowed the helmet, he explained to Nipper that he was going to attack and destroy a bee hive, Nipper didn't believe him thinking that in the pitch black and no known honey producers locally that Grudge was just being typically crazy Grudge and ignored him. However Nipper was proved wrong and Grudge did find a hive and for reasons unknown to us he crazily angered the bees and someone, easy going J.J, got stung. This was one of many strange pointless ruinous japes that Grudge did. Likeable as he was, we couldn't reason with some of his thinking, he seemed to have two personalities at variance and ended up losing the plot one day and spending time at Her Majesty's Pleasure, which avoided him being 'sent to Coventry ' by us for some of his misdemeanours and maybe sadly we saw no more of him. No doubt he had a recurring spasmodic mental disorder, which at the time, society would not accept and on a bad day or moment, he was classed as a 'wrong'n'. However such a bad day is known now as a psychotic episode and is so commonplace that help and understanding is available. Maybe the bees thought they had got suitable revenge, but unfortunately they chose the wrong person. This saw the death of some harmless bees which automatically die when they sting you, maybe the Grudge did not know this and put them in the same class as the hated wasps, who sting for the hell of it. Bee stings aside and after the thrilling evening, we all rode off into the warm summer night to our various homes within a five mile radius, looking forward to the next biking day.

PART NINE

THE ESSEX COAST IN THE SIXTIES

SOUTHEND'S ETERNAL PLEASURE

A typical summer weekend evening ending with a girlfriend would be a breeze down the A127 Southend Arterial Road ending up at Southend's rather long four-mile seafront, part of it being called 'The Golden Mile'. There was plenty to do and see and a good time was always guaranteed, starting the evening with an ice cream, spending plenty of small coins in the amusement arcades, enjoying the thrills of the legendary Kursaal Pleasure Ground, or the fresh air on The Pleasure Pier, rounded off with a bag of well salted chips or a hot dog before the ride home. The ride home would often be a pleasant cruise during a warm summer's evening with hardly more than a zephyr to cool you. The homeward ride always started with a cruise along the seafront through the spectacular illuminations, which were like a smaller Blackpool. In the longer light evenings of June and July we might, after the seafront cruise enjoy a very rapid A127 ride and a final blast down Rayleigh Cutting, call in at the 'Owl' to round the day off talking with other bikers and their girls about bikes, music and bikes.

The Southend Police was a provincial force their white helmets and fast cars and bikes were always moving us on or pulling us up. There were police everywhere in the summer and you did your best not to attract them and stay within the law, but if we were on bikes, we were their eternal targets.

Three times within fifteen or so years, the pleasure pier, the longest one in the World, caught fire. After the second fire, the corporation replaced all of the fire fighting appliances and equipment at great cost on the mile and a third long pier. In this department's planning they replaced the entire water supply piping from the mains on the land to the pier-head's fire reporting point more than a mile out to sea. In a moment of brilliance it was decide to save cost by using a large diameter plastic pipe to carry the fire brigade's water for the entire length out to the seaward end. It didn't need a scientist to see that in the event of a fire that the pipe would totally melt, and on the third fire, that is exactly what happened leaving no water supply to the Fire Brigade. The Essex Fire Brigade had no option but to call for The Port of London's Fire Boats that were thirty miles and maybe two hours sailing away in the London Docks. Why did they not just install a submersible salt water pump and just pump sea water that was in abundant supply at the pier-head onto the fire instead of pumping it a mile and a third through very low melting point plastic pipes. Brilliant! Just Brilliant. What a brilliant piece of strategy! The Pier-Head was ruined. The plastic pipe noticeably drooped on every hot summer's day let alone in a fire when it melted altogether. Maybe it was the same responsible plastic wizard that designed the Plastic Fire Engine that lost a head-butt with a pre war wooden Austin horsebox that is mentioned earlier in this book. Keeping plastic for toys and electrical appliances seems a much more sensible attitude.

There was another rather embarrassing set of circumstances when a ship hit the pier in June 1986. It turned from a near fatality into a farcical event that could only be created by an East End Londoner having a good day out and more than a few beers in his belly. It was a good summer's day at Southend, plenty of sunshine, warm air, crowds and the usual happy go lucky feeling that such an environment puts into local residents and tourists alike, but particularly so visitors from the East End of London who had drunk just too much either in the seafront pubs or the pub at the seaward end of the pier.

And typically after plenty of beer washing down copious amounts of jellied eels, shellfish, pie and mash or fish and chips, all being Southend-on-Sea culinary delights, there is often a very necessary desire to head for the ablutions to rebalance ones stomach. Southend has ample ablutions (public toilets) of a reasonable standard, well above that of the Blinking Owl, including a large wooden Victorian structure positioned towards the far end of the pier. On this particular day a medium size ship, the MV Kingsabby, flying a foreign flag and crewed by some foreigners who were apparently asleep or drunk at the wheel of the ship, let the eastward bound ship exiting London crash into the pier at speed. They said that the sun blinded them and that they could not see this sixty foot high pier that is over a mile and a third long, nor saw it on the charts where it had been adequately marked for nearly one hundred years. A later marine investigation showed that they were one and a half miles off course in clearly charted and buoyed water in clear daylight and no fog in the area. Carelessness or lack of good Navigation was to blame and the Skipper charged.

However they did hit bulls-eye by crashing bow first into the clearly painted large white ornate Victorian wooden toilet block. Fortunately, the only occupant at the time was a gentleman from the East End of London who was considering his immediate future whilst seated on the throne in the privacy of his cubicle when the virtually silent ship took two side walls and the roof of his cubicle to one side and threw them into the sea, whilst he did the only thing that came to his mind, and that was to vacate the cubicle pronto, pronto with his trousers around his ankles, swearing and cursing in the most colourful language and eventually laughing off the event, as only an East Ender can do.

The ship, the 1,860 feet long, MV Kingsabbey, a sugar tanker weighing nearly a thousand tons empty crashed into the pier in broad daylight and caused substantial damage. It cut the pier in two leaving a seventy feet gap and destroyed the historic lifeboat station, as well as totally reducing the large ornate toilet block to matchwood.

Marooned visitors at the Pier Head had to be ferried back to the land end by the lifeboat that was fortunately not in the Lifeboat shed at the time of the impact.

One thing was certain, we would always have a good time at Southend in the summer months where the East Enders called the natives 'Saarfenders'. Even if the wind was holding the sea out, over a mile away across the mudflats, or it was raining, we always had a good time in Southend-on-Sea with its saucy girls and its Golden Mile, fuelled by the 'out to have fun at any price' East Enders.

TORNADO SMITH   The Wall of Death dare devil

Southend-on-Sea had one of Britain's earliest Theme Parks, the famous Kursaal, the Kursaal consisted of some twelve acres of fairground rides, some under cover, on the seafront. Some unusual entertainment was given by a 'Tip The Lady Out Of Bed' that was basically a coconut shy type of operation where young lads threw a hard ball at a target and if it struck lucky, then a scantily dressed young lady was ejected from a bed that she was occupying to a big cheer from watchful teenage lads. There was also a wooden roller coaster called the Mouse that was advertised as being the longest and fastest in the country, it was a totally wild experience that encouraged you to have a second ride, if you could suffer the next queue. There was also The Dyno that was a rotating vertical drum that you stood in with maybe a dozen others and when it got up to a good rotational speed, the floor would drop away beneath your feet and you would be held, pinned against the vertical wall of this scare machine being held by centrifugal force alone, and nothing else. Sure, you got dizzy and spooked and it was a strangely disorientating experience, maybe like being inside Mum's twin-tub washing machine on the dryer cycle, but a heck of a lot more fun, noisier and seemingly faster. Most fascinating however was almost certainly The Wall of Death. This also consisted of a wooden drum, some twenty feet high and maybe twenty feet in diameter within which a dare devil rider or two, often one being a young girl would ride around horizontally on an old motor cycle at speed with the drum swaying on its guy ropes and steadying braces. The spectators stood on a narrow platform at the top perimeter of this wooden wobbling tower, looking down on the stunt riders. Usually there would be two BSA A7 500cc motorcycles rotating together at a frightening speed in avoiding ellipses making the entire structure wobble. In the earlier years, the owner, a bespectacled lanky character by the name of Tornado Smith, would ride inside this vertical wall with a twelve stone Lioness by the name of Briton riding on a motorcycle and sidecar outfit, or even in an open bodied Austin Seven car. Tornado Smith would often be seen promoting his event by riding an ancient Penny-farthing bicycle around the Southend streets. At some time in the early sixties, Tornado was called to the Magistrates Court in Southend, accused of speeding and therefore dangerous or reckless driving in his car. He was fined the grand sum of £10.00 for dangerous driving, which was about a week's basic wage to a bus conductor back then and he took it as an insult considering what he did for a living. He showed his disdain by offering to pay off the fine in tiny Farthings, four to a penny, nine hundred and sixty to a pound and a mind boggling nine thousand, six-hundred farthings to ten pounds.

The clerk of the court wanted to show authority and refused to accept so many tiny coins saying that beyond one-pound sterling they were not legal tender and accused Tornado Smith of contempt of court. Always looking for free publicity, Tornado stood firm and invited the local weekly press, The Southend Standard, to witness and photograph the Court refusing to accept the ten pounds worth of farthings. At a pre-arranged time, Tornado turned up on his penny-farthing bicycle with the press and the nine thousand, six hundred farthing coins in money bags at the courthouse, where an embarrassed clerk was photographed accepting and tediously counting, no coin counters then, this so called illegal tender to avoid further ridicule. Tornado eventually was said to be bankrupt and emigrated to South Africa. Being the colourful individual that he was, it came as no surprise that after he'd emigrated it was reported that he had an estate worth more than one hundred thousand pounds which back then was a considerable amount of money, no doubt he didn't keep it as farthings under the bed.

THE LEGENDARY DERRY PRESTON-COBB

The uncatchable speedster of Southend-on-Sea

As I have mentioned earlier, I had a super-smooth and super-quick Greeves motorcycle. It was built in a factory in Thundersley not far from Southend-on-Sea. It was in this factory that the World famous Greeves Competition Motor Cycles were built. It was an offshoot of Invacar Ltd, a motorised invalid carriage builder that was owned by a Bert Greeves from Devon. His inspiration came after building a one-off motorised invalid carriage from a basic framework and a lawn mower engine in 1946 for his very disabled and extremely overweight quadriplegic cousin, Derry Preston-Cobb. They could see a market for such an invalid carriage for the many badly disabled servicemen returning from The War and went into production, soon winning a government supply contract. Being a relatively small concern, they did not have enough land to carry out prolonged endurance testing of their Villiers proprietary power units that were however extensively used in the motor cycle and construction industries, and were mounted within their own produced invalid carriages. They figured that the best way to thoroughly test a 250 cc bike engine to a destructive point was to overload it in a heavily loaded road vehicle that could be held at full throttle for reasonably long periods of time. All they needed was a suitable vehicle and a hell for leather if not near suicidal, pilot. By good fortune they had such a combination on the company payroll . . . Derry Preston – Cobb and his archaic three-wheeled invalid carriage. Derry was an unfortunate very heavily paralysed invalid who was however jolly but had a fantastic brain and was conveniently the Sales Manager at Invacar Ltd, and subsequently also at Greeves.

His invalid carriage was a crude affair that in essence was an open-air chariot. To what I remember it had no seat, just a rear ramp and small platform for his crude ministry supplied basket woven and metal frame wheelchair to climb and accommodate. It had tiller steering and a blue canvas apron giving some weather protection to his legs and lower body and a flat glass windscreen. The carriage seemed to be based on a pre-war motorcycle sidecar chassis with a single small front wheel and two parallel rear wheels maybe five feet apart fitted with the drop down ramp at the back for his hand propelled invalid chair to climb so that it fitted within the open body on a floor maybe one yard square, and was propelled on the pavements or roads by a small 147 cc air cooled single cylinder British Anzani two stroke engine that was bolted alongside the occupant giving off a lot of noise and smoke as the speed and revs increased whilst driving one of the back wheels. Heath Robinson would have looked at it with much amazement and possible envy. It may have appeared rather crude but there was absolutely nothing else on the market at the time that was suitable for the disabled who wanted, or needed, more than a pedestrian hand propelled wheelchair, so it had to be a success with maybe some attention to detail.

One day, the police nabbed Derry after many failed attempts, for breaking the speed limit on the A127 Southend Arterial Road in his invalid carriage. Many an 80 mph police car had failed without success to apprehend this well-known and very disabled speed lunatic in a three-wheeled open invalid chair that was reputed to often pull a wheelie on a pull away, and there were several incidents where the police recovered him from his crashed upturned contraption, whilst he was apparently often laughing. When indeed the Police did actually snare him it was with much embarrassment that they reported the recorded speed in excess of ninety miles per hour, the Magistrates almost laughed out of court the claim as being ridiculously unbelievable to the extreme. But alas it was true, as he was testing the Greeves Motorcycles latest 250 Griffon 32 bhp racing motor-cycle engine that could propel it at speeds in excess of 100 mph. Derry, after receiving so much astonished free publicity, gladly paid the fine and not only became a legend to this day, but the consequent sales of Greeves Motor Cycles fitted with that engine ended up with a healthy order book.

THE GHOST OF THE A127

There was a story, maybe anecdotal but certainly it became of a legendary status of a young girl hitchhiker who was picked up alongside the A127 dual carriageway just half a mile east of Kent's Hill Corner and A127 crossroads in Eastwood, in the fifties by a motorcyclist on his way to Southend-on-Sea. On the ensuing journey, there was an accident in which she unfortunately lost her life. The legend continues that some lads have since individually reported seeing her (spirit) on the same spot on the event's sad anniversary, and if you see her and she/her spirit climbs onto your pillion seat, then by the time you reach the Southend Seafront, she will have vanished, you would have lost her, just as they have before.

The Ghost's Sonnet...The Ode of Southend

Where are you now? I eternally sigh, seeing you beckon, I should have rode by,

Road-side bend, you waving your thumb, hitching to Southend, the seafront and some fun.

Quickly I stopped, and at each other we smiled, you boarded my bike to the Golden Mile.

Your golden locks flowed, a dream so supreme, a cruise down the front, sunshine and ice cream.

I stopped and you'd gone, nowhere to be seen, had you fallen off? . . .God, I'd lost my Queen.

Like a spirit you'd vanished, into thin air, all I could find was a truss of blonde hair.

A legend is born, of the vanishing Queen, who fell off a bike, without even a scream,

To the August spirit forever trapped in that bend, you'll always be here, in this sad Ode, the Ode of Southend.

Beware the hitchhiker on that Arterial bend, A127, two miles from its end,

When at the Pier you finally arrive, don't look then because she'll be gone . . ., whisp'ing her way back o'er the Prom' (15)

Well let me tell you about her, and the way she died,

So let me tell you about her, so many people cried . . .

But its too late to say your sorry, how should I know, why should I care, please don't bother tryin' to find her 'cos she's not there

Well let me tell you about the way she looked, the way she acted and the colour of her hair, Her voice was cool and soft, her eyes were clear and bright.
                                       ...but she's not there
(16)

THE GHOST'S HIGH NOON

The Haunted House of Cold Norton, 1965

During 1965 the lads from South Woodham Ferrers had gathered at the Four Aces Café and were discussing the A127 Ghost legend and the conversation turned to a long abandoned Manor House close to the nearby village of Cold Norton that was supposedly haunted despite a rumoured exorcism, and as it was approaching Halloween it was thought a good idea to evict the stubborn ghost with the roar of a gang of motor bikes on Halloween night. It was thought it could be a bit of a hoot.

We arrived in the dark of that autumn evening and rode up its long dark drive of High Elm trees and parking the bikes we shut down the engines. After a brief look at its semi derelict state of few doors and hardly an unbroken window on the ground floor, and with an embarrassing autumnal shiver down ones spine, we decided on a course of action.

The Eviction

The Bear quipped that we should knock on the dislodged front door and await a reply, at which point he went for the old front door knocker. .

> *Knock, who's there, now that the night is falling, come in the door is open wide . . .Knock, who's there . ?. .(17)*

It was a very quiet and worrying ethereal dark country night, the silence only disturbed by the occasional hooting of a Barn Owl calling for a mate. It was dark, very dark, and in the darkness . . . .

> *When the night wind howls, in the chimney cowls and the bat in the moonlight flies, and a black cat wails in the autumn gales and the Oh! such a midnight sky.*
>
> *Ghosts in the graveyard rise from the dead, under their arms carrying their heads,*
>
> *It's fun in hell at the toll of the bell, and the air goes cold in this shadow of hell,*

For this is the Ghosts High Glory-i and this is the Ghosts' High-Noon, High-Noo-oon, Hi-Noo-oon For this is the Ghosts' High-Noon . . (18)

The Vincent was positioned at the now open front door, a large Velocette Venom at the rear door, each was accompanied by a very smoky two-stroke, a Greeves Sports-Twin and an equally smoky two-stroke Ariel Leader. Flanking the side doors were a large BSA 650 Golden Flash ridden by Derek, The Bear, as he was affectionately known and another two-stroke, a James Captain and a 350 Matchless G3 of Ted Harris. All of the bikes faced with their exhaust pipes facing the doors and Nipper's side-valve 750 Harley Davidson Blackpool Illuminations Special, providing the lighting. It was a grand ensemble.

At the decided moment, all the bikes were kicked into life and the considerable noise filled not only the building but the surrounding countryside as well. The building was filled to capacity with the swirling blue smoke of the two-strokes and with the burnt cabbage smell of the Vincent's Castrol 'R' engine oil. With most of the throttles being held to around 4000 rpm, the noise reached a deafening crescendo with the deep baritone of the BSA twin complimenting the powerful bass notes of the Vincent and Velocette with the cacophony of some laughing hyenas from the two-stroke twins on the overrun, and the waffling of the flat-head Harley Davidson. Enough was enough and Nipper flashed his lights a few times on this Harley and we all shut down. All was very, very silent now, besides the Barn Owl's casual hooting as she was still calling for a mate, and a lot of racket from the flock of rooks in their rookery high up in the Elms that we had unwittingly disturbed. Turning the bikes round and switching on their lights and seeing the drifting voluminous blue smoke that no ghost could exist through, it was clear that we had issued a fumigation of the highest order. We planned to leave, but hey, is there still movement in the old building, we looked agog as slowly through the drifting mystique of the blue two-stroke smoke, very gently strode a cloaked figure, maybe not the grim reaper, but was it a man of the cloth?.

We stayed silent as it seemed that every bike had a rider, so nobody was missing, yet for a moment it was eerie, ethereal even. Up to that point none of us admitted to sensing any para-normal activity, indeed I was not aware of any of the lads being hyper receptive as an artist, clairvoyant or visionary and therefore finding extra sensual activity (ESP) nor claiming telepathy. The usual feeling of a brush of cold air followed by a shivering veil leading to an intensive connection was not there, however eventually the figure lobbed an exploding bird-scarer (firecracker) at us and we realised it was no disturbed ghost, but the Grudge who was pulling one of his crazy pranks on us after finding an awful old blanket in the house to use as a spooks cloak, and a misfired bird-scarer.

> *As thunder claps and lightnings flash, leafs dance like a mischievous child. Temperatures ease in the zephyric breeze and the haunted skies turns wild,*
>
> *As dark clouds cover The Moon. and gone is the Ghosts' High Glory-i, and gone is the Ghosts' High-Noon. High Noo-oon, High noo-oon and gone is the Ghosts' High-Noon . .(18)*

With the deep sonorous rumble of the large four stokes and the accompanying ratatatat, pop popping of the smoky two strokes, we left the old house, lonely and dark and desolate in that cold spooky night,

Ghosts ? What Ghosts . . .

Gary the Grudge was one of the Four Aces gang. He was often up to capers that we didn't necessarily agree with but was a likeable local lad who we went to school with. We would often ride as a group on the bikes, The Grudge, like JJ, often didn't have a bike but was a sensible pillion and helped to make up the party and occupied any spare pillion seat. Our weekly routine included visiting from The Four Aces Café, the A127 Blinking Owl, The Long Bar at Chelmsford, The South Woodham Ferrers Village Hall, Maldon Promenade and The Vineyards Community and Dance Hall near Brentwood. At weekends we would visit Southend Seafront or Brands Hatch, which was just a fifty mile run which included a deliciously noisy blast through the Dartford Tunnel. The ride to the Vineyards from the Long Bar was often done with a group of like minded lads including Gulp, a crazy individual that could open his throat and down a complete bottle of Coca Cola without a pause, and Bonk, a 5ft 2inch biker that not only had a new Honda Monkey bike but an extremely expensive, new and unreliable BMW R60 that kept suffering with cracked gearbox casings. In later years I was to learn that the German super reliability assumption is a myth that so many people strangely want to believe.

We'd meet at the Long Bar Café at Chelmsford and it always included a 90 mph high-speed dash along part of the totally unlit A12 dual carriageway known as the Ingatestone By-Pass. It was as a bit of a shock to me when during one particular night trip whilst I was in the middle of the bunch and at speed, that my lights totally failed when the Miller Dynamo Shellac insulation overheated and failed, not an unknown event as it was mounted like on so many bikes, directly behind the engine's cylinder where it was ideally dry but subject to lots of heat, especially at speed. It was a test of nerves to stay with the group with no street lighting and very little visibility at such speed, knowing that if I slowed to a more manageable speed of maybe 30 mph that I would be plunged into a very dangerous sudden period of darkness as the pack disappeared into the moonless distance, so I held on and hoped. Soon we arrived at the Vineyards a record player was always playing, this was the pre-tape and pre-CD era and a favourite was a little known 'B' side of one of Cher's 1964 Number One hits, it was called 'Waltzing the Quintez' A lovely moving piece, that deserved to be a Number One by itself.

I never knew my mother, I hardly ever knew my Dad, I've been in town for eighteen years and you're the only boy I've ever had, Baby don't go, pretty baby please don't go- o. I love so-oh!, pretty baby please don't go . . (19)

The recording industry eventually realised this mis-labelling and re-launched it in 1965 with the easier to remember title 'Baby Don't Go' and it shot to Number One. Eventually at the end of the evening we would return to South Woodham Ferrers and swop thoughts before going home. South Woodham was a sleepy Essex village on the banks and fens of the upper reaches of The River Crouch. It's only feature besides the very attractive riverside was the large Marconi Radar Research Scanner and control station on its highest hill. Apparently it could trace the movements of bird-flocks as far away as The Mediterranean, but it was joked that it could not spot the details of amorous birds of the human type that were up to high jinks with their boyfriends on the nearby South Woodham riverside each night, or could they? we will never know.

FUN IN THE RAIN

The autumn weather of the following weekend in South Woodham was not too promising. There was still the need for bike adventure in the air, and we hoped that a ride on our bikes into Southend for an evening on The Golden Mile might find a drier weather slot. Either way, if it did rain there, then the bright lights of the Illuminations and the out of the weather arcades and amusements would be more fun than The Four Aces in the rain. The thought of finding some fun by travelling in our cars was not a very convincing option. Gogsy with his rapid Matchless G12 joined us and we headed for Southend after going through nearby Wickford to get some petrol and with the splendid roar of the many bikes climbing Rayleigh Cutting from the yet to be opened Fairglen Underpass at speed was a joy to listen to and be amongst. After a couple of hours of undercover fun at Southend we went back to our bikes and discovered that it was indeed now raining which did not impress us. If we went home straight away then we were sure to get a thorough soaking from the twelve-mile ride. We decided that it would be better to take shelter from the weather in one of the ornate Victorian seafront shelters for an hour or so until the weather hopefully abated. So that is what we did, and encircled ourselves and the shelter with our bikes, to cut down the cool breeze coming off the sea. We laid on the wooden slat benches and after a short chat we all started nodding off, laying comfortable and cosy out of the weather in our leather jackets, denim jeans, riding boots and not forgetting our crash helmets, face scarves and leather gloves. It was gone eleven with everything shut or shutting down and it was still raining. We were cosy preferring a kip in our leather gear in the shelter to a soaking on the A127, yes we were very comfortable and not wanting to be interrupted, hmmm!

> *Listen to the rhythm of the falling rain telling me of what a fool I'd been (20)*

"Come on! What are you lads up to, you can't stay here for the night, you must be on your way" barked a voice of authority. Raising ourselves from our nap, we see a couple of Southend's larger than life coppers towering over us complete with their capes and white police helmets dripping rain. Oh bugger, we were quite comfortable and we aren't doing any harm was the unanimous response. But the police just wanted us gone, with our bikes, in the rain. Nipper, being tall, self-confidently sensible and of the nature that he was, as normal tried to argue our rights, but we knew the odds were against us and after starting our bikes and passing more than a few moans, we rode off towards the A127 in the persistent rain but making a fair bit of noise about it to show our objection and disapproval, like passing voluminous wind when leaving a lah-de-dah party.

After eight miles from Southend we approached the Blinking Owl biker's café where we hoped that we could dry out a little, but it was close to a late autumn midnight now and The Owl had closed early because of the rain. Less than half a mile further on was the almost completed Owl (Fairglen) underpass, where we parked out of the rain under one of the underpass structures after ignoring the road closed signs and shut down our engines. With almost total shelter from the weather Brinnie suggests again that we form a circle again with the bikes and now that the engines are rather warm we can dry out a bit, and so we did. It got a little cosy out of the rain and with the warm engines until a little while later. Before long, the peace was shattered by Nipper, who with too much noise and laughter was descending one of the forty five degree concrete slab embankment walls, rotating out of control sitting in an upturned metal dustbin lid that he had found. It didn't take much for us to see that this was a hoot of an idea and before long we had found other suitable toboggans such as discarded road signs and plastic container lids and had a whale of a time wearing our crash helmets to avoid collision concussions and jackets and gloves and careering down this 25 feet concrete block ramp crashing into each other and the concrete support pillars of the yet to be opened underpass. It was great fun while it rained but eventually the rain decreased and we decided that we'd had enough fun and tomorrow would be a fifty mile bike ride to Brands Hatch with a stirring blast through the Dartford Tunnel, if it was dry and preferably warm, so we called it a day and went home to get some decent sleep for an early start the next day, which we were all looking forward to.

Brands Hatch was always a favoured destination for us especially if it was hosting a motor-cycle racing event. However it was very open to a cold and sometimes rather wet wind especially around Clearways. If it threatened to be a rainy or a cold day then we would travel reluctantly by car and enjoy the heater and general banter, with passing through the tunnel being a total non-event, but we always had a great day at 'Brands' as we use to say. The atmosphere was always terrific there, so we always went home happy and with many good memories and wanting more.

VIVA JAYWICK

VIVA JAYWICK INDEED, 1964 and 1965

Every year, a group of us bikers would rent a holiday chalet for a summer's week in Jaywick, some sixty miles away on the coast and enjoy a brilliant bikers' week in sunny Clacton and the surrounding area. To get there we would ride the bikes through a very picturesque part of central and eastern Essex. After leaving our early Saturday morning gathering point at the Four Aces Café' we would pass through a very pretty Bicknacre or East Hanningfield and then over the Eves Corner crossroads with its weeping willow tree graced pond at the highest point in Essex in classy and expensive Danbury, down the very long hill to the nearly sea level Chelmer and Blackwater Canal at Little Baddow's picture postcard Paper Mill Lock. Then, over the bridge and then we climbed, to the main A12 near Hatfield Peverel. The A12 is the very busy road that links London to Colchester and East Anglia. The A12 was always a good road that was spoiled by passing through many small or medium sized towns, one every four miles or so. Every summer Saturday the A12 would have a 15 mph crawl for all of the thirty mile distance between Chelmsford and north of Colchester, with holiday maker's traffic to the many seaside towns of Essex, Suffolk and Norfolk and holiday camps such as Butlin's and Pontin's. However to ease matters in 1964 a new three-mile long by-pass, among the first of many nationally, had been opened to avoid the busy town of Witham, and as it was almost to motorway standards it was the first time it was possible to really open our bikes up and beat the magical 'Ton' and hold it there for a distance before the bypass ended, Wow. To someone who has never ridden a powerful bike without streamlining at speed it is almost impossible to relay the exhilarating sensations of holding very tight to your handlebars whilst your body is fighting against the incredible force of the wind that is trying to blow you off your saddle at such high speed. The wind, the noise, vibration and the thrill of seeing the speedometer climb relentlessly from an indicated sixty to seventy to eighty, and march on to ninety and then to one hundred miles per hour and more while you pray nothing is going to break or cause you to unexpectedly swerve or to have an impact with a bird or rabbit or any other wildlife, yes life is thrillingly on the brink at that speed. The next twenty miles to Wivenhoe, north-east of Colchester was a pain, as the continuous slow queue was forcing us to ride too slow under circumstances that most of the bikes were not designed for. Even by filtering the traffic, hedge-hopping the slow moving cars overloaded with families and holiday luggage and slipping the bikes' clutches to allow for the very high first gears on some of the bikes, the bikes' magnetos and ignition coils and fuel systems started overheating. Also the bikes' clutches start to overheat and drag causing sticky gear-changes, petrol in the overheated carburettors and fuel lines started to evaporate causing misfiring for the next half hour after the slow ride from the Witham Bypass, before we got to Wivenhoe, just past Colchester and at last, a chance to rest our tired clutch hands and pick some speed up to cool the air-cooled engines. We took the superb B1027 from Wivenhoe to Jaywick, enjoying the rises, falls and many fast sweeping bends and a thrilling ride all of the way, (very similar to the B1010 that links Rettendon (near Wickford) to Burnham-on-Crouch, (also in Essex.) Through, Alresford, Thorrington Cross, and St Osyth we rode, and finally to our sunny rented Chalet on stilts in Essex Way, Brooklands Estate, lively Jaywick.

During the summers of 1964 and 1965 Jaywick was spot on for us, not how it is now sadly projected on the TV. Back then we classified Jaywick as Upper Jaywick and Lower Jaywick. Upper Jaywick was on slightly higher ground, mostly bungalows of which were privately owned, attractively built in brick and had colourful gardens, that we passed through every time we journeyed to and from our chalet in Lower Jaywick. We stayed in Lower Jaywick which was below sea-level and consequently there was no main drainage as all of the properties were designed for summer occupation only. All of the properties in Lower Jaywick were built on stilts or piers to avoid flood damage, should there be excessively high tides or winter storm surges from the North Sea that was separated from the area by crude, low sea walls and earthworks. This area was known as The Brooklands Estate, named after the car racing circuit in Surrey and all of the enclosed roads were low standard concrete treeless avenues that were named after various car manufacturers, including Essex Way, which was named after the American carmaker, Essex. Regardless of the image portrayed by later TV in their programme 'Benefits by the Sea' we thoroughly enjoyed our annual stay there as the chalets *then*, were by council decree, left unoccupied in the winter months whereupon the owners refurbished them and they were fit, healthy and happy for the next new season and all of the summer occupiers were happy holiday makers, many returning from previous happy years. As a low cost holiday centre with its beaches and proximity to Clacton and it's attractions, it was ideal.

The Jaywick chalets were mostly wood and asbestos, of low build quality and mounted high on five feet high brick legs. They were always pleasant each spring, and always sold out every summer. With the low rental charges demand was understandably high.

THE AWFUL LAVENDER CART

JAYWICK'S ONLY UNPLEASANT RESIDENT IN THE SIXTIES

However, as the holiday estate was built within some low sea walls and below sea level there was no main drainage. This necessitated each chalet to have an outside toilet in a small shed that was called the thunder-box, which contained an Elsan chemical toilet. Each morning at 07.15 sharp, a most unpleasant small collection tanker (that we called the Lavender Cart) would pull up outside our chalet and a small gang of arguably delightful environmentally friendly but nevertheless heroic men, would walk to the thunder-box sheds around the rear of each chalet, and with a quick deft heave, hoist the chemical toilet chamber and it's less than pleasant contents onto their individual shoulders, they then marched to the front of the chalet to the awaiting Lavender Cart and with gay abandon and in one quick and deliberate action, and with such dexterity to ensure accuracy and avoid spillage, heave the chamber up and over spewing its evil contents into the tank. If that was not bad enough, they would leave the odorous cart, smelling heavily of lavender disinfectant amongst other things, outside our chalet for ten minutes or so every morning whilst they had a cup of tea in the adjacent chalet. No doubt after a quick wash, and then continue on their delightful daily round. I'd sooner be a much hated traffic warden than do that job, mused The Bear, Yuk. We assumed that the rather smartly dressed lady occupant of the rather tidy adjacent chalet, either had absolutely no sense of smell or was a very close relation of one of the crew, why else would anyone entertain such foul smelling workmen into their home?

How things have changed, In Essex and elsewhere in the UK everything besides over-crowding has improved immeasurably since the sixties, but alas, Jaywick, since the sixties has sadly got noticeably worse as so many of the chalets have run into serious disrepair as they are no longer occupied by reasonably fussy holiday makers for just part of the year, and are now owned by private landlords that previously maintained them well in the quiet months, but are now rented all year round with declining maintenance standards, to the unfortunate less well off.

Yes, with Jaywick as it was, the Essex summers in the sixties were excellent. Viva Jaywick (1960's that was) So sad that it has now fallen from favour.

The group of us, usually eight or so, would base ourselves at this otherwise harmoniously friendly chalet every August, and from here make visits to nearby Clacton-on-Sea on the bikes. Clacton and the Pier always attracted us with its permanent fun-fare, saucy girls, ice creams and sandy, mud free, golden beaches where, unlike Southend-on-Sea (or mud, depending on the state of the tide) There was only a small tide effect and therefore enough water on the beaches of Clacton for a dip, no mud, just sand and sea.

The area of Clacton, nearby Frinton (where Winston Churchill once lived) and a little further on Walton-on-the-Naze is the Bournemouth of the East Coast with very high sunshine levels, golden sand beaches, two Victorian Piers, slot machine arcades, dodgem cars and most of all to us lads, Pretty Girls, plenty of pretty girls, complete with mini-skirts, kiss-me-quick hats, squeaky giggles, and all slim enough to make you smile. There would nearly always be a group of them waiting at our parked bikes awaiting our return from our walk around. On our return some of them would dare each other to ask us for a ride on the bikes. They didn't need to ask twice, but we always asked them if they had ridden pillion before and based the length of the ride on their claimed experiences. We didn't carry spare crash helmets as they were not a legal requirement back then and they were awkward to carry on the bikes. Our aim was to please, so a quick ride along the front with skirts blowing high in the breeze and shrieks of nervous excitement from the female passenger was a joy to behold with the deliberate use of full throttle briefly in a high gear to make the most impressive noise without a crazy speed, is where matters started. When we returned to the pick-up point, cheeky chats would lead to not a lot really, as most of the girls were or acted too young to spend valuable time with, or they obviously lied about their age, still, it was a laugh, as we often said. To the other extreme, we later found much to our initial delight, that a group of slightly older girls were staying in the chalet opposite us and invited us in. We did not however expect their completely different characters to the Essex seaside and country girls. This new group of girls had come to stay from Nottingham and were all brassy barmaids. Large they were not, but larger than life in ambitions they certainly were, and loud, Good Grief, talk about shell shock, hold on to your hats lads! They're Nottingham Barmaids, and they don't take prisoners, nor fools, lightly. They were more East Enders than Maid Marions.

Can I go home please? No, not yet lads, us girls want some fun, so we shared them in their two-bedroom chalet . . .hmm, best forgotten I think.

Although never to forget, is the memory of the tall dark haired girl returning to the lounge after twenty minutes or so with Clyde, straightening her hair whilst wobbling as she tried to put on her remaining high heel shoe, with a untidily buttoned blouse complaining that we didn't warn her that one of the lads could be so rough. Strange that she wanted to meet up again in the next day!

> *Common, dirty, she looked about thirty, I wanted to run away but I was on my own. She told me later she was a machine operator, she said she'd like to be with me all alone. . . . . My, my, my, like a spider to the fly, one more step and your dead! (21)* Oh heck!

The next day we decided to visit Walton-on-the-Naze on the bikes, without the over the top barmaids and on the way popped in to The Happy Valley Golf Course in Holland-on-Sea, and after a fun game on their small hilly Links we then continued along the long sun soaked Holland-on-Sea cliff-top to a boating lake at Walton-on-the-Naze. An hour or so on the lake soon showed us the need to learn tacking to get us back to the boat-house to avoid over-stay charges without paddling in the wooden sailing dinghies that we had hired. On the return journey to Jaywick we were enjoying the many sweeping bends of the Holland-on-Sea marshes after passing the Lion's Den public house, an empty but very substantial heavy duty folded empty coal sack bounced off the flatbed of an unladen Austin coal lorry as it became briefly semi airborne passing over a dyke bridge and narrowly missed Derek the Bear on his heavy BSA Gold Flash, he was not amused at the near dismounting.

BEING INFILTRATED BY MOTORCYCLE POLICE

We were then returning to our rented chalet at Jaywick after the outing to Walton-on-the-Naze and Clacton Pier and were riding along the sunny coast road and planning to pass Butlins Holiday Camp and then the Clacton Airfield. Malcolm had already said that he wanted to give his BSA 650 Super Rocket a bit of a blast in second gear to hopefully clear a hesitation that the bike had developed by purging the carburettor and fuel system with a few heavy blasts at full throttle. When passing Butlins and approaching a half-mile of open road passing the airfield, Malcolm did his ballistic blasts. Almost in the same instant our group of bikers all travelling at 55 mph or so suddenly felt the intrusion of some other bikers by a drone of rolling thunder of decelerating heavy bikes and shadows into our midst. It was very unusual but not totally unknown to find a few other bikers join us without prior warning when we were out on a ride. This attachment seemed a whole lot more sinister by its aggressive suddenness. A quick look around showed that a pair of smart Triumph Speed Twin Police Bikes had joined us and were now part of the ensemble, and with a few hand gestures they had stopped our group before arrival at Jaywick. A series of questions, ticking offs, lectures and a request to see documents, led to a Police Motorcycle escort back to the chalet to inspect the documents there.

After everything was found to be in order and the Police officers had spent their assertiveness on our group, relationships changed and they spoke as fellow bikers rather than disciplinarians. One of the motor-cycle cops then sat astride Brinnie's Velocette and having difficulty getting comfortable with riding positions with the clip-on handlebars and rear-set footrests, he said "how the bloody hell do you ride this?" "With a little difficulty" was Brinnie's humorous reply. They explained the finer skills of riding bikes at speed around corners, braking and off course the perennial reason why speed limits exist and the possible consequences of going too fast in the wrong place at the wrong time.

A radio call, and with the hectic sound of Triumph engines starting in a hurry, they were gone. All in all it did help the understanding between the motorcycle police and us bikers. After this we carried on riding very fast and enjoying ourselves as before, but with a little more care and skill and therefore safer.

It was actually a worthwhile reminder in safety that their lecture did not go unnoticed, indeed we are still talking about it more than fifty years later.

A good day out was completed by seeing the sun go down with some cans of beer whilst laying on the remarkable white sand beach of Jaywick, chatting about bikes, birds and burn-ups with Clyde, Malcolm, Brinnie, Nipper, Dick, Jed, and Derek the Bear, or 'Singer' as he was also strangely known.

THE BRIGHTON MOTORBIKE SHOW, a sad turning point

During 1965, three of us, Nipper, Brinnie and I rode to Brighton to visit the British Motor Bike Show. We had already ridden some long distances from South Woodham to The Santa Pod Raceway and Woburn Abbey for various events during that very sunny summer and we enjoyed a good ride going through the then new Dartford Tunnel and then, fortunately, as it was before the M25 had been built, a scenic and enjoyable ride through Otford with the duck pond in the roundabout, The Sevenoaks Weald, Royal Tunbridge Wells, Haywards Heath and finally to Brighton. The Harley set the pace cruising where possible, at a steady 55 mph woofle, followed by Brinnie's Velocette Venom and my Vincent that were both biting at the leash to go faster. At least at this slower pace we were able to soak in the relaxing sights of the extensive South Downs before arriving at Brighton on the South Coast. At the normal faster speed of the Venom and Vincent we'd be too focused on the state of the roads, traffic, cambers, bend apexes and low sun blindness to admire the scenery, so for once we enjoyed the slow cruise of the Harley Davidson.

Brighton with its glorious Georgian and Regency terraces and architecture with a sun soaked setting it was a delight but had an unbelievably stony beach. Even its railway station sat in historical splendour with museum piece Pullman electric trains, the 'Brighton Belles' whisking you the fifty miles to London in *apparently* less than five minutes, that is seriously fast, faster even than today's Euro-star, But you could experience the journey free, at least four times a week as the BBC in the fifties and sixties used the cab view journey as an interlude filler between programmes on the TV. How the Lobster Soup managed to survive the journey without spillage in the parquetry adorned dinning cars, I often wondered. However the Brighton Belle's dinning cars, were the last vestiges of Kippers or was it Smoked Herrings, for breakfast on British Railways at the time and deserve a mention, God rest their Dover Soles. I would watch with fascination this journey every time that it was transmitted, it was only when I was nearing ten years of age that I was made aware that the film had been speeded up to significantly reduce the apparent journey time, and then I realised why, north of Clapham Junction, this high speed flier was overtaken by an even faster tube train that vanished down a distant hole at speed like a rat down a drain, very impressive.

Wherever and whenever we parked the Vincent, the Velocette and the Harley Davidson in Brighton, we were sure to have a small crowd when we returned, mostly of girls, usually giggling girls, wanting a breeze along the seafront on something more exciting than a scooter. We stayed overnight in a pleasant Victorian Terrace guesthouse and the next morning visited the memorable show, which was full of glamorous bikes from all of the famous British makers and a few much smaller displays from the Japanese. Sadly however, it was a turning point where many of the British manufacturers were showing their magnificent Swan Song models before cutting down production and eventually closing their factory gates forever over the next six years. The British Government, unlike the French, did not have a protectionist policy to prevent the Japanese from enjoying and taking unfair advantage of the exchange rate that favoured them, and was caused by the collapse of the Yen after WW2. It led to British unemployment, with most people lamenting the passing of our world leading industries, blaming the government of the time or the unions, and resulting in the industrial strife of the seventies that followed. Sometimes we should learn from, and not sneer at the French way of doing things. We eventually shed tears for the Velocette Thruxton, the BSA Lightning, the Triumph Triple and various stillborn models from AJS, Matchless and Norton that were on display, it was the swansong of the Roaring Brits that were sadly soon to be replaced by Buzzing Japs.

The next day after an English breakfast we had a lovely scenic Harley woofle led ride home through Sussex and Kent to Essex in the sun with many fond memories of the short but enjoyable visit.

Our country won the war on May 8th 1945 against Germany and the Japanese, but we lost our trading values with both of them for the next half-century or more. They both had new post war factories and machinery built at the British and American expense and with powerless German or Japanese unions and low value currency, whilst we soldiered on with dark Victorian factories, using machine tools worn out by high volume wartime production and over-active unions partly funded by the Eastern Bloc.

Tragedies

TED HARRIS (RIP) A Giant Among Men

Ted Harris was always one of the lads and often brought his long time girlfriend Brenda with him to our meetings. He was thick set with a square chin, with a gruff and somewhat loud voice when he spoke or more likely joked and took the rise out of his mates, he stood just five feet four inches tall whilst Brenda was nearer six feet tall. Ted was seemingly of an Anglo Saxon or indeed a Viking bloodline with his blue eyes, fair hair of many tight curls, high jowls and living in East Anglia. He always held his chin high and with a grin.

In his young years and before his birth his doting Mum named the unborn babe, Edwina, yes, Edwina, a girl's name. His mother desperately wanted a girl and was sure that she would be blessed with one. So sure in fact that when the village ladies commented on her buying *girls* baby clothes *before* the child was born, Ted's Mum told them that she was definitely carrying a girl, no question of it. She said that she could feel it in her water, so a girl it was to be and may well have been anyway, so who can blame her desire,

They say that an unborn child in the later weeks of development can sense the sounds of the outside world and so may have heard the ladies chat.

When *Edwina* was born and was able to look around its unblemished naked form it would have realised that contrary to what it had heard from inside its mother's womb, (she) was actually a BOY and not a girl. Edwina was a Boy!

Edwina, later to be accepted as Ted, at that very precious moment when born into the world, if able, would have almost certainly loudly and rebelliously celebrated the event by stretching out his arms and in his first breath bellowed out . . .

> *I'm a Boy, I'm a Boy and my mother won't admit it, I'm a Boy I'm a Boy I'm a Boy'.*
>
> *I'm a Boy, I'm a Boy and if I say I am I get it, I'm a Boy I'm a Boy, I'm, a Boy . . .*
>
> *I wanna play cricket on the green, ride my bike across the street, cut myself and see my blood, I wanna come home all covered in muuudd. . . .*
>
> *I'm a Boy I'm a Boy, yes that's what I am, I'm a Boy, I'm a Boy . . I'm A BOY (22)*

As (Ted) grew up, the farce could no longer hold water and at school he was to be known rightly as Ted, not Edwina, and eventually became a brusque Rocker, Hoorah!

Ted and Brenda, unmatched they may have physically seemed, especially when out riding with us but totally matched they were in devotion to each other. Ted had a lovely black Matchless 350 G3LS and when Brenda was pillion, which was often, she looked clear over the top of Ted's crash helmet and caught the full force of the wind in her face without any protection or objection. Brenda was very easy going and kind hearted while Ted, as short as he was and with his broad country accent would take no truck from anyone and was always ready to stand his corner even though he physically looked *up* to them he would easily *talk down* to them. Ted had a great sense of humour and was welcomed wherever he went. Whilst riding his bike one day Ted crashed into a badly driven van whilst riding his Matchless passing The Whalebone pub at South Woodham. It was not Ted's fault as the driver came out of the pub car park without checking that the road was clear, which was a hazardous move, as the car park adjoined a hump back bridge on a blind bend. It was a strikingly hot Saturday lunchtime and the road surface tar was melting. Cheerful Ted, not the sharpest of riders, came along at around 40 mph on his bike on the de-restricted road from Wickford and went straight into the side of the van, a green Austin 35. Ted was thrown off the bike and the bike and van were damaged, Ted sustained aches and pains and road tar ingrained in his face and ended up in an ambulance to Chelmsford London Road, Hospital. That evening three of the lads visited Ted in hospital where they found him then under observation with a now tar-less but grazed face but in high spirits, the usual Ted. Soon after they left they returned and passed three bottles of Guinness through the ward's window. Ted, battered, bruised and blooded, but not busted nor beaten shrugged the whole matter off with the assisted recovery given by the Guinness. He was back to work on Monday, chin up but grazed and bruised with one of his eternal grins on his face as we will always remember him.

Ted was in later life was an energetic football referee, a tireless village councillor and a member of St. John's Ambulance Volunteer Service. He was an all round do-gooder who was always putting others before himself. He sadly passed away from natural causes. His devotion to good causes was evident in the Eulogy and casual praise at his funeral at Rettendon Church in his middle years, where he and finally *Edwina* were finally put to rest.

Ted, despite his height, was a true giant among men, he was indeed larger than his environment and often larger than life itself.

THE BEAR (RIP) Sadly missed

Derek (The Bear *aka* S*inger*) was a gentle giant of the first order. He was always there, there in the background, never a troublemaker nor rebel-rouser, just a thoroughly likeable fun loving good guy. Bear was all of six feet tall and tipped the scales at fifteen stone or more, he was as calm and as cool as a cucumber, had a good sense of humour with a deep, soft rumbling chuckle when he laughed and was always ready to put anyone's worries to rest shrugging off problems with a couldn't care-less grin and a shrug of his shoulders. He was in some senses a woolly bully and whenever that song 'Woolly Bully' by Sam and The Pharaohs was played on the radio or on a jukebox, Bear would cheerfully and loudly especially after having a few drinks, join the chorus lines, albeit some of the verse left us confused. One night at the Jaywick chalet, the Bear, happily drunk from our evening on the beach after the trip to Walton and the dinghy sailing, started reciting the monotonous Dutch style dialogue from the owner of the Four Aces Cafe', Vic Rainer. Vic was a chubby moustached, middle aged white South African immigrant who had taken exception to Brinnie sitting on the cafe' fence some months earlier and breaking it, declaring "get oorrff of my premisses Boouuey, if you have got six thousand pounndss you can buy my premises" in his archetypal Dutch South African drawl. This got us all falling about laughing, no more so than the Bear, who recited it at every opportunity for many months if not years afterwards. The phrase became so much a part of Derek's routine that when we visited Derek's parents' house and waited for Derek to ready himself for a ride out on the bikes, we would, with Derek's parents absent and Derek in the bathroom, attempt to teach his parents' black Indian Myna Bird, that repeatedly said Larry Greyson's "shut that door", the phrase "get off of my premises", it would cock his head to one side to listen then roll his eyes, and try to say "get oorrff my premises". After several weeks we only got as far as "Get oorrff my . . ." before the bird strangely died, or was he strangled by an irritated listener/owner, we will never know . . . squawk. Derek's drunken repetition of the irritating phrase at Jaywick that bedtime caused mayhem one night in the chalet. Most of the lads had eaten too much curry and there was a little too much flatulence and bravado going about. The three lads that shared the bedroom with the Bear decided that enough was enough as they couldn't get to sleep with his continuous drawling Dutch dialect recitals, and decided to mischievously mug him in his semi comatose state and clear the air by igniting the unwanted methane that had built up after being emitted from an unnamed person's backside into a sudden blue flash, that literally cleared the air. Bear was extremely easy going but very strong and resisted all efforts to mug and mute him until matters turned into a full blown pillow fight that got a little out of hand with holes being knocked through the chalet's thin asbestos inner walls and breaking them with elbows flying in full recoil. That evening of rough play in the chalet where The Bear was the affable, if unfortunate target, there was so much hilarity that Easy Dick couldn't control his laughter to the point that he was getting breathing difficulty, possibly due to Asthma as he had a hoarse but happy laugh. Dick vacated the crazy chalet with its tomfoolery and spent the remainder of the night in the sanctity of his Hillman Minx that he had travelled to Jaywick in. Sanctity, Oh, Sanctity! he cried. Where there was fun, there was always The Bear. We laughed so much that we were in extreme pain of laughter.

The next day was spent buying repair items and hiding the damage that was done to the bungalow. So typical of the Bear, there were no hard feelings, just a load of laughs and yet again, more recitals, "get off of my premises" Thank God I thought, that we will be on the bikes again soon and he can recite to himself inside his soundproof crash helmet 'til the cows come home.

Derek (The Bear) was a great guy, a feeling that came home to us even more so some thirty-five years later when he died of natural causes in middle age and we attended his cremation. The respect for Derek was evident by the large number or mourners present, eventually with standing room only. His remorseful son read a beautiful eulogy and chose the music 'The Living Years' by Mike and the Mechanics. I don't think many of the mourners had listened to the words of that song properly, until that very day, words that were so very poignant. There were many tears.

I wasn't there that morning when my father passed away, I didn't get to tell him all the things I had to say, I think I caught his spirit later that same year, I'm sure I heard his echo in my baby's new born tears, I just wish I could have told him, in the living years . . .. (23)

As we gathered afterwards outside the chapel there was a sudden gentle gust from the Crematorium's chimney. Derek was having his last burn up and heading for the Angels. I bet he was looking down at us jesting. . .Get off of my premises! See you another day Bear.

THE WORLD of MICKY CRAVEN (RIP)

Micky Craven, not to be confused with obnoxious Mad Mick the butcher's boy, both of Wickford, was a true rough diamond, maybe the only rough diamond amongst us. Although he was not tall he was thick set with a square chin and a rugged gruff demeanour, however he was sincere and would never let a mate down and was someone that you would always want on your side in the thick of troubles. Mick liked his drink and although sometimes a little wild, he was never mad, crazy or a fool. He was a building labourer by trade but his heart was that of a dreamer. He could never hold a job down no matter what the circumstances. If he awoke in the morning to the dawn chorus of the wild birds at daybreak and if the sun was shining, he was just as likely to leave home with a catapult in his back pocket and a home made fishing rod and without saying anything to his wife Sandra other than thanks for his lunch-pack, head for a long walk in the countryside, leaving his shotgun in the loft, while whistling and enjoying the morning's glories without turning up at work. With such a laid-back attitude to life he never saved a bean, all of his wages went to his wife Sandra and kids and in the winter months when building work was affected by the weather, his money was rarely enough. He had no enemies, just frustrated employers and many, many very good friends. He was a great lad that had a lifestyle of his own that we all at sometime envied. He only ever had one motorbike, a smoky old James 197cc Captain, but abandoned it as it was faster, easier and more fun to be a pillion on one of the many bikes or combinations that would always have a spare seat for him if not for anyone else, and where he could travel after a pint or two. As time went on he often had a memorable used older car with a bit of status but had no financial ambitions, we all thought that unfortunately he had drawn the short straw of life in this matter.

 By chance I met him again at a building site at nearby Shotgate where he was working. I'd been sent there by my employers in the cumbersome Bedford mobile workshop to replace a hydraulic power ram on a Drott digger and also to replace a drive chain and sprockets on a Benford cement mixer. It was after Friday lunch on an August Bank Holiday weekend, and unusually the clerk of the works had paid the men their weekly wages in cash late in the morning. Normally this would be done during a Friday afternoon to avoid absenteeism during the afternoon after wage packet time. Being a Bank Holiday weekend the clerk of work did his round early so that he could be off sharp at the end of his day. I arrived at the site to much hilarity going on with chuckling Mick running at speed across a pile of sand, hotly pursued by an enraged and rather filthy looking Irish labourer. There were always plenty of Irish labourers on the building sites as they were very hard working and capable men, however, they had a strong desire to drinking, especially at summer lunch times and would overstay their lunchtime in the pubs, hence the late Friday afternoon pay-packet practice. As was said, this being a Bank Holiday weekend, the wages were paid out early and so the men did spend lunchtime in the local pub. The site foreman was a no-nonsense toughie and all of the men returned to do a reasonable amount of piece-work between them after their lunch break. But what was not uncommon after a lunchtime pub visit was for one of the men who had drank more than he could take, to visit the 'thunder-box' mobile chemical toilet (WC) on returning to the site, and sometimes fall into a deep drunken sleep in there. This enraged the other labourers as not only did it mean that they would have to use the ditch and hedges as a latrine but also that the sleeping drunkard was not putting any effort in to finishing the job in the time allotted. So action was taken and straws were drawn, whoever drew the short straw was given the task of creeping up to the occupied WC and sliding a peg or similar into the outer hasp of the WC door, effectively trapping the deep snoring sleeping beauty inside. The next move was for a Drott or JCB driver to start his machine, drive up to the WC and very gently push it over sideways, whilst the sleeping beauty was still inside and retire with his machine, vacating it quickly to a safe distance. Amid the following much violent cursing from within the toppled thunder-box, he who drew the short straw would have to remove the peg from the hasp and run, run very fast indeed, as he would certainly be chased by a very irate and tough and now smelly Irishman, and that is how I found Mick that day, he'd drawn the short straw once more in his life and it was total mayhem, but this was all part of the building site fun he loved so much. When working on the building sites or as a navvy roadman Micky would cheerfully dismiss sarcastic criticism from passers- by with an impromptu remark and laugh the matter off. Typical of his reaction would be. .

> . . . *There was I, diggin' this hole, hole in the ground so round and sorta deep, the bottom was sorta' flat and the sides were steep, when along come this bloke in a Bowler which he lifted and scratched his head, who had never dug a hole before and he said . . . 'Don't dig it there, dig it elsewhere, your digging it round and it ought to be square, the shape of it's wrong it's much too long and you can't dig a hole where a hole don't belong' to which I leaned on my shovel, lit a fag had a drag and replied,' If you disagree it*

> *doesn't bother me, That's where the hole is meant to be'*
> *Well it's not there now, the ground's all flat and beneath is*
> *the man in the bowler hat, And that's that . . .(24)*

Unfortunately and sadly Mick passed way in middle age before his time of natural causes, in a caravan where he lived in later years in a breakers yard in the quiet village of Steeple, long after parting with his loving wife and grown children. Skint but always with a grin on his face, he left absolutely nothing material to this world, he joined this world with nothing and left with nothing, just bucket-loads of priceless, hilarious memories. We miss you Mick.

Even though motor cycles were often blamed for road deaths however of the large group that we mixed with, only two (if that is not already two too many) of the bikers I knew had a fatal accident on a bike, both at sub 30mph and both when riding alone when they were just seventeen.

GARY

Gary was a student that studied with me Motor Vehicle Technology at The Southend Municipal College. He was thorough, caring, intelligent and enjoyed life, but one morning he pulled away from his house to go to work on his 350 AJS and after less than a hundred and fifty feet on a clear dry morning on a road he used daily, a local paper boy witnessed him ride straight into a lamp-post at low speed, which was fatal. The coroner could find no fault with Gary and nobody could understand what went wrong. My guess is that either the bikes side-stand was still down and threw the direction of the bike, or his steering damper was for whatever reason, was set too tight and once he noticed the problem it was too late to overcome and avoid what sadly happened.

TERRY

My other friend who suffered was Terry Sharpe, who riding his Ariel Colt misjudged a parked car in a poorly lit Swan Lane, Wickford that was facing the wrong way at night in the pouring rain. Clearly the car driver was at fault especially as he was parked on the wrong side with his headlamps on main beam, which blinded the motorcyclist and it appeared that Terry misjudged the situation and passed the car on the wrong side and went straight into a ditch and died instantly. I was driving a car in the same road and by chance arrived moments after the accident happened and being in the era before mobile phones I drove quickly to the nearest phone box and called for an ambulance and the police. I returned to the scene and only then, and after a few minutes had passed did I recognise the motorcyclist, as being Terry, who was a good friend of mine. I felt so bad that as he lay there, ashen faced with his mouth agape in the pouring rain, that I didn't recognise him immediately. He left a very sad girlfriend.

> .... *He rode into the night, accelerated his motor bike, I cried to him in fright "don't do it, don't do, it don't do it".. He'll never know how much I cried for him to live. Please wait at the gates of heaven for me, Terry ... (25)*

RAY WHITE...A HOUSE FIRE

The only other tragedy that we experienced was one evening when we were gathered at The Four Aces Café, when a fire engine from Wickford passed with its bell ringing and we soon heard that there was a house fire in South Woodham Ferrers where there was no fire station. We decided to jump on our bikes and follow it and give assistance if possible. We thought that half a dozen motor cyclists dressed in leather with leather gloves, leather boots and crash helmets and some self ego, are sure to be of some assistance, so why not. We caught up with the fire engine and followed it to Albert

Road in South Woodham Ferrers and suddenly we were all stunned and disheartened, the house fire in front of us, a large wooden bungalow that was owned by the family of one of the lads, Ray White, the youth club organiser. We parked our bikes and were appalled by the fact that the bungalow had burnt so quickly and all that was left were some standing and much collapsed framework timbers and a large glowing pile of yellow cinders and ashes, so many of them glowing so brightly that they lit up the otherwise very dark night. This was partly due to the delay caused by the time it took for the Wickford part time Fire Crew to get to their station and then further to drive the six miles to the burning home.

We were totally powerless to do anything, there was absolutely nothing that six fit lads who were ready to take risks and help, could do. Very soon out of the blinding glow a figure came over to us and much to our surprise it was Ray. All we could find to say was "are you alright Ray?" He replied with much controlled excitement in his breath as he'd obviously been dashing around hopelessly in a losing battle with a hose and slow filling buckets of water... he replied " Yes I am OK, but I have lost everything... *we* have lost everything...it's all gone." We were speechless.

We privately realised that besides the home itself, treasured memories can be lost forever, there was nothing left, such a sorrowful evening. We were left absolutely gutted and after a while and ensuring that there was absolutely nothing we could possibly do to help, we quietly started our bikes and hoping that Rays family was reasonably insured even though some priceless possessions are gone forever, we left without speaking to each other and went quietly, very quietly, on our own way home. This was not the time to show off or make a statement with a handful of throttle. We were humbled, solemn and remorseful that a fire station at South Woodham would have possibly created a much different outcome, but that was not to happen until another ten years had passed and South Woodham Ferrers was to become a busy centrepiece of a New Town and have a permanently manned fire station.

RETURNING TO JAYWICK

After our memorable visit to Brighton we once again returned to our annual break at Jaywick. We had plenty of time to spare at Jaywick and spent some of it spent fettling our bikes. Brinnie, trying to locate the reason for a flat spot when accelerating his Velocette looked into the large open bell-mouth of its Amal Monobloc carburettor only to find to his amazement that a large section of the carburettor throttle control piston was missing and he couldn't understand to where it had disappeared. I said to him that logically only one thing could have happened to it, and that was that the engine with its very large valves had consumed or eaten it. He was a little puzzled when I said to prove the point we should remove the bikes exhaust system and give it a good shake when inverted, which we did and hey presto, out fell the rather battered remains of the carburettor piston. Fortunately spares were readily available back then and within a few hours the bike was flying again.

Another day saw me resetting and balancing my Vincent's very powerful four-brake system. The system with air scoops and high-grade materials was the same system that was used on the heavier one hundred and fifty miles per hour Vincent Black Lightning World speed record model, and even when the system was out of balance it was extremely powerful. I spent a couple of hours, or so it seemed, setting up the system to perfection and then without a care in the world I gave it a low speed emergency stop test. I simply rode the bike the fifty yards to the cul-de-sac end of our chalets location, Essex Way, I then turned the bike and gave it a brief but firm twist of the throttle and in a moment it was at thirty miles per hour at which point I grabbed the front brake lever with a little trepidation and was promptly dismounted in front of an audience of my biker mates. The bike's brakes responded powerfully to my careful application by standing the bike virtually on its nose, which caused me to instantly slide forward off the front of the dual seat and then ending astride the fuel tank only stopping when I am most uncomfortably perched astride the four-inch steering damper. With my wedding tackle in danger of being rendered beyond further use and whilst under excruciating pain the whole ensemble of me mounted high above and my beloved bike below, keeled over and crashed with great humility onto the concrete outside our holiday chalet, Bah Humbug!, I thought as I dusted myself off to a certain amount of mockery.

  Far too quickly the week was over and sadly it was time to return to the south of Essex and work again. The journey, consisting of eight motorbikes, began with the twenty miles to Colchester on the sinuous and enjoyable B1027, a part of the journey that we always really looked forward to. However, Malcolm, whose Dad owned the chalet we rented each year, took the lead out of Jaywick and led us into the first garage at the Clacton Road junction. Due to some extra mileage that he had covered that week his BSA 650 Super Rocket was dangerously low of engine oil and we had a rapid sixty-mile journey in front of us in high summer. I said to Malcolm, "seeing that you've been looking for a specific oil (Total) all week without success and travelled quite a few extra miles visiting your unwell girlfriend then don't risk the engine on the relatively long journey home to South Woodham Ferrers, put another good make of oil in such as Castrol" I said that *"any oil is better than no oil"* However, Malcolm, never a lad to compromise, stayed faithful to his Super Rocket engine builder's dictate and would not see reason, and Forty minutes later, having enjoyed a good hard ride on the B1022 to Colchester, and now travelling in excess of ninety mph on the fast stretch of the B1027 near Great Totham on the way to Maldon, I am at the back as the Vincent's upgraded suspension made that second rate road a bit too lively without a pillion at high speed, I see a big puff of smoke in the distance ahead from a leading bike. Very soon I am pulling up as all of the bikes had stopped and after dismounting I ran back along the line with Clyde on his Bonneville calling to me that Malcolm's engine had blown. As I then pass

Brinnie on his stationary Venom, he said" look at by bloody nose" which I did, and could see a moderate lump of dark grey metal stuck into it. Brinnie pulled it out, exclaiming "bloody ouch!" while blood poured out of the wound in his nose. Malcolm was understandably unhappy that a big end on his BSA had failed big time so soon after an engine rebuild and the subsequent flaying broken connecting rod had smashed through the crankcase throwing lumps of metal everywhere and one hot and oily piece had become so airborne that it met Brinnie's nose, that was three bikes back and at ninety mph. After surveying the situation Malcolm said that his tax disc and holder had been lost and thrown clear by the calamity. We started looking for his tax disc without success in the greensward. Fifty years later, as I sometimes pass the spot, I still have a glance at that stretch of greensward in case I see its chrome holder shine through the long grass. Crazy I know, but some-things, no matter how trivial, you never forget. Not compromising on oil branding cost a seriously broken engine, a sticky plaster and a lot of pride . . .and a tax disc and holder. At first I suggested towing Malcolm and his busted Super Rocket home, some twelve miles away with the Vincent, a small matter was that we needed a tow rope, time for a little ingenuity. A quick tot up showed that although there were eight of us, only four had non-elasticated leather belts, holding our trousers up. We needed at least eight 34inch waist leather belts that each would be 40 inches long which when doubled to give enough strength would equal about thirteen feet. From experience, elastic would just not do as if it lets go at one end or breaks, the biker on tow would get heavily smacked in the face by a projectile buckle and may lose an eye. With the very steep one-in-three Maldon Hill to climb, it would be an accident waiting to happen. The key was to do everything gradually, especially when accelerating out of a slow bend with a solo on tow. Maldon Hill and an elasticated section of the towrope was a no-go however, and a van was commandeered from a friendly villager and Malcolm eventually arrived home, more than a little cheesed off, and without a valid tax disc to reclaim from.

The moral is; 'Never ever run low on oil, *Any* oil and an easy throttle is better than no oil at all'. We did feel sorry for him, an expensive lesson learnt. Eventually our holiday by the sea was over, but the following year the Super Rocket now proudly showed its replacement power unit, a very rare Triumph 500 all aluminium Grand Prix engine. The bike now became an attractive and very desirable 'Tribsa'.

The fun filled sunny biker holidays, just like the Super Rocket's tax disc, the Nottingham barmaids, the pillow fight with the Bear, and Clacton Pier, The Motorbike Police and the lavender cart, will never be forgotten.

PART TEN
GIRLS, GIRLS, GIRLS

POLICE OFFICER GEORGE COLLIER, DEFENDER OF THE WOODHAM FERRERS VIRGINS

Due to the much more rural nature and very much smaller population, the policing of the Dengie Peninsula was done by a handful of small police stations usually with a single policeman, being a sergeant and/or constable in each village, or a Sergeant with a small staff at the towns of Burnham, Southminster and Maldon who gave us bikers little trouble as they knew us all from our developing years.

The policemen in the Essex villages found it very useful in crime control to know virtually each young family in the village especially any of the boys that were about to become teenagers and may well be tomorrow's high testosterone mischief makers. Nearly all of the local teenage boys were known to the Police Officers, George Collier and Bill Pepper by our first names, even if we didn't live on the peninsular but were frequent visitors. Officer George Collier was in charge of the South Woodham Ferrers Police Station and Sergeant Bill Pepper was in charge of the smaller Rettendon, Battlesbridge and Rawreth Police Station. Rettendon really did have a Sergeant Pepper at the time that the Beatles released their album of that name. Sergeant Pepper had a habit of hiding behind the Rettendon village phone box when he heard a bike approaching so as to be unseen, and build a record of frequent speedsters. Both officers would patrol their countryside beats in a grey Morris

Minivan, or on a grey Velocette 'Noddy' bike, which was an almost silent small motorbike that had some weather protection. (This was the type of machine of PC Plodd from Enid Blyton's Noddy and Big Ears) or finally, an ordinary police pedal bicycle.
Understandably, the pedal bicycle was rarely used, except by George Collier of South Woodham Ferrers on a clandestine duty that he enjoyed patrolling during the evenings of Spring, through September and into early October of each year.

In the Essex countryside during the sixties, there was very little evening entertainment other than the once weekly village hall youth club or a visit to one of the many thriving and traditional local pubs. Often during a Saturday evening in the village hall there would be a dance with the music supplied by a rock and roll band of local lads or an unexciting disco, which was a cheaper and sad sign of the future. A trip to the Ritz or Odeon cinemas at slightly distant Southend-on-Sea, Maldon or Chelmsford was an expensive night out when money was tight for a lad and girlfriend, as few girls went Dutch back then due to low wages and traditional manners. The extra journey was worthwhile for the latest James Bond or Carry-On films, or when we went to the Coronation Hall at Maldon to watch The Tornado's playing their instrumental 'Telstar', their latest hit, live and totally terrific. Free entertainment of a more natural type was found by spending a warm summer's romantic evening on the Crouch riverbank car park at South Woodham, watching the sun slowly going down until suddenly it has gently gone, but returning brightly the next morning.

It was at this point that the moustached Officer George Collier whose portly stature somewhat but politely resembled Noddy's Mr Plod, would carry out his dusk patrol suitably kitted out with regulation rubber hand-torch, police pedal cycle and regulation police plimsolls instead of his usual Police heavy black boots which were definitely of the PC Plodd image. Fifteen minutes after the sun had slipped below the evening horizon George would quietly leave the village Police Station aboard his pedal bicycle and make his way unobtrusively to the riverside. He would precisely time his police station departure to avoid waiting unnecessarily at the level crossing gates at the Railway Station if a train was due, which might risk exposing his frequent clandestine mission. Between 8.00 and 9.30 pm there was the Southminster bound passenger branch line train followed by a sand train, followed by a nuclear flask train, both from Southminster, and then the returning passenger train, from Southminster and now Wickford bound. After clearing the level crossing George, nodding a sign of respect to Dennis Potter the elderly village resident railway crossing gate keeper, and in 'black out kit' George would then cycle poste-haste on his trusty steed through the sleepy and dimly lit village and would finally approach his due destination and the point of about to be much mayhem, the totally unlit River Crouch riverside car park, about a mile and a half from the Police Station. The journey through the village, particularly after a heavy summer rain was often through air that was heavy in the uncertain aroma created by the mixed fragrances of wild flowers, roses and cesspits, that almost every house had as there was no main drainage. Some cesspits would overflow their liquid contents onto the gardens when overfilled with the excess rain-water, which then enriched the clay base soil and created award winning roses for the local annual flower shows, especially the well known Southminster Flower Show. It was often joked that George Collier kept a heavy moustache to act as a scent filter to prevent him sneezing and giving away his whereabouts when on a stealth patrol. Cesspits were often not emptied when full due to money shortages that still existed. Dennis the gatekeeper knew full well of George's plan being a village resident whose family through the generations had always been gate keepers, he and his family were strong Church people of the small but well attended local Evangelical Church. As such a centre of village life, Dennis Potter knew most of the residents and their gossip as they waited at the closed gates and chatted with him whilst awaiting the often late running branch trains to allow the gates to re-open. He therefore whole heartedly supported George's valiant plan to protect and indeed defend the purity of the young girls of the village, and would quietly cheer George as he gently but purposefully put pressure on his bicycle pedals and climbed the small incline away from the crossing on his way to his valiant deed as defender of the virgins. At the peaceful tidal riverside there was a stone and sea-shell hard and an ancient ford that was now used as a launching ramp that sat harmlessly alongside the muddy 'between tide' area and marshes of the upper reaches of the River Crouch a mile or so away from the level-crossing. It was an idyllic spot with the fast running tide with a range of some seven metres, gurgling and rippling and eventually rushing once it had got into its stride an hour or so after each tide had turned, to the twenty mile distant North Sea. The chatter of the wild fowl settling down for the night amongst the reed covered marshes, were accompanied by the gentle rhythm of halyards clanging gently to some obscure erratic musical melody against the aluminium masts of the thirty or so yachts that were riding out the night out swinging at anchor. The South Woodham riverside has a view of the opposite village of Hullbridge with its active waterfront and Anchor Public House some hundred yards or so away, on the river's Hullbridge south bank, giving it a distant focal point and a dimension that attracted the courting couples to the desolation of the unlit South Woodham car park that was at the southern end of Hullbridge Road. In the evenings and in the winter it was indeed desolate, not a soul except the amorous goings-on inside a few young couple's cars, and a dark cloaked and bulky character that was seemingly acting as a Peeping Tom. However, this was no Dracula nor Peeping Tom, no this was a member of Essex Constabulary's finest, Police Officer George Collier with his worrying photographic memory, on his self-indulgent dusk patrol. George's routine was to quietly and slowly cycle along the Hullbridge Road towards the riverbank, avoiding the many loose pebbles near the road end that may warn of his coming. With his bicycle lights firmly switched *off*, he would soft pedal quietly the final fifty yards or so towards the foot of the riverbank car park's approach ramp, making a SAS type silent approach. He would then dismount the bike still some fifty yards from the small number of lovers' cars in the car park that sits higher on the sea wall. Leaning his black police pedal cycle against the dark blue engineering brickwork of the water boards under-river water supply tunnel access shaft. He would then deploy the stealth approach afforded to him by the uniform issue plimsolls and keeping a low profile against any moonlit riverside horizon to avoid giving away his silhouette. He would then creep up in his dark blue uniform in the unlit car park without the occupants knowing, to the first car parked in the line. Without saying a word, George would very gently rest the rubber lens end of his powerful police issue torch against one of the car's rear side windows and so very very gently, and without any formality, silently press the 'on' button of his torch. Immediately, all hell would break loose as the startled occupants, amid much swearing and screaming busily and assumedly quickly dressing themselves, often with the lad violently swinging a door open to angrily confront the assumed Peeping Tom. But it was no Peeping Tom, but was the rather imposing figure of Officer Collier filling the car doorframe, complete with moustache about to defend the village girls' decency and humiliate the boyfriend who nearly always came from another town or village. The local village boys knew only too well of George's dusk patrol and had their fun elsewhere. If you knew of Collier's stealth patrol, there was a method however, to spend time with one's girlfriend in that car park's and avoid the arresting intrusion of the local constabulary's rubber torch on your side window. The plan was to only visit the riverbank car park when there were at least two other occupied cars already there and to park up between them. Hopefully with moderate gaps on both sides, in the privacy of darkness the two of you could discuss the worlds affairs, listen to the erratic but latest music from Radio Luxemburg or the more lately, the better reception of the then new Radio Caroline, watch the goings-on of Hullbridge on the opposite riverbank, or failing all else, find something else to pass the time whilst being tactfully observant of the goings-on of the neighbouring cars. The moment that you heard a commotion, some loud swearing and when torch beams and car headlights started spoiling the black or star-filled night, it was time to be off, very definitely off, don't stall the engine and don't compromise yourself by looking out of the side windows, be gone young man and don't look back at the mayhem that you had left behind. Tomorrow's another day.

It was time to pull up elsewhere, review the situation, and after having a laugh at the expense of the other couples that you had left to the clutches of the long arm of the law, re-plan what was left of the evening. A quick waive to Dennis as you used his railway crossing to escape the village and wonder to ones-self, did he know what was going on? He did have an odd wry smile as he waived back. We always wondered why it was that the evening romantics were never reported in the news starved local Maldon and Burnham Standard or Essex Chronicle weekly newspapers, as all of the authorities were always too keen to ostracize us young lads. We even had a Magistrates Court at Southminster, but still no reports of riverside evening mischief in the press. It was often thought that Officer Collier enjoyed his patch too much and didn't want the promotion to Chelmsford HQ that improving his already low crime rate almost certainly would lead to. So he felt that an informal warning and an extreme embarrassment that would certainly make the lady very cheesed off with her boyfriend's plan of a romantic evening would do the trick, without many reams of paperwork. What a perk of the Job.

Another of Officers Collier's plots was to tap on the side window of any parked up suspicious van where he could not identify the contents, which was often if occupied, which was nearly always the case, The window would be partially wound down and he would politely ask for a light for his cigarette, and in a well planned minute or so, or more if he *accidently* but deliberately duffed the lighting and asked for a re-light, the interior, its contents and occupants were totally lit up and George had got the clear view of all that he wanted and scared off any romantics. A very cunning move by a country bobby.

WHO MAKES THE FIRST MOVE?

It took a brave lad to try to date a girl up in front of her defensive and envious mates. The country girls were always well able to answer back, humiliatingly so to an admiring lad, whether she wanted his attention or not. So many girls left the dance hall disappointed as they, or their mates, had either scared the lads off, or were not suitable pillion passengers because of their dominant or unbalanced nature. Very very rarely was a girl turned down due to their physical size. Girls were always slim and proud of it.

A girl's "Vital Statistics' of a 36 inch bust, with a 24 inch waist and 34 hips and cup size C were bragging rights, but far more importantly to us lads, a balance of good looks, a soft voice, and a less than dominant but brave nature, was what was wanted. Girls regularly gathered wherever there was a group of parked motorcycles and sweet romances sometimes started quietly or ended brashly there and then.

Hey there baby, how about a date, don't get too excited, you will be delighted,

Let's not stand here wasting time with words, You seem a lot better than all the other birds,

Will you let me take you walkin',

Will you let me hold your hand then, **Will I What?**

I will tell you what my game is

if you'll tell me what you name is,

Will yer? **NO I WILL NOT!** . . .*(26)*

Bah, Women!

Where's my bike, oh there it is, great, BRRRRMMMMMMMMMMMM,

Oi, come back 'ere !

Not likely! Your too late girl.

BOO HOO, HOO, I'm going back to my Mum.

Hello lads, fancy a burn up down the bye-pass, come on then...BRMMM BRMM, 95 96, 97, 98mph, feel the wind and that noise, TERRIFIC! who needs girls. Hey, what's that ringing jingling noise? what's that black blur in my mirror? Oh heck it's a Met' Police Jaguar, Drat, Drat, Bugger!!

To avoid mental, financial or physical scars you approached an unknown pretty or attractive girl very carefully, as you would approach a stray but purring cat. A bad response was always feared and in an instant you could be ridiculed, sometimes embarrassingly in front of your mates. One outspoken girl managed by a crazy act to reverse this often no-win trend, and she actually ended up marrying me some years later.

THE RISKY GIRLS OF ESSEX . . . The Mistress

> The wind is your mistress, that drives your boat on . .
>
> so soft in the summer, so warm in the sun, through
>
> winds of change in autumn, she may happily sail . .
>
> But keep an eye wary, for a true winter's gale,
>
> So beware of your mistress, Beware you are warned,
>
> As Hell hath no fury, as a woman's scorned. (27)

A guide that us young lads had back then was simply;

A teenage lad's guide to a girl's nature by her hair colour

Red Head - Can be Glorious, may leave mental and physical scars.

White Hair - Too old, or maybe not, but why not?

Blonde - A trophy for sure, but sometimes an air-head.

Mousey Blonde - Interesting, level headed and sometimes exciting.

Brunette - Intelligent and warm hearted, usually trustworthy.

Black (Raven) - Mysterious and exciting, but was her Mother a witch? After all, England's last Witch master General came from not so far away Manningtree,

So again, was she a witch?

Saturday evenings however was when most things took off. The Village Halls, in our case The South Woodham Ferrers, Danbury or Purleigh Village Halls or The Vineyards at Brentwood, would be the centre of a weekly dance where there might be a rather good rock and roll band, some soft drinks, and lots of girls in miniskirts. No drugs, back then, only the purple heart was occasionally mentioned but never seen, but to buy some would mean a difficult thirty return mile journey to a music event at 'The Corn Exchange' in Chelmsford, and only then if a top group such as 'Herman's Hermits' or 'The Who' were playing and attracted London drug dealers. So No Drugs, and No Alcoholic Drinks were the safe options that prevailed with the bikers. During the winter months most of the bike lads would arrive in cars and then we would break the no alcoholic drinks rule a little. We were looking for the right type of girl, 'Talent' as those girls were known in the summer or 'Crumpet' as they were known in the winter, very rarely were the girls too large in the sixties for us lads to be interested in them. It was not until 1974 that the first American style fast food outlets came to the UK, and that started the trend of Burger Bars and eventually overweight teenagers and then obese adults and sadly followed by obese children. *Thanks a lot Uncle Sam, Thanks a lot!* Was it Popeye the Sailor Man's sidekick Wimpy, the tubby bowler hat wearing office worker that encouraged the burger craze that Mcdonalds seemed to prosper on? Pre-teenage youngsters were obsessed with the American Popeye cartoon series week after week on the television in the late fifties, and besides his arch-enemy Bluto and his girlfriend Olive Oyl, there was this chubby bowler hat wearing office character called Wimpy. At every opportunity when Wimpy was lost for words or an idea, he would stop, turn a control on the side of his bowler hat that opened up on a hinge and exposed a small barbeque, with a well-cooked sausage rotating and ready for slipping into a bun, a bun that Wimpy always carried in his coat pocket and created a seemingly mouth-watering Hot Dog. Until Wimpy arrived on our TV screens with Popeye and Company, us English kids had little idea what a burger or hot dog was. So can we blame the start of the current obesity problems on TV's American Popeye cartoons of sixty years ago, and the fashionable fast food outlets that followed.

It was unwritten back then that you did not have sex with a girl unless you was prepared to marry her if the condom split and you made her pregnant. Few lads dared sex without a condom. If she became pregnant it was a major crisis. Her Dad might make it a 'shotgun wedding' after possibly beating you up, humiliating you, ruining your ego and future, and banning you from seeing her again, and you selling your beloved motorbike to make ends meet. There were no contraceptive nor 'morning after' pills and single mums were seriously frowned upon, shotgun licences were almost ten a penny in the countryside where most of the girls lived with their parents. To make matters worse as it was not very long after the war and National Conscription had only just finished, so many Dads had military experience and had a gun or shotgun, were over-worked, tired, short tempered and angry, and hence a desire for the odd brawl. Although rarely used, shotguns added to the no-go thinking.

Most teenage girls were slim, fit and attractive, noticeably less than nine stone or dress size twelve, only their differing nature, mood swings and expensive tastes might prevent a lad from getting involved with any particular one of them. So yet again, with no strings attached, a motorbike *without* an expensive girl pillion passenger was the favoured fun in the summer for many lads, however, girls with a good temperament became good mates in the following winter when the cars came out and might have developed the friendship towards wedding bells in the next or subsequent summer. Girls who regularly lost their temper were left out, didn't get loved and so didn't get pregnant no matter how pretty or curvaceous, unless their suitor was drunk, and even that was often naturally self-controlling.

Like many lads in my teenage years I often had a so called girlfriend, that was just that, whoever she was there was no deep romance nor long term plans, at least not from my point of view, and she was just a friendly girl who wanted to take part in my varied and active lifestyle. Rightly or wrongly girls were classed as a bit of an accessory. Looking back it sounds like an insult but it seemed that most were only after fun, not security nor long term relationships.

As the months and eventual years rolled by it seemed obvious that a longer relationship with a suitable girl was the most sensible way to go forward, as I would not be a motorbike tearaway for the rest of my life and I should start thinking and planning more maturely for the future, as I had not forgotten the effect that 'Shangri La' in London Road Wickford had on me some years earlier. I needed to return to my long-term plan for a Shangri La. I needed a long-term girlfriend that may well become my wife one day. Autumn leaves beckoned and the future became warmer and more and colourful.

THE SAD CASE OF MISUNDERSTOOD LINDA

Among the various girls that I was developing a relationship with was Linda from Gay Bowers near Danbury. I first met her at the Danbury youth club where we lads regularly went each Friday evening, bikes in the summer, cars in the winter. There were always the regular local girls and lads present, but one autumn evening seemingly out of no-where appeared Linda, lovely brunette Linda. She was well dressed, well spoken, intelligent, tidy and pleasant with an attractive build. Somehow she didn't fit the Essex country style or scene. She was almost too straight-laced and correct for it. Was she from the softer Buckinghamshire, Surrey, or Berkshire? I never did find out. She was so polite, considerate and not opinionated without being a shrinking violet and her personality and looks took me by total surprise. On our first date I collected her from her home next to the phone-box in Danbury where I was greeted by a lovely homely small family, smart and easy going without any ulterior motives, who welcomed me in without hesitation.

After the rough and tumble way of life that I and the local lads and girls had led, it was a very pleasant surprise, but not so as to be alarmed, far from it. Linda and I went to a local pub and then had a walk along the nearby scenic canal towpath at Paper Mill Lock at pretty Little Baddow. On the second date a week later, matters were just as pleasing and instead of spending some time at a local pub and enjoying a drive around the nearby beauty spots we stopped at Danbury Common and started talking about each other. I wasn't acting pushy as this girl was of a rare nature and worth spending some extra time with. She gently admitted to me that she was in care at the home of the local family from where I collected her, and that they were caring and didn't have children and she was very appreciative of the way that they tolerated her intrusion into their lives. I was in no position nor frame of mind to prejudge her or her carers indeed I could only take my hat off to the situation. I did not have the temerity to ask of her previous problems. I felt that l should let bygones stay bygones unless she felt compelled to tell me and then I would give her my ear.

On our third date we went to the River Blackwater's riverside at the Millbeach near Goldhanger as the Sun went down early, being late October it got dark rather early and our conversation slowed to the point that maybe a bit of romance was in the air. Suddenly and unfortunately she freaked out and not only lost the plot but was in a state of terror. I calmed her without finding out what the problem was and drove her to her home and took her to the door and explained to her carers that she was very distressed by the dark for reasons that I did not really know. They seemed understanding and asked her if she wanted to see me again to which she said yes, and apologised unnecessarily to me. The next Tuesday came and after a lovely evening, a sweet kiss in the earlier sunshine was fine but darkness alone in a car with a lad freaked her out again, Linda said that even the darkness of a cinema was too much for her and she always slept with the bedroom light on. I again took her to her home and left my phone number with her and her carers in the event that she might overcome her worrying phobia. I said that I understood that maybe I was not the right type for her. She again apologised but didn't want to explain her problem, nor did I press her. Her eyes welled up a little and tears started to fall, I felt helpless, what was she trying to tell me? I felt totally out of my depth and hopelessly inadequate and unable to help her, what awful experience was she trying to hide, life can be so unkind.

> *I know all there is to know about the crying game, I've had my share of the crying game. First there are kisses, then there are tears, and then before you know where you are, your love disappears... (28)*

Over the next year or so I would often think of her, trying to understand her dilemma. I never did come to an answer and sadly never heard from her again. I reflected that maybe I was at fault and didn't give her enough time and understanding as all girls were not the same, but it was too late now to help matters.

> *It was only a winter's tale, just another winter's tale, why should the world take notice of one more love that failed, a love that was not meant to be, though it meant a lot to her and me, on a world wide scale it's just another winter's tail.* **(29)**

Many years later, and after seeing so much more of life as I grew older and the exposure of so much harm to some youngsters in some institutions, I wondered whether she was a tragic victim of some misdeed in her younger years. I will never know, such a waste, such a pity. I wish her well.

> *She called out to the man in the street, Sir can you help me, Its cold and I've nowhere to sleep, is there somewhere you can tell me, You can tell from the lines on her face, you can see that she's been there, probably been moved on from every place, 'cos she didn't fit in there, Just think about it, Oh think twice, it's another day for you and me, you and me in paradise, Just think about it. (30)*

I can only hope that with the passing of time that she is now Miss Understood and no longer, misunderstood.

> *"I'm just a soul whose intentions are good... Oh Lord! Please don't let me be misunderstood"* *(31)*

Take care Linda.

SOFT SYLVIA

Who is Sylvia, What is she

It was at the weekly village Friday evening social club that I met my first truly steady girlfriend. A true sparkler of a girl, pretty as a picture in her yellow top, was young Sylvia with her blonde hair and brown eyes, soft complexion and even softer nature. She dated well and soon got the hang of being a very good pillion rider on my bike, and often Brinnie with his just as pretty girlfriend Jenny would join with us for evening or weekend rides, we became the envy of many.

> *That yellow dress you wore when we went dancing Sunday nights, that smile you gave me in the movies when they dimmed the lights, I tried in vain to rid that memory from my brain, I can't forget you and that's what love will do. The spins together on my beat up motorbike, the look your mother gave me when we turned up late one night, what can I do, I can't help thinkin' of you (32)*

I explained to her that to be safe on the bike she would have to be totally relaxed at all times and act as my shadow whilst holding but not gripping my waist, and not to pre-judge riding matters to the point that she would subconsciously steer the bike from the rear and contribute to an impending problem, I further explained that only if I shouted "Hold Tight" did she need to do just that and grip my waist very tight, otherwise relax and enjoy the often very fast ride. Even though Sylvia was little more than eight stone in weight, as most other girls of the time, her ability to flow with the bike was paramount and at that she was very good. My Vincent had probably the most powerful brakes by far of any road vehicle and therefore an accident was most unlikely. However if we were to fall off, then tuck your arms in and roll, was the advice that I gave her. Fortunately it never came to that.

However, we had several very near misses where her obedience to my instructions contributed to us not being involved in an accident at speed with a much slower and badly driven car. The problem was always predictable if I was really alert, which being a teetotaller when biking, I always was. It was at a time when direction indicators, (flashers with their noisy but effective clicking flasher unit inside the car) were replacing the old fashioned and very unsuitable semaphore trafficators on all new cars built from around 1958/1960. The not very noticeable trafficators, that were somewhat like a miniature semaphore railway signal, served the same purpose as the later effective flashing indicators but were lit by a dull low wattage bulb, did not flash to attract attention and were often poorly positioned on the car bodywork, just one on each side instead of two or three, and due to not having a clicking flasher unit inside the car, they were often carelessly left *on* for many miles until the next sharp bend might cancel them. If ever I approached a small Austin, Standard, Morris or Ford that was possibly built before 1960 and it was cruising sedately in the road, I was always on extra guard as I was about to overtake it. Often the left hand trafficator would still be wrongly switched on and overlooked by the driver until the next turn at a junction or into a drive that might be to the right, even though the trafficator, if seen, was suggesting a planned left turn. When you was approaching this dilemma at speed on a heavy motorcycle you had to take immediate and extreme pre-emptive avoiding action. The only successful avoiding action when approaching from the offside rear and are virtually level with the car's rear bumper and ready to finally overtake was to instantly lay the bike almost flat to the left and then before that split second action had completed, heave and flip the heavy bike and pillion passenger back upright again and swerve the bike around the back of the car to the left and pass the car down the nearside still at speed, to continue the journey whilst cursing hidden and dull trafficators. Some drivers, usually older accompanied women, had not noticed that they had left them on for several miles indicating erroneously left, because they were chatting to their passenger/s possibly about the previous night's Coronation Street, and then turned right into their drive or another road and naturally but a little late, cancelled their misleading trafficator before checking their mirrors in good time. The then new Mini, Ford Anglia and Triumph Herald soon flooded the market and eventually saw the end of the Standard Eights, Austin A30s, and the dreadful Ford E93A 'sit up and beg' Ford Populars, or 'puddle jumpers' as they were commonly known, and so many other older cars with their dreaded trafficators and six volt electrics, and thank God the roads became a little safer.

With the exceptions of these occasional but nevertheless unwanted near misses, the four of us had a fine time together in that particularly warm sunny summer. Brinnie had a noisy, rapid and lightened black and chrome Velocette Venom and I had a similar natured Black Vincent in Grey Flash spec, a very, very rare bike. We made quite a sight and sound when together, but that was not the point, we just lived life while we were young, and life was thrilling.

One day at the Owl, while the girls were powdering their noses or whatever else girls do in the ladies, Brinnie surprised me and asked me if I might one day marry Sylvia, maybe he was considering marrying Jenny. After a little deliberation I quietly replied 'no', when asked why not, I replied that although she is an ace of a sixteen year old, she may be a very pretty and pleasant young girl for too long, and maybe some years before she develops into a young lady with her own agenda or is mature enough for the commitment. I needed someone who was more than just a lovely little sister to me. I will need a stronger girl, a no nonsense girl, but nonetheless one with some passion, not as tomboy as run-around Sue, but she needs to be a little softer than Sue, and tougher than young Sylvia was at that time to be a good future wife and mother of any children, and that she was out there, somewhere.

I should have remembered that walls have ears.

Soon after that discussion and after a scary short chase with an ever roaring black Austin A60 Police Car opposite the Basildon Bowling Alley with Sylvia unusually on the pillion in a pursuit, Sylvia, also influenced by the sudden prominence of the Mods' styling, Pirate DJ's and Discos visiting the village hall, and the forward thinking nature of The Who and the music scene generally, reasonably suggested that I smartened myself up from motorbike gear and bought some Mod style clothing and joined the modern trend.

I explained that even though I didn't actually object to the softer styling, there was no chance on earth that I could wear a Mod's Parka on a 100 mph Vincent. I would have invented Hang Gliding with a quarter ton Vincent between my legs and a girl on my back some fifty years before hang-gliding was invented.

So no, I was not going to change my clothing style and my Vincent for Sylvia nor anybody else for that matter. Fancy clothes and fast bikes just don't mix.

Soon after this, and after being together for a little less than a year and when walking her back to her Mum's house in Hullbridge Road and after a good day watching the regular motor-cycle scramble on The Radar Hill at Woodham Ferrers, Sylvia dumped me, Boomph, Just like that, as Tommy Cooper would say and left me up the creek without a paddle. It seemed that she preferred the ways of a slower and softer Mod culture to the very thrilling motorbike way of life, shucks, she wanted to slow down and I didn't. She, without looking at me, quietly said that she didn't want to see me anymore and that it was over . . . . *"Who is Sylvia, What is She, Is she kind as she is fair?"* (obviously not on this occasion} are words from Shakespeare's ballad.

> *Think it over what you just said, think it over in your pretty little head, are you sure that I'm not the one, was your love real or only fun, yes think it over, think it over, the mind grows old and cold, (33)* . . . but her mind was set.

Oh dear, Oh sod! Oh bugger, I didn't try very hard to save the situation, as I believed that when a door is shut in my face, it's best to let it stay shut, just find another door that opens easier and leads to a better tomorrow, after all, she was a very nice sweetie, but not a wife for me in the foreseeable future, so on with the next, whatever, whenever, however, whoever, Oh Sod, I thought, and turned to the piano, maybe Beethoven's soothing 'Fur Elise' was played a few times, and then his sad 'Farewell to the Piano' which Beethoven composed whilst going blind in old age. I had to choose between the ways of life of the Vincent or Sylvia, I chose the Vincent, I didn't try hard to re-open the door with Sylvia but in anger I did put my fist through the village hall window which dared to show my cheesed off image, and that cost me a pretty penny. I paid, disgraced, to the Hall's Treasurer who happened to be run-around Sue's Dad, whatever next. Bah Humbug. Brinnie asked me if matters were recoverable, I said I will never get on my knees to a girl, it's bad practice, there's more chance of a successful re-love by throwing three coins in the Trevi fountain.

> *So tell me something have you met an Angel, someone too lovely to live on earth, well yesterday I thought I'd met an Angel but she wasn't worth all she seemed to be worth. So oh what a fool I have been, I was sure taken in, but I'll find another, and we'll start anew. It'll be easy forgetting you. You're no good, you're no good. Baby you're no good, I'm gonna say it again. You're no good, you're no good, Ba-by you're no good. (34)*

But, I did still have my terrific bike! Sod it again, *I had won*, the piano sprung into life with the Dam-Busters March, three times over, followed by The March of the Gladiators, both of which could be played with much verve and gusto, Boom! as Basil Brush would say. Maybe the future was to be even better, I hoped, *and indeed it was*.

> *Walk like a man, talk like a man, walk like a man my son, No woman's worth, crawling in the Earth, so walk like a man my son. (35)*

.and then it happened

STRIKING PAMELA,

When a firework replaced a sparkler

From page six ...Many, many, months later, after the arrival of winter and whilst reviewing the past events and considering the current situation bought on by my impatience and stubbornness, I am leaning on the evening coffee bar of the unusually quiet South Woodham Village Hall, head in cupped hands and my mind is in the doldrums without a current girlfriend, just my Vincent motorbike as company

> *Only the Lonely, know just how I feel tonight, Only the lonely know that things aren't quite right, maybe tomorrow, a new romance, no more sorrow but.(36)*

...at which point I was startled by a very sudden and dramatic 'Splash', and a very cold wet head and face. 'Oh what now I think to myself, Drat, it's a cold winter's night and I am soaked through. What now, who has dared to chuck cold water over me? I cleared my eyes, fists clenched and arm muscles tense, expecting a fight or full-on confrontation with a visiting bad lad or Mod, and there, giving me a verbal lashing was a sure fire talking, but very attractive, well proportioned and well dressed 5ft 6inch brunette, by the name of Pamela, Pamela had struck. Pamela was a brunette that I previously never had the pleasure nor indeed the displeasure of knowing. I had occasionally noticed her and reasonably assumed that she was a no-go to a biker, an unapproachable type of girl. She was a girl who held her head high and was assertive, often holding court among other girls and usually casually leaning against the hall's centrally mounted wall radiator with a couple of girls each side of her. In the summer she was often to be seen walking in the village very admirably in a miniskirt and occasionally bare feet, with her own very noticeable driven charisma and never with a local boyfriend, an out of reach stunner, or so I thought.

> *Pretty woman walking down the street, Pretty woman the kind I'd like to meet, Pretty woman, You are lovely as can be, are you lonely just like me, Pretty woman will you stop a while, Pretty woman will you talk a while, Pretty woman give your smile to me . . .(37)*

Apparently she was part of the South Woodham Ferrers Carnival Queen Court. Whatever does she want of me, it can't be the bike, can it? and surely not the way I dress nor for some more confrontation, maybe she's just mischief.

This no-nonsense blue-eyed brunette had ambushed me, telling me in no uncertain terms whilst looking me directly in the eyes, that this coffee bar might not have music nor coffee, tea, nor the Cola that I had requested tonight, but it does indeed have cold water and plenty more of it, If I want it... I have just met Pamela, Pamela Mary that is. Our eyes, in a moment of surprise, were fixedly aligned and I just hoped that I could calmly break the deadlock, do I run or take up the challenge, this girl, she who dared, is certainly no shrinking violet, more of a striking rose, complete with some threatening thorns. After all I'd been through I was in for the challenge. No More Fairies for me, after all, I'm a biker and can take on anything, anything within reason, take a chance I said to myself!

> *If you change your mind, I'm still free, so if you dare, take a chance on me, if you'll let me know, I'll be around . . (38)*

A few minutes earlier I had innocently popped into this village hall, and as usual went to the coffee bar to warm up being a cold unpleasant night. The evening organiser, Ray White, was running late and had not yet arrived and until he did, there was no music, no cola, no juice, no coffee, no tea, but an abundance of water, cold water, straight out of the cold tap. So when I asked the leading young lady behind the counter "what sort of coffee bar is this?" she responded in the way that I was soon to learn, was her only way of dealing with a problem. Full On! Was this a moment of serendipity or disaster?

I responded with a bit of bravado . . .come outside?

> *Come outside, come outside, there's a lovely Moon out there, Come outside, come outside, come while we've got time to spare, . . .(what for? its cold out there) (39)*, she retorted, keep trying I thought, this girl's a minx.

I had lost a sparkler and gained a firework, not a full-size banger like run-around Sue, but a complete box of tricks including the odd short fuse. I decided that her strange sense of humour and the challenge of taming her could suite my future.

> *Pamela, Pamela, remember the days of inkwells and apples and books and school plays, but you was so young and everything was new, impatient to do things you couldn't do (40)*

... Just don't chuck cold water over me, OK,

Yes, I had just met Pamela, a true enigma of a girl, she just needs re-training . . . if I dared to try, so take great care I thought. I didn't realise until later that she was indeed Sylvia's close friend and looking back it seemed that from a distance she had created and watched matters develop and unfold with Sylvia, and after the dust had settled made her chess type move and successfully ambushed me, a really clever one-move check-mate. Probably the only time in my life that a check-mate move against me was actually in my favour...perchance a good move indeed.

As time passed It turned out that our ambitions experiences and thoughts were surprisingly alike, and a little while later, I realised that maybe I had found the pathway to my 'Shangri La' as she was no Southend-on-Sea or Jaywick 'kiss me quick' tart nor Nottingham Barmaid, but a girl to be proud of.

My six-year search was over, my jigsaw of life was complete, I never gave up.

TYING THE KNOT

Two years later in September 1968 a happy, determined and attractive Pamela and I became married in the ancient Anglo Saxon Saint Mary's Church on the hill, in Woodham Ferrers. It was a beautiful autumn day complete with Church Bells, a Choir, bridesmaids and smiles, and a beautiful black MG Magnette ZB as a bridal car. The very popular, inebriate and local Reverend Stone was happy and shiny eyed after his usual pre wedding service drink, (or several) in the Bell Public House opposite the church, and gave us an excellent free flowing, colourful and memorable, probably whisky inspired, service, seemingly part Church of England and part Roman Catholic.

A lace adorned and lovely Pamela with a tiara and veil was escorted down the aisle with so many friends and family in attendance . . .once Pamela was standing alongside me the vicar said "say after me" *"I do", which we did and it was done.*

He raised my left arm into the air and then took Pamela's hand and interlocked them and then whilst chanting, he bound them together with his colourfully embroidered religious scarf, ceremoniously tying the knot, I was moved.

I wondered, had Jack the Lad won a Carnival Queen?

> *From a Jack to a King, from loneliness to a wedding ring, I played an ace and I won a Queen, She is the queen of my heart. (41)*

I had achieved my goal.

And I sold my treasured Vincent to my Best Man Richard (Easy Dick) and moved to Southminster in the Dengie Hundred with Pamela at the start of our long and adventurous life together.

PART ELEVEN
A VOYAGE OF MEMORIES

Memories,
I can dream of the old days,
life was wonderful then.
Let the memory, live again

Some 31 years after our wedding and some years after the Caroline's Mi Amigo's sinking, I am sailing my Seawolf Bermudan sloop sailing yacht 'Carioca' between Margate and Burnham-on-Crouch over the wide and unpredictable Thames Estuary, passing through the remote Edinburgh Channel on a rising tide and with a stiff breeze and then over The Black Deep, when I spotted the isolated, desolate, haunting and worryingly troubled looking top end of the transmitter mast, some fifty metres (165 ft) of it, of 'Mi Amigo' apparently rising and falling amongst the waves and swell in the Knock Deep Channel. The transmitter masthead, still attached to the sunken Mi Amigo, was sticking abandoned and defiantly erect through the waves as an index finger's symbol gesturing towards London and the Government's one-time Post Office Radio control department of the sixties, whose duty was to protect the BBC's much out of touch radio monopoly.

The ship sits there deep and alone amongst the fish and seaweed on the seabed, in the Knock Deep, like all Pirate Ships, abandoned but not forgotten. She is full of swirling murky seawater, with immersed and imaginary echoing music and memories, and the music of the sea, but the DJs are long gone.

They had abandoned ship some years earlier, and went ashore in the Sheerness Lifeboat taking their chances with the taxman and the authorities, before she slipped finally and unceremoniously below the waves.

With one hand on my yachts tiller and the other holding my binoculars and with an eye on the compass, I raised a wry smile and remembered a snapshot memory of it's musical heyday. The only transmission from my yachts marine radio was the boring but important Channel 16 Shipping Forecast. Mixed feelings indeed. And I sailed on by.

I then ceremoniously opened a can of beer, and raised a smug cheer, in memory and respect of the background of the cheerful swinging music that Mi Amigo and Radio Caroline gave through tens of thousands of radios to the young at heart throughout the nation, in the swinging, memorable sixties.

Something the government of the day and 'Auntie BBC' tried very hard to stifle, and humiliatingly failed. Caroline had helped in no small way to create the Swinging Sixties and advance pop music to the advantage and enjoyment of all and helping to spread the English language as a standard throughout the World.

LAUGH OR REMORSE

The Pirate Radio stations, having proved their point, eventually and inevitably lost their battle with the authorities and to coin a phrase, vanished below the waves. However, their memories will never be stifled. You could not accuse the Pirates of giving up.' They fought to the end, they Never Gave Up.

Most people are likely to name at least four Disc Jockeys and twenty hit records from the sixties but not many will remember the Prime Minister, nor the Telecommunications Minister of the time.

And from a love-less conception, Radio 1 was born...

> *Music was my first love, memories we'll forever keep, while Mi Amigo is quietly sleeping, sadly rusting, in the deep.*
>
> *Music is the future, and will always be in the past, once silently transmitted, invisibly from her mast. (42)*

IN LATER YEARS

Some of the era's DJs and personalities are held in 'Her Majesty's Pleasure' having been accused of earlier wrong doings with some of the girls and young ladies of the sixties.

NEARLY FIFTY YEARS LATER

After a career as an experimental mechanic on the dynamometers at Ford Motor Company's Research centre, and then working with Lotus and Subaru, I then earned the crown jewel of owning a top Lancia dealership. I drove The Flying Scotsman, and took two First Prizes in the 1985 Nore Race of more than two hundred yachts in the Thames Estuary, becoming a Commodore of Brandy Hole Yacht Club, and recently designed a totally pollution free bus for London. I eventually found my Shangri La. Shangri La was no longer a pipe dream, a pie in the sky Utopia nor a Chimera, but my own Shangri-La.

In early 2016 with five adorable grandchildren in Norfolk UK and Oklahoma USA, Pamela and I retired to Holland-on-Sea on the Essex Sunshine Coast.

During the following summer we visited Pamela's Mum's grave in the hillside churchyard of the same church, Saint Mary's, where we were married nearly fifty years earlier in Woodham Ferrers, with its beautiful views over the rolling hills to the west to Rettendon and beyond and to ancient Edwin's Hall to the east. As usual for our visit to our parents' graves it was midweek but unusually there was a lot of activity going on, which were community service lads attending to the grounds and so the church was open for the day. Curiosity got the better of me so I took Pamela's hand and led her into the thousand year old church and we were greeted by the current lady Vicar and I asked her if Pam and I could walk down the aisle to bring back some memories. The Vicar was happy to allow us, and discretely followed at a distance behind us. Pam and I stopped at the altar and revisited some distant but moving memories. The Vicar then approached us and asked what our interests were in her church. When we replied that we were married here nearly fifty years earlier, which was probably more than her age, she was taken by surprise and shared a brief chat with us and said that we probably pre-dated everyone who was in the church on that day and instantly offered to bless our marriage, which we gladly accepted. As she did, I am looking through the same centuries old magnificent stained glass window high up in the church's eastern gable with the same ancient Yew tree and vast blue Essex sky beyond, and the inside of the church was just the same as it was fifty years ago and maybe a thousand years ago as well. Whilst holding Pam's soft cool hand which was just as then, for a moment she was the same stunning nineteen year old bride in a laced white Wedding Dress and a Tiara with a veil as she was on that day back in the autumn of 1968. As the present day Vicar turned her back to us and faced the Crucifix, for a moment again, time stood still. A tear rolled down my cheek just as then. Anyone who has not shed a tear at their own wedding has missed a magical moment. Again, we were blessed.

 I said to the Vicar that at our wedding the church had the same large hand powered pipe organ that had a recess in the rear where a young lad did the pumping, the vicar replied that the lad was actually present today, and called over an elderly looking chap who now remembered our day well, and told us that the organ has since received an electric air pump giving him a much easier life. The routine visit to Pam's Mum's grave turned out to be anything but routine. I was humbled. You just never know what is around the corner.

BEING TELEVISED

In April 2016 The television company Shiver TV invited me to revisit some of my nostalgic memories with Robson Green at Clacton Sea-Front. I participated with my 1959 Velocette Viper motor bike that was nearly new at the time of the riots, with the production of his 'Tales of The Coast' Series, 'Mods and Rockers, Clacton 1964', recorded for ITV at Clacton's Martello seawall, in glorious sunshine and televised nationwide in the Spring of 2017. There was quite a crowd as it had attracted a lot of public interest. Two weeks or so previous to the filming, the television company had asked me to gather a group of Rockers to add material interest and mix. Surprisingly, up to the evening before the filming, I had not found anyone within a reasonable distance who was old enough to have a bike licence in 1964 and who was also still alive and had a suitably aged motorcycle. After trying the local vintage and veteran motor cycle clubs, the motorbike cafés and other contacts, I visited the local motor cycle dealership, Manley's in Clacton and asked Sean there, if he could try and get a link into their computerised customer base to find some suitable candidates. He apologised saying that whilst he would try, there was little chance of success. This was at 16.30 on a Monday afternoon with the filming starting at 10.00 am in the following morning. The next morning, Tuesday, whilst walking Tess our dog early on the beach and pondering my failure to find any old rockers that still had a bike, I got a panic call on the mobile from my wife Pam urging me to contact Manley's immediately, which I did. Sean at Manley's was in a state of semi panic as he had seen more than thirty-two thousand hits on his computer overnight and it was still climbing as we spoke. If just ten per cent of these hits turned into visits, then three thousand two hundred people and their companions were likely to descend onto Clacton within the hour. If just one per cent would visit then that would be three hundred and twenty people and companions arriving at Manley's and either way he was understandably worried. So Sean did the sensible option and attended the gathering at the Martello beach on an old Royal Enfield Bullet that they had in stock at the dealership, and left his staff to cope with the possible crowd, which really meant re-directing them down to the beach. Regardless how it seemed on TV, I was the only person there who was also at the riots and problems of 1964 besides a disabled character that I found in the crowd just five minutes before filming, who had a trike. Thank God for him. All of the other present 'Mods and Rockers' were look-alikes and younger if not considerably so than me and certainly were not on bikes at the 1964 riots. After the initial discussions and filming I did an impromptu performance singing 'Just for Kicks' in front of the TV cameras but there was nowhere near enough time to include it within the programme's time slot, if indeed I was in tune, which was doubtful. What has the world missed?

Robson asked the vexed question, why did the two groups of us hate each other so much, to which I replied "that everything was well until the Mods came on the scene with their flash scooters, fancy clothes and money to spare and started stealing our girlfriends" to which he responded whilst grabbing my forearm "Get over it Peter, you will get over it!"

The last laugh was had by the owner of a very old Big Beeza, a BSA M20 side-valve motorbike with a very large three-seat sidecar of similar vintage. When the camera crew needed to take some filming of Robson riding a mod scooter amongst others along the promenade, they turned to the seventy-year old sidecar outfit for help to be used as a camera platform. Indelibly etched into my mind is seeing a group of a dozen or so scooters, led by one being ridden by Robson Green, pop pop, pop, ratatat-tatting along the promenade emitting the usual copious amount of blue smoke, and in their midst is the ancient motorbike and sidecar just quietly muffling along with a suitably dressed cameraman, complete with a futuristic giro body mounted camera-frame, standing through the wooden sidecar's open canvas sunroof taking film of the procession on the move in the Clacton sunshine for posterity. The old BSA had its day over the newer scooters and was a star if laughable performer. As they say, every dog has its day.

THROUGH THE RIVER MIST, AN APPARITION

A la' Marie Celeste

In April 2017, I crewed an Evolution 26, 'Non Sequitur' (Latin for 'doesn't logically follow') racing yacht on an eleven hour early season passage from Bradwell-on-Sea on the River Blackwater to Hullbridge on the Upper Crouch also in Essex, and as we left Bradwell Quay, out of the swirling early morning river mist we noticed like an apparition, that there is one of Radio Caroline's ships, 'The Ross Revenge' no less, apparently pushing through the sea mist and the incoming tide that is rushing past her hull. Just as the Marie Celeste, abandoned and seemingly moving, but actually sitting quietly at anchor.

Some of 'Caroline's' sister ships continue to exist in the summer of 2017, looking fresh but mothballed, basking in the Essex sunshine in their bright red hulls and white superstructures, in the East Coast Estuaries. They serve as a reminder of their musical heyday in the past. An ex-lightship (LV18) now named 'Caroline' was acting as a public museum that successfully displays the pirate radio story and was permanently tied up afloat but with some hull reconstruction, alongside the Ha'penny Pier at Harwich Waterside, River Stour. Another, 'The Ross Revenge' is resting off Pewit Island, Bradwell Creek at Bradwell-on-Sea, River Blackwater, looking ready to literally drop anchor and sail (or steam) away where, defying the passing of time and legislation, and attached to a mooring buoy, she continues to swing like a youngster to the sea breezes and the tides of change. Apparently she will be changing her name, like others have been temporarily, to 'Caroline' in readiness for an Ironic if not hypercritical final story to be filmed by The BBC for later broadcasting. Already a fascinating film has been made based on the reality of it all, called 'The Boat That Rocked' a highly recommended watch and an accompanying book to read is also available.

As you approach her, the bow of The Ross Revenge at Bradwell-on-Sea proudly but sadly watches over you in your lower, smaller boat as if to say... *Help me, help me, help me, sail away, Give me two good reasons why I ought to stay, well I like to live so pleasantly, live this life of luxury, lazing on this sunny afternoon, in summer time.(43)*

Oh the pleasure of reminiscing the sixties when there was a suitable song for almost every occasion.

Radio Caroline will remain an influential iconic legend of the sixties for eternity. It changed the acceptance of pop music in a way that is totally unmatched, and *who* was the Prime Minister then? strangely I can't remember... *But I had achieved my dreams of sixty years ago...*

When walking our forever-youthful Springer Spaniel Tess each evening, I look out over the sea from the cliff-tops of our current hometown, Holland-on-Sea that overlooks the North Sea. With The Wallet Seaway, through the Gunfleet Sands, The London Array wind-farm and over the East Swin channel to the distant Black Deep and beyond to The Knock Deep channel, with the occasional mournful calling of a foghorn in the sea mist over Radio Caroline's 'Mi Amigo's' final resting place. The ship's three hundred foot transmitter mast has since collapsed in a storm and lays underwater but still attached and across her sunken deck, and now only visible by sonar. The mind wanders.

Tess then brings reality back and with a bark of impatience she runs down the high cliffs to the beach eighty feet below and a hopeful swim. No Tess! Please   let my mind continue to wander, its a special moment, a very special moment indeed. '*What if?*' comes to mind

What if. .

May 2019. Similar thoughts pass me by again when I revisit a little while later, the riverside at our previous home town of South Woodham Ferrers at high tide on a fine early summer's day and see many of the same unchanged yachts still swinging happily on their same moorings, their GRP hulls being defiant against the ageing suffered by their owners and myself some fifty years on. Their masts still standing erect and defiant just as Mi Amigo's mast did for so many years. For a moment time seems to have stood still. I think '*what if?. .*

June 2019. *I have just returned from an unexpected journey to Oklahoma,* USA where I was rather surprised to see one of my grand-daughters as the lead ballerina in a ballet production of Disney's 'The Little Mermaid' in Tulsa, again, *what if?. . .*

. . .***what if*** *that crazy girl* had not chosen to chuck water over me during that cold winter night in 1966, I might now be changing yet another truck axle on the centre lane of the M1, at night, in the rain. Now there's a sobering thought.

LOOKING BACK

Now that I have completed this book, I can start reading and reviewing this mixture of fun and mischief and relive every one of those events, the bikes, the people and of course, the swinging sixties. It certainly brings back many fond memories.

There are places I remember, all through my life though some have changed,
Some forever, not for better, some have gone and some remain,
All these places had their moments, with lovers and friends I can recall,
Some are dead and some are living, in my life, I've loved them all.
(The Beatles).

To quote Robson Green,

"Get over it Peter, . . .you *will* get over it."

A Lesson Learnt

Should you ever have a deep desire

that seems to be an impossible dream,

or should you face a terrible crisis, and your chips are down

then remember;

Never, Never, Ever, Give Up

(Sir Winston Churchill)

Anything is possible.

Appendix

The dying Flying Enterprise *from Brinnie's Story, Chapter five*

The stricken cargo ship 'The Flying Enterprise'... About to be towed fatefully but to hopeful safety in an Atlantic Storm by Her Majesty's Rescue Tug 'Turmoil' some Three hundred miles from Falmouth, January 1952

The Captain refuses to abandon her and her secretive atomic cargo until after more than two hundred miles of being towed on her side in the storm a final and fatal wave entered the tilting funnel and she is doomed. The five-inch tow-cable breaks from the immense strain and she sinks to the bottom. After keeping the hovering salvors at bay for more than two weeks at sea, Virtually in sight of Lands End just twenty miles away, she slips below the waves and Captain Calsen swims off her disappearing funnel into the stormy sea to the rescue tug Turmoil   Brinnie's Dad was the Radio Officer of Tug Turmoil.

Despite extreme winter exposure, the thirty seven year old Captain Calsen **never gave up**

Search on the Webb 'Flying Enterprise" to see much dramatic film footage of the event. There are some fantastic images that can be seen in the records, alas copyright does not allow me to share them here.

Autumn 2021 addition

A tableau appears in the Holland on Sea promenade naming a certain beach as 'The Pirate Beach' due to the infamous radio history of the area and eventual Radio North Sea International (RNSI).

With anchorage break-aways, running agrounds and conflict with the authorities, Radio Caroline was eventually succeeded in 1970 by RNSI and RNSI Mebo 11.

It seems that during 1970s, the British Labour Party were concerned with the minimum voting age being reduced from 21 to 18 years, and the new pro pirate younger electorate would vote Tory in the approaching general election. The Conservative Party, who were pro-free enterprise and anti-public ownership, were understandably favoured by the pirate radio companies and given good publicity. The BBC under the guidance of the worried government actively jammed the broadcasts of Radio Caroline and its successor Radio North Sea International (RNSI). RSNI responded by switching its transmissions to wavelength 244 metres that was so close to BBC ONE's 247 metres. With it's powerful transmitter, more than twice that of previous Radio Caroline, in a stroke RSNI virtually wiped out BBC ONE's coverage of Kent. One might cheer, "Own goal!"

It is then said that the salvage tug 'Husky' with the launch Viking, was sent by adversary Radio Veronica to cut the RSNI Mebo II's anchor chain, setting it adrift and then towing it into territorial waters where it would then be breached of maritime radio laws and the crew arrested. When the invasive tug pulled alongside with three frogmen, the Mebo II's disc jockey, Andy Archer, pleaded 'on air' for immediate public help. The public bombarded the authorities blocking their switchboards in London, the Hague and Zurich. Petrol bombs were exchanged and vessels in the area rushed to help. A Royal Dutch Navy frigate was sent, but not before the Husky had aimed a destructive water cannon at the transmitter mast of the Mebo II. The tug's crew however was warned by Mebo II not to fire, as it was claimed that the very high 105 KW power of the transmitter would electrocute the entire tug and it's crew. Embarrassed, the Husky withdrew to Dutch waters.

Then in 1971, Mebo II was fire-bombed in those waters, a Mayday was issued and the crew assembled for a lifeboat. However, the severely burnt ship did not finally sink. It appeared that 12,0000 gliders had passed hands for the aborted sabotage and five of the attackers were arrested and given custodial sentences in Holland for their 'Totally inadmissible gangster methods."

In 1977 it is further said, that the Mebo II, renamed El Fatah and its sister ship were sold to Libya to transmit the Quran from the Gulf of Sidra, off the coast of the Libyan Coast. It was eventually used for target practice by the Libyan Navy and sunk, joining the distant cousin 'Mia Amigo' on the Seabed.

The Radio Caroline saga seems endless.

After several read throughs, I have realised that there is almost no mention whatsoever of foreign products in this book. Almost without exception all of the cars, motorcycles, commercial vehicles, buses, fire engines, railway rolling stock, ships and yachts were British built. This book is written and compiled by me as a reflection of 'as it was' at the time, the period between 1953 and 1969 when Britain was proud and very self-dependent. It leaves me a little disappointed that we import so much now, but we didn't need to, then.

Flying Scotsman

After a few hours of driving and firing this 100mph beast, this giant motorbike on steroids, one is left both mentally and physical exhausted. Having gone deaf, bodily shaken, filthy dirty and so dehydrated that you have lost your voice through shouting, it is no wonder that the days of steam, at every large terminus you would find a railwayman's bar. An unpleasant and dark refuge, emitting the constant smell of beer from its damp carpets with snoring, sleeping but heroic enginemen, seeking salvation, slumped in the corner.

Headings and Lyrics
Typical artiste/s

The Sixth Sense

Foreword

It is Said

Viva the Sixties

Memories

PART ONE The start of my world   1946

L   Any dream will do (1)   Lee Mead

L   The Desert Song (2)   Stigmund Romberg

The make-up of the Islanders

The Canvey Flood of 1953   1953

Hope springs eternal

Wickford Junction

The Beautiful Dengie Peninsula

Is this East Anglia's 'Shangri La'

PART TWO **The decision is made**

L	Walk Tall (3)	Val Doonican

The Wickford Flood **1958**

Vic Pliopa

Final School Days

The Smoky City and the Sunshine Coast

The World's first pollution law of 1285 AD

London's Railways

Jock the Scot

The old guards van

We arrive at the Ilford Milk Depot

L	Freight Train(4)	Joan Baez

PART THREE **A new world begin** **1960**

RAF 1474 Squadron

A Rather Long Cycle Ride

Walking Back to Happiness

A Driving Licence at last

Troubled Graham

PART FOUR   **My first Employment**

The Big Freeze Winter   **1963**

New Frozen Arrivals

M1 Breakdown in the Snow

Taming the Raging Bull

The Deadly A127

On with the next

Out of the Frying Pan

The Summer Weekends

Cricket Match with the Rettendon Rabbits

L   Run rabbit (5)   Flanagan and Allen

PART FIVE   **Tales of the Turnpike**

Welcome to the house of fun

L   Welcome to the House of Fun (6)   Madness

L   There's Magic in my eyes (7)   The Who

The Arrival of Nipper

L   Tired of waiting (8)   The Kinks

Brinnie's Story, A sailor's son

Night Run to Bournemouth

Just for Kicks

L   Hold Tight (9)   Dave Dee Dozey Mick & Titch

L   Just For Kicks (10)   Mike Sarne

The Notorious Blinking Owl

No Condoms

Arson of the Vending Machine

Re-cycled doughnuts

PART SIX An epitaph of the sidecar world

The Return trip to the Isle of Man

More sidecar madness

Easy Dick

Clyde Cardy

PART SEVEN Icons of the Swinging Sixties　　　　　　1964

Radio Caroline and the Mods

L　　I'd Listen to the radio　(11)　　　　　　Carpenters

L　　I'd sit by the radio　(12)　　　　　　　Queen

The Making of the Mods

The Scene is set for Trouble

PART EIGHT The thrills of the Bikes

Built Like a Gun, Goes Like a Bullet

The Chase

| L | Now that I can dance (13) | Dave Clarke Five |
| L | Hit the road Jack (14) | The Overtones |

Jack the Lad

The arrival of the Thunderous Vincent

Birds, Bikes and Burn-ups; and Thunderbird John

The exciting Open Road

PART NINE The Essex Coast in the Sixties

Tornado Smith - The Wall of Death Dare Devil

Derry Preston-Cobb - The uncatchable paraplegic speedster

The Ghost of the A127

	The Ghost's Sonnet (15)	Author
L	She's not there (16)	The Zombies
L	A Ghost's Hi Noon/The Haunted House	

The Eviction

L	Knock, who's there (17)	Mary Hopkins
L	When the Night Wind Howls (18)	HMS Pinafore
L	Baby don't go (19)	Cher
L	Rhythm of the falling rain (20)	Neil Sedaka

Fun in the Rain

301

Viva Jaywick

The Awful Lavender Cart

L   Common Dirty (21)   Rolling Stones

Being Infiltrated by the Police

Brighton Motorbike Show

Tragedies

Ted Harris RIP

L   I'm a BOY (22)   The Who

The Bear RIP

L   The Living Years (23)   Mike and the Mechanics

The World of Mickey Craven RIP

L   Hole in the ground (24)   Bernard Cribbins

L   Terry (25)   Twinkle

Terry

A House Fire

Returning to Jaywick

PART TEN **GIRLS, GIRLS, GIRLS,**

Who makes the first move.

    L   I will tell you what my game is (26)   Mike Sarne

          The Risky Girls of Essex . . . The Mistress(27)   Author

A Guide to a girl's nature by hair colour

Linda

L	The Crying Game (28)	Dave Berry
L	Only a Winter's Tale (29)	David Essex
L	Sir can you help me (30)	Phil Collins
L	Don't let me be misunderstood (31)	Eric Burdon

Soft Sylvia

L	That yellow Dress (32)	Joe Brown
L	Think it over (33)	Buddy Holly
L	Have you met an Angel (34)	Chris Andrews
L	Walk like a man (35)	Four Seasons
L	Only the Lonely (36)	Roy Orbison

Striking Pamela

L	Pretty Woman (37)	Roy Orbison
L	Take a Chance on me (38)	Abba
L	Come Outside (39)	Mike Sarn
L	Pamela Pamela (40)	Mindbenders

Tying the Knot

L	From a Jack to a Queen (41)	Elvis, and others

PART ELEVEN **A Voyage of Memories**

Laugh or Remorse

L   Music was my first love (42)   John Miles

 Some ten years later

Nearly fifty years later

Being Televised

Through the River Mist

L   The Taxman's taken all I've got (43)   The Kinks

 A Lesson Learnt

LOOKING BACK

LYRICAL CREDITS *above are often recorded by more than one artiste and have been re-worded or abbreviated to suite their application, and are **highlighted with an 'L'***

THE LADS

Afro Trevor: Trevor Sullivan
Car Sprayer Supremo

Author: Peter Williams
Vincent 500

Barry: Barry Hathaway / Rally Cross Champion
BSA 500 Shooting Star

Big John: Johnny Dones
Triumph Thunderbird 650

Bonk: Very Short, Long-Bar biker
BMW R60 / Honda Monkeybike

Brinnie: Brian Woodman
Velocette Venom 500

Clyde: Clyde Cardy / European Champion
Triumph 650 Bonneville

Colin Selvage: Likeable girl puller
Triumph 200 Tiger Cub

Crazy Pete: Peter Bird the sidecar jockey
BSA 500 M20 and sidecar

Easy Dick: Dick Schmeig
AJS 500 and sidecar

(Edwina): Ted Harris (RIP) and Brenda
AJS 350 G3 LS

Gogsy: Alan Williams
Matchless 650 G12

Grudge: Gary The Grudge (Robert)
Likeable but troubled pillion

Gulp: Long Bar, Could swallow a Coca Cola
without a pause!

J J: James Anthony Jay, no less
Lost in the Canadian wilderness

Jed: Jed Cooper
Greeves Sports Twin

Graham: *aka* Crash Kavannagh
Thrashed and trashed cars.

Mad Mick: Mad Mick the butcher
Norton Jubilee

Malcolm: His beautiful red haired Linda became so very, very unwell God Bless Her, and then his bike engine exploded 1965 was a very unlucky year for Malcolm.
BSA 650 Super Rocket/Tribsa

Micky: Mick Craven RIP, a likeable toughie
James Captain

Nipper: Adrian Emberson
So tall, only his lazy Harley Davidson was big enough

Ray White: An organiser, always busy.
Phoenix Scooter

Speedy Reedy: John Reed
BSA Bantam 175 Super

Terry: Terry Sharpe
Ariel Colt

The Bear: Derek Pinnock RIP One of the best
BSA 650 Golden Flash

306

THE LASSES

Brenda Shepherd

Ginger Sue

Jenny Seaman

Pamela Blackshaw

Run-around Sue

Sad Linda

Sylvia Firmin

Publisher's Notes

Firstly, I want to say thank you for purchasing this book. This book is different from the usual publications that come from The Book Nut Publishing, and is a little bit special, as it is a book written by my father, Peter Williams.

Peter has achieved so much throughout his life, because of his unwavering optimism, confidence and determination. He spent years running his own car business, working more hours than he should, provide a loving home and environment for his family. It comes as no surprise that in his retirement he still needs something to keep him busy. Writing is a passion he has discovered and thrived on.

He is so many things to us, but one thing always stands out, he is a natural storyteller. As children, he weaved tales to us at night. A mix of memories and fantasies but always delivered full of heart and warmth. As we grow older, he continues to gather stories to share with us and the generations after us.

When he started writing down his stories, the initial shock of how much he would need to write to create the book he envisioned almost knocked him sideways, but in true Peter fashion, he quickly took the challenge that seemed impossible, and made it possible. We have had so many discussions about this book. Hours spent looking over details, discussing copyrights and musical lyrics, the photos, the people, everything we could think of was considered.

My Father has gone over everything he has put in this book with a fine-tooth comb. Even now, as I type this, he is sending over edits (I have lost count of how many we have done now), as he pours over the manuscript time and time again, working to make it the best it can possibly be.

Therefore, we would hope that by now, the errors are few. The stories he has shared are from his past and are as accurate as his memories will allow and so we hope you, the reader, will forgive any inaccuracies.

The most important part of this story to me is that he is telling his story. He is sharing his voice.

This book is a love-letter to Essex in the Sixties. It is full of anecdotes, providing a personal view of what life was like growing up in that decade, with the music keeping a constant beat in the background.

What an achievement, one my Dad can be proud to have accomplished.

Father Bear, you did it. You finished the book.

I am so, very proud.

Hazel x

P.S. Dear readers. Standby. He is already writing another book...

www.ingramcontent.com/pod-product-compliance
Lightning Source LLC
Chambersburg PA
CBHW060457090426
42735CB00011B/2014